# THREESCORE

*This is a volume
in the Arno Press Collection*

# SIGNAL LIVES
## Autobiographies
## of American Women

*Advisory Editors*

Annette Baxter
Leon Stein
Barbara Welter

*See last page of this volume
for a complete list of titles.*

# THREESCORE

THE AUTOBIOGRAPHY OF

SARAH N. CLEGHORN

WITH AN INTRODUCTION BY

ROBERT FROST

## ARNO PRESS

A New York Times Company
New York • 1980

Editorial Supervision: RITA LAWN

———

Reprint Edition 1980 by Arno Press Inc.

Reprinted from a copy in The Pennsylvania State Library

**SIGNAL LIVES: Autobiographies of American Women**
ISBN for complete set: 0-405-12815-0
See last page of this volume for titles.

Manufactured in the United States of America

———

**Library of Congress Cataloging in Publication Data**

Cleghorn, Sarah Norcliffe, 1876-1959.
    Threescore.

    (Signal lives)
    Reprint of the 1936  ed. published by H. Smith &
R. Haas, New York.
    Includes index.
    1.  Cleghorn, Sarah Norcliffe, 1876-1959--Biography.
2.  Authors, American--20th century--Biography.
3.  Reformers--United States--Biography.  I.  Title.
II.  Series.
PS3505.L58Z5  1980      818'.5209 [B]      79-8783
ISBN 0-405-12831-2

# THREESCORE

WHEN I GRADUATED FROM THE SEMINARY

# THREESCORE

## THE AUTOBIOGRAPHY OF
## SARAH N. CLEGHORN

WITH AN INTRODUCTION BY
ROBERT FROST

NEW YORK · MCMXXXVI

HARRISON SMITH & ROBERT HAAS

TO EACH ONE
OF THE MANY
WHO OUGHT TO BE IN IT
AND AREN'T,
THIS BOOK IS
AFFECTIONATELY INSCRIBED

# ILLUSTRATIONS

# INTRODUCTION

SECURITY, security! We run in all directions for security in the game of Pussy-wants-a-corner. I find security chiefly in proper names —the thought of certain people, I mean people I can be certain of at their posts or postoffices. I am like Childe Roland on his way to the Dark Tower: I need someone pleasant to think of. They that are against us should be more than they that are for us by all present-day accounts.

> "May be true what I have heard:
> Earth's a howling wilderness
> Truculent with force and fraud."

It will not do to underestimate the relative strength of the enemy. But neither will it do to overestimate it. That, I take it, is one lesson of Grant's greatness as a general. It is necessary to keep in mind in a campaign just whom we can muster in an emergency. We in Vermont are taken care of on the north by three great ladies up the valley, three verities who can be depended on to hold Vermont true to its winter self against all summer comers. And one of these is wise and a novelist, one is mystic and an essayist, and the third is saintly and a poet. This book is about them all, but principally (and charmingly and naturally) about the poet. It is her own story of her life told with a beautiful unconsciousness of its beauty.

Saint, poet—*and* reformer. There is more high explosive for righteousness in the least little line of Sarah Cleghorn's poem about the children working in the mill where they could look out the window at their grown-up employers playing golf than in all the prose of our radical bound-boys pressed together under a weight of several atmospheres of revolution. The reformer has to be taken with the rest of it. And why not? Some of us have developed a habit of saying we can't stand a reformer. But we don't mean it except where the reformer is at the same time a raw convert to the latest scheme for saving the soul or the state. The last we heard of him may have been two or three fashions ago as one of the ultra-arty insisting that we join him in his minor vices at his wild parties. Now he turns up at our door to ask without ceremony— You don't mean to say you don't love God or you don't mean to say you don't love humanity.— Don't you believe public confession is good for the soul?—Don't you believe so-and-so died a martyr to the cause of humanity?—Let me recall you to your better self.—Have you given anything any thought?

I don't know what makes this so nettling unless it is that it ignores so superciliously the strain we may have been under for years trying to decide between God and the Devil, between the rich and the poor (the greed of one and the greed of the other), between keeping still about our troubles and enlarging on them to the doctor and—oh, between endless other things in pairs ordained to everlasting opposition. No, it is not the reformer we object to. Nor is it yet the convert. The convert has his defense. It is the rawness, the egotism, the gross greed to take spiritual advantage of us. We have all had attempts on our self-respect of the kind, and we cringe at the memory. I have had four, one of them lately that would afford one scene in a comedy. But a reformer who has all her life long pursued the even tenor of her aspiration, is no one to resent. On the contrary she is one for me to claim friendship with and, if permitted, kindred spirit with. Pride enters into it, as may be seen.

Just after the great Democratic victory of 1932 I made occasion to bring the election into conversation with a Negress who had come to our door soliciting alms for a school for Negroes in the deep south.

"My people don't very much like the Democrats in power again," she said.

x

"Surely you aren't afraid of them any more!"

"I wouldn't just say we weren't afraid of them. You wouldn't think there was much they could do. But there's small things an outsider wouldn't notice."

She was a poor creature, poorly clothed, but she touched her wrists with a pretty pathos for this:

"Here a shackle, there a shackle, and before we know it we're back in slavery."

"Not while Sarah Cleghorn lives in Manchester, Vermont," I answered. Then I went on to explain that Sarah Cleghorn was an abolitionist as of 1861. One of her best poems was about a Negress who personally conducted troop on troop of runaway slaves northward. Many lightly argue that since we have tolerated wage slavery and child labor, we might as well have tolerated Negro slavery. She reasons the other way round: that since we have abolished Negro slavery we are bound in logic to abolish all other slavery. She is the complete abolitionist. She has it in for race prejudice and many another ignobleness besides. Some time I intend to ask her if she isn't bent on having the world perfect at last.

Did I know her?

"Yes, very well," I said with effect.

I have just come indoors from boasting among the egrets of the Everglades of Florida that I was acquainted with the lady up north who by writing to the papers (see page 110) had done more than anyone else to get them free of the terrible yearly Minoan tax on the flower of their youth and beauty. I don't know what impression I made in this case. The egret standing nearest me in the water simply lifted stiffly and withdrew further into the Everglades, as unresponsive as a bank clerk with whom I should have attempted to establish credit. The fact remains that I do know one or two people who have done measurable good. And I think I have a right to speak of them when the chance offers.

You get some notion of Sarah Cleghorn's range of beneficence—all the way from pure black to snow white—which may sound danger-ously like being an extremist—and typically a New Englander. But you have only to read to find out that she was not born a New Englander nor of wholly New England stock.

We can't all be judges. There must always be a thousand *ex parte* lawyers for one judge, sitting out impartial till sides have all but wiped each other out in encounter and judgment has all but pronounced itself. A philosopher may worry about a tendency that, if run out to its logical conclusion, might ruin all; but he worries only till he can make out in the confusion the particular counter tendency that is going to collide with it to the cancellation of both. Formidable equations often resolve into no more information than that nothing equals nothing. It is a common question: What has become of the alarming old tendency to come to grief from each one's minding his own business? Oh, if I remember rightly, that bumped head on into the tendency to come to grief from minding each other's business. The philosopher values himself on the inconsistencies he can contain by main force. They are two ends of a strut that keeps his mind from collapsing. He may take too much satisfaction in having once more remarked the two-endedness of things. To a saint and a reformer like Sarah Cleghorn the great importance is not to get hold of both ends, but of the right end. She has to be partisan and even a trifle grim. I heard a clergyman say she is the kind we need most of to get the world forward. Well, here we have her, her whole story from the first dawning on her in childhood of the need of goodness and mercy.

ROBERT FROST

# THREESCORE

# 1

CARL, Fanny and I were playing in front of our house, Fairfields, in the middle of the morning, when Aunt Jessie, our mother's younger sister, came out on the piazza.

"You children run round to the back of the house," she said, "and then come back, and you'll find something." We faithfully went and returned, expecting maybe a gumdrop, and there were three big saucers of strawberries on the steps.

I felt an onset of pleasure the strawberries alone couldn't account for. I was enraptured by the unexpectedness of the treat. Coming on a weekday morning, uncalled for by any festival or birthday, it was almost inexcusable kindness!

It set up a kind of standard in my life. It was the way people ought to be treated. Something like it, as a social principle for everyday life, has ever since been fluttering over the world in my imagination, and tantalizing my heart.

Almost on the same spot, and in the same year—my fifth or sixth— I had an impressive setback in my endeavors to regulate the conduct of my little brother Carl. I can't remember what he was doing, perhaps getting his feet wet; something, at any rate, that I had been taught to disapprove of; and I made a threat that if he didn't come back to the gravel path at once, I would throw my ring into the long grass. I still feel dumfounded when I recall the jolly indifference with which he allowed me to carry out my vow, and didn't even watch me doing it. Having solemnly thrown the little gold band into the grass, I went over and tried, long and anxiously, with a sense of dreadfulness and doom, to find it. I thought over that experience a good deal, and owing partly, I am sure, to it, I came quite early by a dim notion of the foolishness, *and something more*, of trying to regulate other people. This something more, I gradually understood, was the indignity of receiving, and the indignity of exerting, arbitrary control. I grew up with a strong dislike for witnessing "implicit obedience"; a wish to turn away my eyes, as from people who are making a painful spectacle of themselves.

Both my sister and my brother occasionally offended my own sense of independence. I remember at seven telling Fanny, who was nine, that she was "getting dictatorial." It was a satisfactory mouthful of a word. Carl, at no more than five, picked up an offensive habit of throwing out his stomach and declaring,

"I'm a man, and I can do what I please."

Fanny never paid any attention to this, but it threw me into a pitiable fury, which greatly tickled my brother, little as he was.

The first of many thousand enchantments I remember feeling was due to Aunt Fanny's manicure case, a tiny leather barrel, which it gave me the greatest delight to play with. To me, as to many others, anything in miniature is extremely attractive. Aunt Fanny was evidently wise enough to keep the fairy barrel from falling to the rank of an everyday plaything; at all events, I never became disillusioned about it.

This sense of enchantment, though so much shallower, arose in me before the conscious sense of beauty. I was first aware of the presence of beauty when, in the hymnbook my mother had given me, I read,

"The Son of God goes forth to war."

I took delight in the towering dark spruces which lined the oval driveway up to the front door at Fairfields, the first home I remember. Lights and colors in the sky, the beauty of woods and water, I believe I never noticed in those years. But there were crimson peonies under the spruces, "globéd peonies," and somewhere about Fairfields were locust trees. The triple beauty of a tree which trails white

CARL, FANNY AND I

flowers from its branches and throws out clouds of fragrance, especially through open windows at night, filled me with wonder and joy.

This Fairfields was a little farm near Madison, Wisconsin, which my father had oddly, almost accidentally, bought "for a song." We moved there in 1877, when Fanny was three and a half, and I was one and a half, and Carl was born there the next year. Our Scotch father knew nothing whatever about farming, and our town-bred American mother knew nothing about being a farmer's wife; but the place was so lovely, and Madison people so delightful, that all our family loved it, and we managed to stay five years.

There were eight in our family; besides the five Cleghorns, Grandmother Hawley and her two unmarried daughters lived with us. Grandmother Hawley was a blue-stocking, the only one in the Hawley family. Her parents, Troy people by the name of Mallory, had been strong backers of Emma Willard in establishing her Troy Female Seminary; and this daughter of theirs, graduating there at seventeen, was sent by Mrs. Willard to teach the planters' daughters in Camden, South Carolina, a little over a hundred years ago. She might have married there, but that she had been seen, at thirteen years old, standing up at a public examination in Emma Willard's Seminary, by a young man from a Vermont farm, who never forgot her afterwards.

Grandmother's love of learning was reverenced by her husband and all her children, not one of whom inherited it, though all her daughters duly graduated from Emma Willard's school, where Aunt Fanny was the *enfant terrible*. With all Grandmother's bookishness and religious, charitable temper, she never took the smallest interest in women's public activities. She was indifferent or hostile to woman suffrage, the crusade for temperance, Fanny Wright's leadership in the spectacular rise of labor, and even the abolition of slavery. She was of a placid, tender, docile disposition, and though she followed public events in Europe and America with "intelligent interest," nothing roused her from the mellow glow of private thought. So unquestioning was her acceptance of the *status quo,* that her life-long affection for her South Carolina friends, after one of whom she named my mother, seems never to have been troubled in the smallest degree by scruples about slavery.

It was Grandmother who taught me to read; and her room at Fairfields was the spot I remember best of anything inside the house.

Death came into our household three times before I was ten years old. I was between six and seven when Grandmother died. She was ill in bed a long time. I understood as well as anyone else what happened when life went out of her body. I can't remember any time when I didn't understand (as we strangely call it) about death. And though a number of children have asked me questions about birth, none of them ever asked me anything about death.

But now that I have written thus solemnly about what were memorable events in my childhood, it seems to me that I have perhaps been unduly solemn. Is this because accidents are so frequent now, and violent deaths so common? Or does death seem more normal than it used to seem? Can it be only age, that brings it nearer?

Perhaps a little of all three.

Soon after Grandmother died, we sold Fairfields, our aunts went back to the east, and we moved to Minneapolis, where my father, ceasing to be a farmer, began just as ignorantly to be a business man. We soon had a little house, 1706 Laurel Avenue, a house which could have been tucked into a pocket of the house at Fairfields. We called this the Snuggery.

I remember chiefly a lot of romping, inside and out, of this little house. On Sunday afternoons three or four young men came out to see our parents and played and romped *ad libitum* with us. Mr. Wylde was exceedingly reckless and exciting to play with, tearing wildly round and round the lawn. Mr. Martin, too, a Scotchman, was great fun, and once when we tore off his coat wasn't a bit shocked. Mr. Knowles, a red-haired young man from St. Paul, was rather dignified, but gave us delightful presents. Above all, our own father loved, beyond every other pleasure in life, to play with children. He was inventive, dashing and gleeful, behind a delicious mask of

18

solemnity, and we resented his ever going down to the office. One morning I locked the front door and hid the key.

When Papa had gone, Mamma had lessons with Fanny and me. The purely bookish type of education was entirely pleasant to us, though I often have breathless glimpses nowadays of what an education with dramatics, plenty of drawing and painting, and wood and cooking crafts would have been to us!—perhaps a surfeit of joy. We had a formal titbit of French every day, spelling, history, geography; and Mamma read aloud to us. We both were beyond having to study reading—we read freely for pleasure, *Harper's Young People, Chatterboxes,* etc.

I made one great leap forward in real education while we were in Minneapolis. On Sundays, we often all went out on horse-cars to the edges of the young city, to walk in some froggy violet fields which we children loved. Once on the street-car Mamma had occasion to say to me,

"Don't stand in front of the gentleman, Sally."

It was a beery-looking man whom she thus described. He was frowsy, unshaven, unpleasantly flushed, and with dirty hands. I was too young to feel the unchildlike emotion of disgust; but I was bursting with astonishment at my mother's choice of words; and in simple wonder I exclaimed, standing still and gazing full at him,

"Why, Mamma, you don't call *him* a gentleman?"

No sooner were the words out of my mouth than I felt how dreadful they were; how much more horrid than dirt or even drunkenness. My wonder all turned in upon myself; as for Mamma, I understood perfectly why she had used the word. I felt all the difference between treating people with unexpected strawberries and doing what I had just done. I still get an echo of that dismay every time anyone says, "I told him just what I thought of him."

Nothing was ever said to me at home about this, the greatest *faux pas* of my life, and so my reflections upon it were all unconfused by anyone else's thoughts. How much value there is in the application to children of the creative Quaker silences!

19

Cleveland's first election was a momentous event in my life, because it gave me that inevitable first revelation of my father's fallibility. All through the autumn he had continued reporting to my mother (in a tone of despair, for he was a strong free-trade Democrat) that "Blaine would carry everything." I never heard him say anything about the "rum, Romanism and rebellion" speech, and my notions about his judgment were knocked into a cocked hat when he finally announced;

"Well, Sarah, Cleveland's elected."

It was a painless shock, however. It caused me no grief, only intense surprise. I still had perfect confidence in his moral judgments, (subject, of course, to my own).

I would recommend to all children that their parents be of opposite political, or better still, religious, faith. To be aware, from the beginning, that of these two trustworthy and indispensable persons, one can be a Democrat, or a Protestant, the other a Republican, or a Catholic, or a Jew, is valuable early training.

It seems to be generally supposed that children of seven or eight years old can have only a fantastic idea of such matters as a presidential election, or any other proceedings of which they know nothing by experience. I believe this is a mistake. Children who learn to read early (and many of those who do not) receive the news of the day with pretty fair comprehension. I certainly understood at six the assassination of Garfield, and I think I knew what a disappointed office-seeker was.

I think, too, that religion comes early into children's lives. I believe there is scarcely a child over three who hasn't discovered and practiced what I call natural religion; who hasn't made, that is, some confiding, hopeful effort to throw the power of his will on the side of his unselfish desires. Isn't this religion?

The language of formal religion is a stumbling-block to children, perhaps; though a child like me, a natural lover of language, takes to it like a duck to water. True, I attached a rather crude idea to one expression I heard every day in family prayers—an institution all the households of our double-dyed Episcopalian family, in Scotland and America, habitually used. Fanny and I had each a triangle of silk, pink for her and blue for me, edged with a tiny frill of lace; these our mother tucked under the collars of our winter coats when we went out. I greatly revered these kerchiefs as objects of art, and always especially referred to them in my own mind when in morning prayers I heard the petition,

"Take us, and all things belonging to us, under thy fatherly care and protection."

But though formal prayers and services may arouse unlooked-for responses in children, and probably in adults, the natural emotions of religion, arising wordlessly in a child's heart, are to be delicately, reservedly, sometimes even silently! cherished by us who are older, and less pure in our emotions.

We were always taken to church, where we were sometimes furnished with paper and pencils to beguile the time; and during the sermon our heads were comfortably pillowed on the laps of our mother and aunts, so that we had a refreshing snooze. While this procedure does certainly form in children the habit of going to church, it also formed in me the lifelong habit of going to sleep there. I always liked going to church, however. I liked, and still do, putting on Sunday clothes. I loved the resounding hymns, and the noble beauty of the Prayer Book, if only that endless Te Deum, with all its chanted repetitions, could have been left out. It was really sickening to hear the choir going back yet once again to a phrase they had already sung twice. But the Litany, which in those days was always included in the morning service, made up for the wearisome Te Deum. It was sweet to hear all kinds of people, in all kinds of situations, prayed for so lovingly, rememberingly, almost by name.

Sunday School, which I first attended in Minneapolis, was a very different matter. It lacked almost all beauty and nobility of language, even cultivating an inferior set of hymns, and this gave it a humdrum, calico character by comparison with church. But if at Sunday School there had only been some direct, informal, realistic consulta-

21

tions about how to live our young lives in great and glorious fashion—
a kind of consultation which I believe human nature at all ages truly
craves—there could have been nothing humdrum about that. Of
course it couldn't have been meek and mild advice. Being good never
to me meant being obedient. Books, especially poetry, which I began
to love before the dawn of memory, were full of reckless, thrilling,
even disobedient, ways of being good. The church service also
touched upon these and glimmered with their brightness. Why not
Sunday School? What you found in Sunday School, instead, was
certain undesired information about the patriarchs and apostles. Of
course it was pleasant to go, for there were other children there. Besides there was a Sunday School library.

I had perfect confidence, when I was writing this, that I remembered the Sunday School books of my childhood clearly, and that
they were practically all about consumptive child heroines and heroes,
all something like Elsie Dinsmore, whose father made her sit on the
piano stool until she fainted away, because she wouldn't play the
piano on a Sunday. Happening, however, to find a letter written by
my sister Fanny in 1884, I was surprised to find that

"Sally and I both got books at Sunday School last Sunday. I got
*Robinson Crusoe* and Sally got *Alice in Wonderland.*"

It couldn't have been as bad, then, as I remember. But there was
certainly a majority of sick heroines. A book was a book, however, and
I never missed getting one.

Two entirely accidental circumstances prejudiced me against Sunday Schools. The rector of our church, a delicate man, had tremulous
hands, and laid them on our heads as we went out every Sunday. I
dreaded this. And then at Easter we were to form a procession, with
red, gold and white banners—something I loved; and Fanny was
the banner child in our class. But when the consignment of banners came, they were one short; and it was Fanny who had to walk
without a banner, our class merely melting into the ranks ahead. I
resented this injustice deeply.

Perhaps I was almost jealous of Sunday School as a rival to church;

22

for up to nine years old, I think church was the greatest element of beauty in my life.

In the summer before my ninth birthday Mamma took us three children to spend July and August with Aunt Fanny and Aunt Jessie in Manchester, Vermont. In that lovely valley, our aunts had a nice little brown cottage which they called Sans Souci. This valley of the Battenkill was the ancestral home of the Hawleys, including my doughty little grandfather, who, after settling and marrying in Troy, had regularly gone up to Manchester for the summers. We always loved to hear how Grandfather, piling his wife and five children aboard, used to drive his black horses (Vermont Morgans) the fifty miles from Troy to Manchester in two days; and how, because the return journey was down hill, "and because your grandfather always took such splendid care of his horses!" he was able to drive them home in one day.

We had a happy time in the little brown house with an ell until my sister Fanny became ill with some mysterious and alarming fever. In the end it involved her brain. She died there at Sans Souci in the middle of August, half way to her eleventh birthday.

Red-cheeked, spirited, graceful Fanny was the fourth of my mother's six children to die. The first babies had been twins and they had only lived a day. Little Jack had died of diphtheria before he was three years old. With all my mother's unbounded devotion and care— wise care, too, very much like the best modern care of children—she had been able to save only her two youngest thus far. We led a happy, calm, cheerful, healthy existence, with regular hours, long tranquil nights and bright days full of outdoor play, softly broken by a noon-day nap; our diet was just about what well-cared-for children have nowadays; and we inherited, one might almost say, nothing but health. In fact we were almost never ailing. Carl was never in bed a day until he had pneumonia at fourteen, and I never was until I was over twenty.

Fanny and Carl were both rather beautiful children. Both had the pleasant combination of dark eyes and fair hair, and both had glowing color. Fanny was the greatest runner and romper of us three.

My father preserved all his life, and I still preserve, a scrapbook of Fanny's little water-color pictures, such as all children like to make. He preserved in his beautiful printing a list of the words she had mispronounced in babyhood. My mother, out of her deep reserve and silence, only said, "I can never live through losing another child."

In September, when we went home to Minneapolis, Aunt Fanny and Aunt Jessie promised my father to come and spend part of the winter with us. They were all three vaguely anxious about my mother. But she continued her serene, practical life, and her children never saw her sitting still brooding, or wiping away a tear. Only once, when I was saying my prayers, she snatched me up and squeezed me tightly to her breast, rocking with me to and fro in her chair. She was the most undemonstrative member of an undemonstrative family; and this one wild, impassioned embrace filled me with long, silent wonder.

After my aunts came out, she was very seldom left alone for any length of time. Occasionally it would happen that she sat alone sewing in the house for an hour or two, while Carl and I played out of doors. After one such afternoon, when my aunts returned, Mamma said she had heard an unaccountable voice calling her by name. "It couldn't have been Sally or Carl," she said, "for they would have called 'M'ma,' not 'Sarah.' And if it had been little Fanny or Jack calling me from the other world," she added, as if it had been a natural supposition, "they would have called me 'M'ma,' too."

Such an experience, befalling our literal, unvisionary mother, impressed our father and aunts and deepened their nebulous anxiety. We children didn't hear of it until much later. If I had overheard anything about it, I shouldn't have paid it any conscious attention. Something else had begun at this time to trouble me. I began to be troubled by the strange coldness of my own heart. I couldn't feel that warm, intimate love for my mother which I found constantly referred to in the books and magazines I was beginning to read so much. And I tried to imagine how I should feel if Mamma fell down the cellar stairs and broke her neck. I could only imagine myself

24

MY MOTHER

MY FATHER

dumb, shocked and miserably shaken out of all my customary ways and doings. The knowledge of my own callousness became a long, secret, familiar, humiliating burden on my heart. If I had been intimate enough with my mother I could have told her about it and she could have taken it partly—not altogether—away. But I could never disclose it, even to Carl, who was six now, and very companionable, and to whom I told almost everything, whether he listened or not.

The emotion of tenderness was at this very time slowly dawning on me, in relation to Carl. The loss of Fanny, my incessant playmate, I had received in a sort of cloudy daze, at first of incredulity. Then slowly there grew up a shadowy feeling that from the beginning my lovely big sister must have been marked for death. All her merry, tranquil life, which I had known and shared, now became denaturalized, overhung as it were by a bluish light. Something ghostly took hold of her memory in my heart, and scared me of death. It was a superstitious feeling, much more full of fear and dread than of love and grief. I truly wonder how much of our general fear and suspicion of death partakes of this superstitiousness. Do we not regard death as something abnormal, invading our otherwise normal lives? until sooner or later, by deeper and more comforting experience, it comes so near us, enveloping a being we truly love better than ourselves, that our eyes are opened and we begin with unspeakable relief to see it as it is, a wonder and a mystery indeed, like birth, yet simply natural, and at moments even homelike. We then begin to surmise that like all other changes, death too must be an onward move.

Some natural loneliness I must have felt after Fanny died, but I cannot remember it. This must have been because I still had Carl, who was not only a companion and playmate, but also a smaller child than I and consequently one I must protect. And partly it must have been because we had a crowd of children in our neighborhood in Minneapolis. I was intoxicated by my first taste of such plentiful playmates. The Burton boys walked on the first stilts I'd ever seen. Rachel

Williams was the first child who ever invited us to supper. Edna Durgin across the street had a big, dazzling birthday party, a thing I'd never even imagined before. I learned with keen delight to play prisoners' base.

When Lent came on my mother often took Carl or me with her to weekday services of St. Paul's Church, where I was impressed by the blind organist and the beauty of the low, swelling Psalms we chanted on our knees.

"Out of the deep have I called unto thee, O Lord; Lord, hear my voice."

"I will lift up mine eyes unto the hills, from whence cometh my help."

Late in March Mamma caught a cold; in the language of those days, it turned into pneumonia. She was only sick a week. Dr. Fairbairn didn't think her very ill; but she became delirious and had convulsions. Early one morning, when the house was strange all over, Carl and I were taken in to see her. I remember her saying, dreamily,

"Who's your Mommie now?"

It was her last day of life.

My father received this ruin of his life in wonderful fashion. He, on whom home life and the companionship of wife and children never palled, not even for an hour, had now one overmastering desire—to make life safe for Carl and me. He asked Aunt Fanny and Aunt Jessie to take us back to Vermont with them. He wouldn't consider a housekeeper for us. In the seven or eight days of my mother's illness he had been changed from a man with a wife and two children into a solitary man, thenceforth to live in a boardinghouse.

My father, of all men! who never said once in his whole life to any child, "Run away, I'm busy," who spent the whole of his free daytime playing, or walking and talking with children, always making them deliciously yet serenely merry, telling them travels and yarns, fooling them in delightful burlesques, and droll, gentle practical jokes; chasing and scrambling them in glorious romps; talking with

26

love of the sea and ships, and sometimes briefly mentioning "Almighty God." In early Sunday mornings we got into bed with him; and when at last he rose, so tall, thin and delightfully homely, in his loose, flapping nightshirt, he used to say;

"Children, here's Venus rising from the sea-foam."

I can't, even at threescore, bear the realization that he felt he had to let us go, at six and nine years old, a thousand miles away from him to live! It was his way of saying, as Mamma had said, "I can't lose another!"

All Mamma's family, for four generations, had been buried in Troy. The journey from Minneapolis took two days and a night. We took a great, carefully packed lunchbox. I remember there were endless slices of cold tongue, which I never liked afterwards; and that when we got off the train on this and other long journeys the landscape moved for hours in front of my eyes.

The inscriptions my father and mother chose for headstones always contained a word of endearment. The one to Fanny said "dearly loved child," and the new one now to be raised over my mother's grave said "beloved wife."

Aunt Fanny and Aunt Jessie were homelike, familiar personalities to us. They had often taken care of us before. We now, many times, heard them say to other grown-ups,

"Yes, my sister's children . . . so glad to have them . . . but no care can be like a mother's."

I would like to dispute this. Remembering well the pure, tireless, passionate fidelity to her children of my fair, immaculate and lion-hearted mother, I would still say the change we experienced, in coming to other arms, was a change in temperaments and personalities, rather than a change in kind or degree of love. In other words, I am a believer in potential motherhood as a quality of the soul rather than of the body. In the case of children coming into the care of aunts or grandparents, there is thrown into this potential motherhood the added force of sisterly or parental tenderness and loyalty.

With every additional year I feel more deeply the desolation of my

27

father's journey back alone to Minneapolis that spring. He had however a comfortable fortune in establishing homelike relations with the Abraham family there. He lived with them for many years and maintained, as long as any of them lived, a close and pleasant friendship.

The only creature now left with him of our Laurel Avenue household was the black and tan terrier. This little dog became the object of intense affection to another man in the Abraham household; the twin brother of General Hancock. Mr. Hancock was a brilliant lawyer, who had formerly been engaged to Miss Mary Abraham. Because he could never leave whiskey alone, she would never marry him; but neither of them ever cared to marry anyone else. He always lived at her mother's house, and his old fiancée looked after his health and kept his accounts in order. As years went on, Mr. Hancock gradually lost his law practice, and his resources became very slender. Five or six Minneapolis men who were fond of him regularly maintained him in comfort and security; and this brilliant, attractive and rather helpless man, with no relatives near him, encountered nevertheless to the end of his life nothing but Franciscan regard and care. Such instances, sprinkling occasionally, as they do, the fragment of life observed by any one of us, seem to point the ideal way of caring for the ordinary infirmities of mankind. That we are moving in this direction is clear, I think, to anyone who has observed the course of public charity for fifty years, especially in the provisions for underprivileged children.

# VERMONT

Wide and shallow, in the cowslip marshes,
  Floods the freshet of the April snow;
Late drifts linger in the hemlock gorges,
  Through the brakes and mosses trickling slow
      Where the mayflower,
  Where the painted trillium, leaf and blow.

Foliaged deep, the cool midsummer maples
  Shade the porches of the long white street.
Trailing wide, Olympian elms lean over
  Tiny churches where the highroads meet.
      Fields of fireflies
  Wheel all night like stars among the wheat.

Blaze the mountains in the windless autumn;
  Frost-clear, blue-nooned, apple-ripening days.
Faintly fragrant in the farther valleys,
  Smoke of many bonfires swells the haze.
      Fair-bound cattle
  Plod with lowing up the meadowy ways.

Roaring snows, down-sweeping from the uplands,
  Bury the still valleys, drift them deep.
Low along the mountains, lake-blue shadows,
  Sea-blue shadows in the snowdrifts sleep.
      High above them
  Blinding crystal is the sunlit steep.
        *—Century Magazine*

# 2

WE'D NEVER KNOWN anything of community life until we went to Vermont. On the farm at Fairfields, and in our corner of Minneapolis, we children had no idea of the human surroundings that framed our family life. In Manchester we soon felt their warmth and expansion. Without naming or recognizing community existence, we liked it even to enchantment. The great community figures, standing up out of the village like the saints and angels on Milan Cathedral—Mrs. Miner, Dr. Wickham, Mr. Swift with his noble, gaunt Puritan face—they were our daily familiars, part of the pattern we formed. I suppose that's why our Manchester childhood years were laid on our memories in such bright, indelible colors.

Manchester seemed to Carl and me exactly right; first in the matter of children. Not so exciting as Minneapolis, where the neighborhood was so filled with children that the afternoons were really rather wild with play. (Maybe we had been overstimulated by it; Fanny, perhaps?) But not like Fairfields, either, where we hardly ever had another child to play with. Here on North Main Street, which was called Pill Alley because both the doctors lived there, we had the big, jolly Hemenway family catacorner to us. Bertha Trull, whose father has been our doctor for upwards of half a century, lived on one side of us, and Walter Hard (the poet), on the other; and there were three more children next door but one. Mabel Cone, the deacon's gypsy daughter, came down from "the village," and in summer little Molly Prentice from Chicago fled the hotel every summer day to come and play with us and our neighbors.

Molly Prentice was a two-generation friend.—How much is there,

(I've often thought) in this prevalent idea (or superstition) that heredity predestines us before we are born to all that life can ever mean for us? that all which we call personality is the pure consequence of the matings and other doings of our forefathers, and like a mosaic derives in fragments from this great-great-grandmother and that great-great-grandfather whose names are lost in unread genealogies?

At all events, we inherited our friendship with five-year-old Molly. Her mother and our Aunt Fanny were girlhood friends; and Molly's three glamorous older brothers, who signified all young manhood to me, were objects to Aunt Fanny of pride and fondness as if they had been her own nephews.

And of all the children running, in their starched Victorian clothes, over the tiny lawns of "Pill Alley," that littlest girl, so delicate but so courageous, who never cried when she tumbled out of an apple tree, or was scratched by one of Bertha Trull's kittens, was to become, despite early marriage and long absence, the most deeply entrenched with me in homelike tenderness before threescore.

Perhaps there's something in heredity.

And then it gradually dawned on me, in the course of a year or two, that this Vermont, where we had come to live, was the very lap of beauty. Disappointed as I had been the previous summer by the mountains, which hadn't been pointed enough, I now found their long velvet roll coming over me as far more lovely and wonderful. And to see the upper reaches of Mount Equinox in winter colored rose-pink by the sunlight on the snow aroused my sense of glory to shouting pitch.

More than anything else, Carl and I received from Manchester a silently warm welcome which we appropriated as unconsciously as it was given. Coming to Manchester was just coming home where our forbears the Hawleys and Purdys had lived for three and four generations.

There were other Hawleys in Manchester, favorite cousins to us all, though no children among them. Cousin Charlie was a slim, quiet

32

MANCHESTER VILLAGE STREET

COUSIN ELLEN

young man, with gentle ways and a softly chuckling sense of humor. Exactly why every child would always tag and follow him everywhere he went, he himself never knew; he had nothing eatable or interesting in his pockets, and he sat quietly in a chair instead of rushing about and romping with us, as our Minneapolis young men had done. He is now an elderly man, and children still swarm about him, and he still does nothing to attract them. I remember following him out to the woodshed whenever he went to get a stick of wood. Something about him always quietly beckoned us to come along and stay around.

I became also very much attached, by gradual degrees, to Cousin Charlie's father's sister, elderly Cousin Ellen. It might have been in the beginning on account of her rich row of bound *St. Nicholases,* but in the end I found her more interesting than they were. Cousin Ellen had had a love affair in her youth, which I now find very touching; her lover had seemed effeminate to her domineering old father, because instead of being a substantial young farmer, he'd only been a school-teacher; and so it was all scoffed and interfered away. The young man married somebody else; but on his early deathbed, he sent urgently for Cousin Ellen, and she went—father or no father, I hope. What they said to each other had never been revealed to a living soul. In my childhood and youth, Cousin Ellen was a complete, satisfying and noble old maid. She lived all alone, in a big house, between Mrs. Miner and "Lady" Wickham, who also lived all alone in big houses; and Cousin Ellen spent but sparingly of her income on her own comforts and conveniences—nothing on "pleasure"!—so that she could give substantial help to the education of southern Negroes, and to missions and charities at home and abroad; about all of which she informed herself intelligently, and kept in touch with her beneficiaries. She had been a studious girl, but her parents had had little sympathy with her aspirations; instead, therefore, of going to college, she had taken seal after seal in the Chautauqua home-study courses, and had traveled about Europe after her loyal long ministrations to these parents were ended.

33

Her spacious, plain, Quakerish, comfortable house was my frequent resort. Rocking on the old settle back of the stove in her livingroom, with her big dictionary in its wire stand at my elbow, I used to argue with her in favor of Charles the First and against Parliament and Cromwell. She had that irresistible charm for young people, that she took them seriously, and with the simple candor of her nature, gave them at all times of her best. It was a best all solid sincerity and faithful idealism, a jeweled gift indeed to a sentimental schoolgirl.

The Augustus Purdys, "our Purdys," who lived on a fabulously lovely old farm, now "abandoned," were fairy folks; for we only saw them once in a while, and besides, Cornelia, the one who was still a child, actually knew how to curtsey—a thing that made her seem to me a creature of pure fable.

Manchester being exactly right, and being a truly Vermontish Congregational town, our ancestral Episcopalianism would have stood up but a short time against the generous hospitalities of the Congregational Church, and the fact that all the other children belonged to it. But round the corner, on Seminary Avenue, was our little summer St. John's, open for morning and evening services for about ten Sundays in the height of the summer, when the hotel was crowded and overflowing prosperity into all the presentable cottages in "the Street" that had a spare room to rent. And these summer services were lovely, in the familiar lovely language of the Prayer Book and in the summer air and light, especially in the late afternoons. Grace and sweetness were added by the fresh and pretty summer dresses of the Equinox House ladies who decorated the pews, and their plumed leghorn hats. Carl and I also wore Sunday best, and I carried a Japanese parasol. One Sunday I sat on the delicate stalk of this parasol and snapped it in two. Thinking such a calamity would bring the service to an end, I stood up and called out shrilly,

"I've broken my parasol!"

When Aunt Fanny sh-sh'd at me, and pulled my skirts to make me sit down, I only thought she hadn't realized, and reiterated, louder than ever;

34

"But I've broken my parasol!"

My aunts were devoted to St. John's, and took us to every service that was ever held there; but from September to January (when we went away) and from April (when we came back) to July, we all went to the Congregational Church every Sunday. And knowing the children and grown-ups there so much better than we knew the brief and fluctuating congregation at St. John's, I grew up with the warmest, most homelike feeling for that huge, not especially attractive building that I've ever felt for any church whatever.

I don't know what Mrs. Miner would have done if we had drifted into being Congregationalists. Mrs. Miner was such a pillar of St. John's that she stood up in the village as high as Trajan's column. She was approaching seventy when we went to live with Aunt Fanny and Aunt Jessie—a spirited, handsome, witty, resolute, impoverished and delightfully generous "adopted grandmother," as she once called herself, to us. There was a quarter of century yet to come of her long, rich life. A gleam and sparkle went out of the village when she died. She came of pure New England stock, but nobody but a New Englander would have recognized her as such. Her wit was swift and audacious, not slow and understating, and she treated the proprieties like a family of kittens she was fond of.

Christmas apparently was a very different thing to Vermonters from what it had always been to us. It seemed to be secondary in importance to Thanksgiving! This was one of the mysteries of life. No services were held on Christmas Day in the Congregational Church, nor were there many family reunions. Our playmates got but casual little reminders for Christmas; a box of writing paper, perhaps, and a Christmas card. How unspeakably "homely" and meaningless were the Christmas cards of those days! A pictured napkin cornerwise, with a winter scene in one corner, and a moss rosebud such as never was on sea or land in the other, the whole frosted over as if with Epsom salts! But nothing could diminish Christmas to us little Episcopalians. We had three or four presents apiece! *Chatterboxes,* jackstones, and a doll's brittania teaset, besides the pleasant jokes like a beet and onion in our stockings, along with the expected orange and cornucopia, and filling toe and heel, a jews-harp, and doll's brush and comb, and a tiny purse with a nickel in it. According to our allowances of twenty cents a month, this was a week's income. Far beyond all this was the widespreading glow of Christmas in the heart. I remember being waked up in the night to see "the star of Bethlehem," (Venus, I think), and on Christmas Eves looking out over the radiant snow in the moonlight, or even when we had a thaw, and it was all warm and rainy, I remember great feelings, not of stockings, nor even of the child at Bethlehem, yet somehow Christmasly deep, understanding, and full of mysterious bliss.

A great Vermont festival for the children was Mayday. Nobody in Manchester hangs Maybaskets any more, these many years. We began to plan for it in the middle of April, buying pink and blue tissue paper at Mr. Coy's store, and going to the woods for birchbark. Aunt Fanny helped us make our baskets; she was very inventive and color-ful. The last great expedition to the woods was to get the flowers. Hepaticas were the right filling for Maybaskets. The right baskets were very tiny and only held a dozen hepaticas. Spring beauties and Dutchman's breeches or squirrelcorn were small enough to be al-lowable; and a violet, white, blue or yellow, was a great find. No-body ever found a white or painted trillium in the "Seminary" or "Sugar" woods which we frequented; as for the crimson trillium, (wake-robin) coarsely called "stinking Benjamin," it was too big, besides its shocking odor, for a Maybasket. Foam-flower or mitrewort would do. "Cowslips," which we had called marsh-marigolds in the west, were sometimes out in time, but far too big and clumsy for the fairy Maybaskets.

The evening of Mayday, when we hung them by ribbons or gold thread on each other's front doors, rang the bell wildly and ran away to hide behind a tree and watch them taken into the house was more of a Valentine's Day than the February one. Girls hung them to boys, and boys to girls, and sometimes young men to young women,

36

and vice versa. But we also hung them to a whole family of boys and girls at once, like the Hemenways, or to an old lady friend like Mrs. Miner, or a childless neighbor like Mrs. Harry Bennett, who gave us cookies.

May was a rich festival month, for Decoration Day was erected into great solemnity for the whole village by our neighbor Mrs. Baldwin. She gathered everybody at her house beforehand to wind wreaths. If Mrs. Miner was a monument of the Episcopal Church, Mrs. Baldwin was a whole Roman Forum of patriotism. Both her husbands had been soldiers of the Civil War, and she usually placed a vacant chair, draped with flag and flowers, in the church vestibule, or on the stage at Music Hall.

For days before the wreath-winding day, children brought their squeezed, hot, wilting little bouquets to her house.

"Mith Baldwin, I've brought you thum honeythuckle."

"I've brought you some daisies."

"I've brought you some lilacs."

Lilacs were the great standby; they were always on their last legs, however, by the end of May, beginning to be brown and dry; and they were always picked at just the blossoms, never on a branch; and so they always drooped and wilted inconsolably, hanging limp from the sides of the wreaths long before they were carried by the school children all in white dresses and best suits down the long street behind the G. A. R., Ladies' Aid and Sons of Veterans, held in hot young hands in the noonday sun on the Skinner lot at the cemetery (while the "Gettysburg Address" was read by the veterans' commander), and laid, quite dead and gone, on the soldiers' graves at the order

"Break ranks and decorate the graves!"

I sometimes took my dolls for a treat to walk in Mrs. Baldwin's crowded flower garden. It was only about fifty feet long, from the red, the white and the lemon-fragrant yellow rose trees squeezed in at the north end, to the April daffodils on the outermost edge of the south end, but it also overflowed a few feet around the corner of the

37

house to the curious money plant, hen-and-chickens, Adam-and-Eve-in-a-carriage, and Mrs. Baldwin's great triumph, water lilies in a washtub by the woodshed door.

Compared with Decoration Day, Fourth of July was nothing—as a day. Our aunts only let us have tame torpedoes, and the neighboring children weren't allowed much more. None of the grown-ups on our street would countenance our firing off cannon crackers under tin pails which were shot into the air screwed up into a cocked hat. None of the children we knew ever lost an eye or finger on the Fourth. But in the evening there were fireworks opposite the Equinox House, and the long piazzas of the Equinox, with their hospitable steps extending the whole frontage, were always covered with spectators from all three villages and many miles around. All the children in the township were there. Subscriptions were open for the expense beforehand, and a number of modest contributions were made by citizens. But whether or not these amounted to much, Mr. Franklin Orvis, the founder and proprietor of the Equinox, *would* have the fireworks. He was by nature a sociable, authoritarian old English squire. The evening was a fearful ordeal to his wife. Mrs. Orvis (a Massachusetts heiress, and a very able consort indeed) never ceased for one moment of that evening to tremble lest the kerosene lamps in the long, low-ceiled parlors within be exploded by some stray fireworks shooting through the windows, and the whole hotel go up in a bonfire. Did this fact of her annual evening of terror, a fact well known and respectfully mentioned in every group, add a keener edge to the general pleasure?

All the Manchester children stood in more awe of Mrs. Orvis than of anybody else in town. When Carl and I occasionally supped at the Equinox with our playmates Mark Willing, the Stokes boys or Molly Prentice, and Mrs. Orvis, in her plain brown dress, came sweeping through the parlors, all unseemly giggles and horseplay were hushed as before the brow of Jove. Not that she ever, that I can remember, reproved us. She was simply one of those human beings endowed with natural majesty.

38

All the more Carl, Mark, Molly and I were impressed by the dare-devil conduct we once witnessed in the Equinox parlor. Sitting there one evening on our good behavior, waiting for the diningroom door to open for supper, we saw a stoutish man, one of the guests, seat himself in a small gilt chair, which immediately gave way under him. We were shocked, and from our hearts we pitied him; momentarily we expected Mrs. Orvis to appear. The wretched man however coolly picked up the broken chair and threw it in the woodbox beside the Franklin stove. We experienced a delicious thrill, like modern children, I suppose, at a crime movie.

Mr. Franklin Orvis had a brother, a diminutive being, a fiery Democrat, highly intelligent and very well informed—every half-inch a man. The verbal battles of the two made village history. Orvis Cottage, where Mr. Charles Orvis lived, was only a few doors north of the Equinox, and on all high and holidays, when the great flag was hung across the street between the Equinox office and the court-house, Mr. Charles Orvis hung one of equal size across the street between the Orvis Cottage and the engine house. In election years, the Equinox flag bore the names of the Republican nominees in large print across the bottom. The Orvis Cottage flag in like manner bore the names of the Democratic nominees.

In Cleveland's terms Mr. Charles Orvis was the postmaster; and the children of the town, indeed the grown-ups too, were apt to tip-toe when they entered the postoffice. In winter we very carefully and earnestly shut the door. I once heard Mr. Orvis, standing five feet erect in his tiny shoes, tell big John Wild that if he left that door open again, he would find himself flat on his back in the middle of the street.

It was this dragon postmaster who qualified, to my mind at least, as the most gallant lover in Manchester. It was said that for all his irascible nature, he had never said one cross word to his serene, gentle old wife. He survived her about ten years; and on every Sunday after-noon in spring, summer and fall, we saw him pass our house going down to the cemetery with flowers for her grave.

When Harrison was elected, Carl and I walked in the torchlight parade, and felt that singular feeling, group glory over something which has nothing glorious whatever about it. I really don't think there was anybody in the parade who thought Harrison was a finer man, or would do anything more for man, woman and child than Cleveland had done. No, it was a conscious piece of foolishness on the part of all of us; and yet it was very exciting, and we all got up our blood about it. But though I gloried in having been in the parade I don't remember ever particularly wanting to join in anything else quite so meaningless as that.

In the village street lived, as I remember, only two Democrats; Mr. Moffat of the Munson House was the other. When Papa came to see us, there were three. But Papa had too little time to spare from playing with us to talk politics in J. N. Hard's drug store, or Cone and Burton's general store, or the postoffice. He came at Christmas, and sometimes also in summer. Before he came, he would say in his letters, "Children, we will be soon be having high jinks." Of the delightful presents he brought us, he would sometimes write, "I will bring Carl and Sally their presents in a pillbox." We had so modern and free an understanding with this endearing man, that I once shouted out to him when he was drawing me on my sled and stopped too suddenly, so that I got an avalanche of snow up my sleeve,

"Here! What are you doing, you big galoot?"

He showed a little surprise, but soon began to chuckle, and pulled me along as recklessly as ever.

We wrote to him every Sunday, and one aunt or the other put in a letter. Carl filled a quarter of a sheet with laconic news, and usually concluded "I am going to stop now and eat an apple." His letters must have been a good deal better reading than mine. I was far too fond of a display of words to remember that brevity, etc. I fear my letters were priggish to a high degree.

The purgatory of the year was going to New York for three months —New Year's to April. Before they took us to bring up, our aunts had

OUR FAMILY AT SANS SOUCI ABOUT 1887

gone there for six months. They liked New York—an extraordinary fact. We lived in a pleasant boarding-house, and Carl and I went quite often by the horse-cars to spend a day with Henry and Walter Stokes in Fifty-Eighth Street.

Cousin Eliza, Cousin Lucy and Cousin Annie Audubon, grandchildren of the naturalist, and much beloved by my aunts, who had visited back and forth with them in girlhood days, were still living in the neighborhood of Audubon Park, and we children always lunched with them once or twice in New York. I remember the enormous oranges they always had, and in general the very good food; but they were far from rich, and if they'd ever had a momentary bonanza, their unbounded kindness to every poor person and friendless cat would have dispensed the whole of it, leaving them still wearing last year's coats and hats.

Their father was Victor, the younger son of John James Audubon. Their mother was Grandmamma's cousin, Georgianna Mallory. She was a second wife; and Audubon's elder son, John, also married twice; but the children of both families ran overwhelmingly to girls. I knew of only two grandsons; but of the granddaughters there were Hattie, Maria, Florence, Rosa, Eliza, Delia, Lucy and Annie whom I knew—perhaps more. Every one of them was clever, interesting and attractive; only a few were handsome. No two of them were alike, except that every one of them had a peculiar sort of Audubon highmindedness, or magnanimity, and an unusual warmth of feeling. About their friends they were never judicial, analytical or inclined to balance judgment, but delightfully warm, credulous, openhanded and uncalculating.

Cousin Eliza, (M. E. Audubon) had for a long time a girls' school in One-Hundred-and-Fifty-Second Street—where we had those big oranges. She was called by the girls, who were largely the daughters of old friends and neighbors of Audubon Park days, "Miss 'Liza." She was an absorbed and enjoying reader, the fastest one I ever saw. Of no one else could I have believed that the pages were really read, which I saw turned over so fast. Her culture was old-fashioned, per-

41

haps, but it was thorough, and she wore it in the mellow, human Audubon fashion.

Of all the Audubons I felt closest to Cousin Eliza. I loved her and could have confided everything in my life to her. When in early middle age I became a pacifist, she first of all my friends sympathized and fraternized with me; and when she died, her sister Mrs. Tyler gave me for this reason a brooch of Florentine mosaic which had belonged to her, with a white dove inlaid in black marble, and the word "Pax."

Cousin Delia, the beautiful sister, it was who married Mr. Frank Tyler of New Haven, a scholar and man of affairs. He combined dignity and geniality in a pleasant fashion. Once when we were staying with them, Mr. Tyler told us with relish how Theodore Roosevelt, then President, had greeted him in a recent encounter. It was shortly after that famous invitation to Booker Washington to lunch at the White House; and it so happened that the Tylers had also entertained Dr. Washington that season. The President hastened across the room to shake hands with Mr. Tyler, exclaiming "Hail, fellow miscreant!"

Cousin Annie, the youngest of the Audubons, and a great friend of Aunt Jessie's, was the most piquant creature I ever saw. She was small, delicate, very dark and plain-looking, intense and fiery of nature, pleasure-loving, hard-working, witty and sharp, loving and fond. She taught huge classes in the public schools of New York for thirty years, and at last received her pension—half pay for life—only to fall sick after a single summer, endure repeated pain and die within the year.

All the middle-aged, highly educated and hard-working Audubons had a bevy of much younger men always gathering at their house, and spent the gayest, liveliest evenings of any people I knew. They could always cast care aside after dinner. Cousin Annie was the greatest favorite with all these good-looking young fellows. When they went off to the antipodes, they always corresponded with her at a lively rate.

The large canvas painted by Audubon, of dogs and pheasants, which now hangs on a stairway of the American Museum of Natural History, hung in my childhood in the diningroom at Cousin Eliza's boarding school.

Papa, who took a month's holiday in winter, came down after our Vermont Christmas to stay awhile with us in New York. He loved museums and galleries, and hated concerts, and this was quite congenial to us. I remember the small beginnings of the American Museum of Natural History very well, as Dr. Chapman describes them in his *Autobiography.* The gangling ungainly building was almost lost in its many-acred lot, which we crossed from the Elevated Station at Eighty-First Street. I can never remember the Museum of those days without remembering my father's great anticipation of seeing the leaf insect, and his satisfied delight in it and the walking stick. He had read of them in the Minneapolis papers. Many years later, my Scotch cousin Frances Tancred, coming on a flying visit to this country and having but two days in New York, insisted on seeing the habitat scene of timber wolves in the Museum, of which she had heard in Australia.

Papa would also take us to the ill-smelling menagerie in Central Park, where bears and lions drearily dragged themselves up and down forever before their prison bars. On the way home he would say "Children, how about a little ice cream?" I was entranced and Carl was distressed with mortification when Papa would take off his hat to some sober, plodding old lady in the street, and say respectfully;

"That's the widow of my deceased partner."

"Sh, Sh, P'pa, people can hear you!" Carl would entreat, in great anxiety.

We all five generally paid a visit to our four cousins, the James Hawley girls, on our way to New York. They lived in Albany, and later in Kinderhook. Papa often instructed the girls to ask their teachers some such question as why they didn't use *Cleghorn's Geography,* or what the "German word umbergrunt" meant. Confidingly

43

they went to school and puzzled the teachers with umbergrunt, and *Cleghorn's Geography,* saying that their uncle had written it, and that it was better than any other. These visits to the James Hawleys gave me my dazzling notions of what fun a big family would be. There were enough of us to dance the lancers! Aunt Annie, Uncle James's wife, often lame with sciatica, and awake half the night with fiendish pain, was always delightfully sociable and played the piano well. She played for us to dance, and I often thought "Oh, if there'd only been eleven children in our family, like Uncle George's in Scotland!"

Julia, Anna, Kate and Jessie (with their mother, of course) paid us a return visit in Manchester in June. Into Sans Souci, which had only four bedrooms, were tucked the whole eleven of us, (counting our two maids). I can't figure out how it was done. Two or three sofas were brought into play, and none of the livingrooms were ever invaded by a sleeper.

One element in the disposition of both our aunts was of exceptional merit in our eyes—they both loved company. Aunt Fanny especially delighted in it. Aunt Jessie's young men occasionally stayed to supper; Cousin Ellen often did; we could always have Molly or Mark; and Carl's birthday was always a party day for all the children we knew; but Aunt Fanny, besides, planned and executed great card parties and supper parties. Two of these were annual events; a big supper party for summer people, like the Skinners, Willings, and Cramers, the Stokeses, Ishams, and Prentices; and a big supper party for the home people, at which the noble old Roman Senator head of Dr. Wickham always rose above the scalloped oysters—it was an October party—and said a noble old Congregational grace.

Grace was nothing new to us—only the impressive length of Dr. Wickham's. Carl or I usually said grace for our family; "For what we are about to receive, the Lord make us truly thankful." Uncle James (a traveling man who in his heart was always a minister) said "Lord, bless this food to our use, and us to thy service."

Carl or I also read one of the Psalms for the day and one of the "Family Morning Prayers" every morning. Though we did it quite naturally, it always remained a dignified duty. Though I knew every one of the "Morning Prayers" by heart, and could have gabbled off one after the other at any hour of the day or night, yet I always read them off the page, never trusting my memory for fear I might deface the occasion by stumbling or hesitating.

In the households of our Scotch and English uncles and cousins, as we found many years later, when Aunt Jessie and I went there, the maids always came in for morning and evening prayers. At the striking of a bell, at Cousin Charlie Dalton's house in London, two or three maids irrupted into the room in military formation, whirled in perfect unison and fell simultaneously on their knees. Cousin Charlie at the same moment ceased his conversation in the middle of a sentence, and began instantly to read the prayers.

Our maids never joined in our prayers. They were everything but Episcopalians. Most of them were Roman Catholics. They wouldn't have liked to be mixed up in Protestant prayers. Or so we assumed. Perhaps we would have had a different opinion if we had invited them, and especially if we had invited them to take charge of the prayers once in a while and use their own variety.

Our two maids were a cook and a waitress, and their pay was the prevailing rate of two dollars a week. It seems to me that our cook was always getting married. This did happen successively, I believe, in the case of three young French girls, sisters, who married swiftly from the top down. The eldest of them invited me (I suppose Carl too) with a regular printed invitation to her wedding. It was the first wedding I was ever invited to, and so intense and joyful was the thrill of receiving the invitation that I scarcely felt disappointed at not being able to go. Edith's inviting me—and in this gratifying formal fashion, through the mail—was part of that loving kindness with which everybody in our ancestral home town always treated Carl and me. But then, perhaps children in general were treated so. It seems to me still, for all the neglect and exploitation of children which I have seen or heard of, in all the sore spots of our economic system, that one of the greatest and commonest pleasures and self-

45

indulgences human beings give themselves is being sweet to children.

I couldn't go to the wedding, because, being a Roman Catholic one, it was of course a church wedding, and there wasn't in those days any Roman Catholic Church in Manchester. The nearest one was in East Dorset—a long journey distant—six miles! We had no horse; my aunts' famous old Billy, who had seemed immortal, had been struck by lightning, and their phaeton sold. No train to East Dorset went at a convenient hour. But it was not long afterward that I was invited to another wedding with equal ceremony, and this one was in the Congregational Church. It was our young neighbor Miss Libbie Bennett, with the rich and lovely singing voice, who was getting married and going to live in Massachusetts. I graced her wedding with my presence.

By the time Edith's daughter was married, we had a Roman Catholic Church in Manchester. Anna was married with a High Mass, and I was there and at the reception. I felt almost as old then as I did last year when I went to Anna's daughter's nuptial Mass.

Carl and I never went to grammar school, though it was just across the way from us. Aunt Fanny and Aunt Jessie taught us, just as Mamma had done. We had lessons every morning; the afternoons were free for play; and in the evenings also we never studied, but read *St. Nicholas* and *Harper's Young People,* and played checkers, beggar-my-neighbor, or Paul Davee, going to bed at half-past seven. I managed, with unconscious adroitness, to avoid learning anything about geography; so much so, that when I entered Burr and Burton Seminary, I couldn't find Spain on a big wall-map of Europe. Aunt Fanny and Aunt Jessie both said *they* had always liked to draw maps— Oh, it was great fun!—all children liked map-making! Carl may have responded favorably to these allurements, though he was as adamant as I was about being told that beets were delicious. I not only avoided learning geography, but also managed to keep well behind in arithmetic.

Now that I am a teacher myself, I can look at the arithmetic ques-

46

tion behind and before. I remember perfectly my own opinions, which were drawn from experience with it. In the beginning, when Grandmamma had gently and as it were subconsciously taught me to read, she had also given me gentle "sums" and *I enjoyed the sums*. But very soon I had reason for beginning to dislike arithmetic. At first I was surprised; I said to myself, "Why, I do, too, like arithmetic! I always have! From the very beginning, I've liked it! What *is* the matter? I don't see what I'm so stirred up about—for goodness' sake —why, I believe I'm going to cry!" And then it dawned upon me, with a sense of unbearable irritation, what was the matter. "Devil take the stuff," I felt, "just as soon as I get so I can *do* the sums, and *enjoy* 'em, this hellish book pushes me along to a new kind, that I can't do, and hate! Can't it ever let me alone a minute, and give me a little peace?"

Yes, it was exactly like Sisyphus, in the odd little book full of wrinkly woodcuts, *Keightley's Mythology,* which I also had lessons in. It was just like him, or Tantalus. Push, push, toward the goal; immediately it was snatched away; you were never allowed to enjoy your powers, but were always being hustled along.

However, the printed page could do no wrong, even when you knew it did. It never occurred to me to find fault with it openly.

It seems to me that Dr. Montessori was in nothing quite so wise as in recognizing this deep desire, on the part of human brains, to practice until weary the new art or skill, before having to drop it for another. If we could but relinquish voluntarily the new thing when it had been realized thoroughly, and its enjoyment fully explored, and not before, we should truly "set our own pace," and though learning slower, we should never stop learning.

I was a slow child; not slow in learning to read or write, not in memorizing poetry, not in realizing human rights and wrongs; but slow, very slow in taking on pure knowledge, in savoring purely informational joys, in finding out, or even remembering, classifications. Separating things into classes always obscurely vexed me; bringing them together in some unexpected category always tickled and contented me. If it's true that each one of us has some ruling passion at the core of his being, this inclusiveness is mine.

The worst fault in the grades, I think, is that they don't yet permit young children to "major." It seems to me that the schools will only become children's true culture clubs when, besides letting in, as they are now doing so fast, all possible arts and crafts, projects and expeditions, and providing, as they do, for the social and achievement satisfactions so necessary to spiritual health, there shall also be sliding scales in every school in the land for children's progress. Not necessarily (for any one child) along the whole front at once, but scales allowing him to be fast in one subject and slow in another—always *slow enough to enjoy his study of it!* This surely is the criterion for all study—that the pupil find satisfaction in it for its own sake. He never begins to be educated in any field until his pleasure in it begins —or so I say!

I often hear educators say "Arithmetic is pushed at the children far too fast." "The multiplication table, which it's so hard to learn at eight or nine, could be mastered with ease in a day or two at a little older." "The wonder and thrill of the world of number is all lost under a load of drill for business proficiency."

In later years, while I, though a woman of forty, was nevertheless a young teacher, there was a brilliant and philosophic youth, winner of the highest prize for mathematics at a great University, who came to our school to teach mathematics. He was so full of the meaning and beauty of number as a means of approaching the universe, that he was able—all inexperienced as he was in the art of teaching—to captivate the older students and hold them spellbound in his classes. But he had left so far behind the number-lore of little children, that he gave the youngsters nothing but the ordinary lessons in the ordinary way; and they suffered (both the quick and the slow among them) the ordinary fate of children studying arithmetic.

"If," so I thought, "Joe could but let his light shine into such matters as the places of numbers; and the way the multiplication tables fold into each other, the twos into the fours into the eights, and the

48

threes into the nines on the one hand, and the sixes and twelves on the other, he would get the same response."

For myself, I remember with pity that when at about twenty I began to read a little philosophy, the deep significance of number was so thoroughly overlaid by ideas of its business uses and its value as a servant of physics, chemistry and astronomy, that I was completely puzzled by finding great philosophers referring to it and using it as a touchstone for their theories! I could conceive of no connection between number and philosophy, and considered the notions of these philosophers as pure personal eccentricity.

There was to come a time, late in my own life, when number, so early obscured, arose like a great luminary over human life. And this was not resultant upon any belated improvement in my mathematical knowledge, of which I still have less than the average graduate from the eighth grade. It was conceptions of space, unfolding one out of another, and leading the mind so far that consciousness itself is expanded and can view the deepest problems of life from outside its ordinary limits.

Since this has taken place in my conceptions of number, I can now, as I near sixty, fully appreciate a remark a young divinity student made to me when I was fourteen or fifteen.

"Not studying geometry?" he'd inquired.

"No—for I hate mathematics, and at our school, if you study Greek, you can get out of geometry."

"Well, if you had a teacher who'd show you the philosophic side of geometry," the young man replied, "you'd love it."

I remembered his remark solely from its queerness, and for a fillip to my vanity which I derived from it. And I remember his face and the odd shape of his nose only by virtue of this remark.

If I lagged in arithmetic and geography, I took readily to United States and English History. Aunt Fanny had us learn Peter Parley and Dickens' *Child's History of England* by heart. Parley I've forgotten, but I remember Dickens pretty well, especially the eulogy of Joan of Arc,

"They threw her ashes in the river Seine, but they will rise against her murderers at the last day."

History has long seemed to me the queen of studies. A recent progressive educator has proposed, as the first item in a humanized curriculum, the study of "Human Relations." History, humanly taught, might be almost purely that. I once wrote an article which *The Century Magazine* printed on the possibilities I saw for teaching history backward, and in relation to children's own Utopian dreams, as these expanded from year to year. I also see great possibilities for hitching history to children's natural liking for drawing and painting, by means of scrolls of historical scenes, made by the pupils, of course, which would hang round the schoolroom walls and insensibly familiarize the children with types of cultures and the lapse of time. Dr. Van Loon is quoted as saying, "What children read, they forget, but what they draw and paint, they remember."

If we must continue to use so much of reading in all forms of study, at least one book should be corrected by another, and no one textbook be allowed, even with youngsters under Junior High School, to have it all its own way with their young impressions. An old Quaker teacher of wide experience once said to me that he thought children ought to read rapidly, as rapidly as they would read any other book, a number of histories of the same country by different authors; adding with courageous faith, *"and let stick what will."*

Aunt Fanny gave us no instruction in English grammar, but made us learn a few French verbs, and unconsciously a conception of the structure of language dawned on us. Her favorite book was an insufferable little volume with some such name as *The Catechism of Common Things*. Here we learned how potash is made, the ingredients of glass, etc. It told all the processes of iron and steel. I could memorize the answers without any trouble, but I never had any lifegiving sense of their meaning. I never had any itch to make glass, potash or pig-iron in the orchard. Like the lists of products in those worst of all textbooks, old-fashioned geographies, this little book used only the passive voice, as if in furnaces and factories and fields, the hot and tired workers were invisible, or indecent and impossible to mention.

"Potash is made by," etc., etc.; "It is then heated, it is then cooled." If for one instant the human effort in all these processes had been brought into the light, with those sharp sensations and that courage and that fate inseparable from human effort—if in talking of coal, some hint had been given of the danger and sang-froid of the miners, their reckless rescues of each other from collapsed galleries, or the pitiable lives of donkeys, ponies and canaries in mines, I should have taken every word of these accounts red-hot into the marrow of my bones.

Nothing in literature seems to me more pernicious than the smooth ignoring of man's (and beast's) sweat, pain and danger, in these namby-pamby accounts still given of industry. Children are certainly led by them

> "—to turn an easy wheel
> That sets sharp racks at work."

It was Aunt Jessie who gave us our Sunday lessons. We had to learn the Collect and a hymn every Sunday. We chose our hymns ourselves, and this Sunday duty was a pure pleasure to me—far more so than if a hymn had been assigned, no matter how lovely. I took no interest in finding short ones, but looked out what I thought the most sounding, the most poignant and the most dramatic.

We gained much insight into pure religion and undefiled, however, from Aunt Jessie's warm, tender kindness to animals. She was the best champion they had in Manchester, befriending all sorts and conditions of them, "though it were to her own hindrance." To be sure, she was very silly about our little terrior, Gem. We were all very fond of this irascible little barker, whose tan was turning white, and who was reaching the patriarchal age of sixteen years.

When I was thirteen, I made my first theological discard—hell. It long had been an indigestible thought to me. One night—it was while we were in New York—I was lying awake, feeling hot and unhappy about it. With heavenly sweetness and coolness came into my heart the sudden realization that it couldn't possibly be true. As long as some living beings were in pain, everybody else would be too, even with a thousand golden sidewalks. No, it was obviously a lie, and there was no occasion whatever for anybody to believe in it. What a refreshing sleep I had that night! I never gave hell another moment's consideration. With joy I told Aunt Fanny and Aunt Jessie that I didn't believe in it. They smiled, nodded and said nothing either pro or con.

That same year I began to read *In Memoriam*. "What do you think!" I said to my aunts, "Tennyson doesn't believe in hell, either! Oho, I'm not the only one!"

Carl was very different from me. He didn't talk about such things as hell, and what he believed in, though he did his own deep thinking, and developed an enduring philosophy. He had a great supply of reserve, judgment and balance. From an early age his opinion was respected, partly because he didn't volunteer it very often, and never jumped with it down people's throats, or dwelt and harped upon it. Having said a thing once, he could be silent. He inherited our father's humor, though not all its inventiveness, and he went Papa several points better as a mimic. He developed early the art of listening, and was very retentive and observing, especially of any humorous tale, which having heard once, he could repeat with all the intonations of the original teller. Once in the diningroom of a summer hotel where he was visiting Mark Willing, he told the Willing family one of those stories which have been originally short anecdotes, but become heaped up with absurdity by being told with snail-like care and particularity. This story he had originally heard in a strong New England dialect, and this he always retained in telling it, being skilled in that dialect, which he never overdid. The total effect was so laughable that people at neighboring tables turned their chairs aside to listen, and the waiters found errands to bring them, one by one, into that quarter of the diningroom until eight or ten were standing near, indulging a not very subdued merriment.

Carl liked the analytical studies which I couldn't bear, and understood their meaning, which I missed. He had natural good taste, and this, with his humor, made him patient with customs which he and I both abhorred, and with the defenders of them; so that he sometimes accomplished by his quieter methods much more than I could by my head-on plunges.

Yet I could never think the fiery explosions of the indignant "do only harm." Too well I remember how much good other people's indignations have done me. Repelling them at first with loud scorn, I woke up in the night and had to endure a sickening acceptance. I once when about twelve, stopped a workingman in the street and asked for a dollar he owed me for my tricycle, which he had bought for his children. It was in front of the house of my greatest friend in those years, Mabel Cone. From an upper window, she heard me. Leaning out like Barbara Frietchie, she said some burning words about my stingy and grasping behavior. Her dark eyes flashed splendidly. In theory I believe strongly in the cool, quiet word or two; but I find it difficult, in my own case, to recollect any very impressive response I ever made to such a remark. Perhaps this is because these cool remarks are often made to cool people off, seldom to warm them up. It was against all my notions, when Mr. Leibowitz at the Scottsboro trial, introducing a Negro witness, warned the prosecuting lawyer, "You take your fist out of my witness's face, and when you speak to him, you call him Mister!" and yet I never think of it without irrepressible thankfulness, and to tell the truth, with a strong sense of beauty.

# 3

WHEN I was fourteen, my aunts bought a house, and we moved from one end of the village to the other.

Sans Souci had been only rented. It belonged to a quaint, lovable eccentric, an old bachelor by the name of Julius Kellogg, whose orchard joined ours, his large mansard-roofed house fronting on the main road to Manchester Center, while our little cottage was on "the west road." In appearance Mr. Kellogg was the ideal Wandering Jew. Tall, thin and very dark indeed, with longish curling hair, he seemed forever youthless and ageless, just as he seemed tranquilized beyond all human passions. Certainly he was incapable of anger, sharpness or severity. He could however administer a mild rebuke. Aunt Fanny had a great respect and a kind of humorous tenderness for him. She told us at breakfast one morning that she had attended service at the Congregational Church the previous evening and that Mr. Kellogg (who was wearing, as usual on Sundays, his famous antique waistcoat covered with gold and silver vines) had escorted her home. "He gave me his arm," she said, laughing, "but he was rather nervous about it, and kept as far away from me as possible." Continuing to chuckle, she added, "I took occasion to speak to him again about getting this house painted, and he put a very sad note into his voice and said, 'I'm sorry to say, Miss Hawley, that you care far too much for outside show.'"

Mr. Bert Willard, who was one day rummaging in our woodshed at Sans Souci after some tool or other, found a rusty old gun in the rafters, and got Aunt Fanny to believe "it was the gun Mr. Kellogg carried at the battle of Bunker Hill."

54

Mr. Kellogg had a sister, Miss Emeline, who looked like a portrait, and belonged to an earlier tradition of life. They led a very secluded life in the big house girdled by fruit trees. I made, many years after, a triple portrait in verse of Miss Emeline, Mrs. Miner and "Lady" Wickham, which *Scribner's* printed with a delightful illustration.

But our new house was three-quarters of a mile from Sans Souci. Though an exciting event, the move was a great upheaval. I had to leave "my corner of the hall," an eave corner upstairs, where I still preserved my dolls and their furniture; and we had to leave the big Greening and Spitzenberg apple trees that surrounded the garden, trees among which Carl and I with Walter Hard, Mabel Cone, Bertha Trull, Mark, Molly and the Stokes boys, each had a house, and "nom de pomme" of our own. We had to leave Mr. Kellogg and all his fruit—his three kinds of grapes and even his peach tree. We left all the North Main Street children for one new playmate, Belle Smith.

We moved on the first of April, 1890, and there was snow enough for all the furniture to come on sleighs. Carl and I rode back and forth on every load, our playmates accompanying us in instalments. We were going to live in the "old Elijah Littlefield house," next door to the new stone house of the cemetery superintendent, Belle Smith's father. My aunts were having a piazza built, and having the barn moved—its old axe-hewn beams creaking slowly across the garden; and having a hammock swung between two old apple trees; and we had both a well and a cistern, instead of having to go to Mr. Coy's spring house every morning with two pails in an express wagon, to supply drinking water. (For the new "drive well" at Sans Souci, which Aunt Fanny had placed such faith in, never had come clear. This well had been started with all possible ceremony, a year or two before. Hearing from the well-driver that a witch-hazel forked twig would "find" water, Aunt Fanny herself, in her firm belief that she "had a kind of second sight," paced solemnly back and forth carrying the twig; and finally said with decision "Dig it here!" And water there was; but permanently muddy.)

55

The best thing at the new house was a piano-box half full of excelsior, standing forgotten in a potato field next door to us, and making a cosy home for an unclaimed cat and three or four kittens.

Beside all the furniture on which I had sleigh-ridden down to the new house, I had brought something down there which was invisible to everybody but myself; a presentiment. It had come out of beholding, for the past year or two, young Burton Swift, Miss Maude Swift's brother, slowly getting thinner and thinner, and knowing that he had consumption. One day the presentiment had darted like a serpent into my mind, "When I am as old as Maude Swift, and Carl is turning into a young man, he will get consumption. Yes," I thought with horror, "something says that at that time he will die!" I struggled against this idea, but I could see that it would be a long struggle, won and lost a great many times. Only if Carl grew up safe could I throw it away, as I had thrown hell away. I wouldn't have mentioned it to anybody for a thousand dollars, because to speak of it would have made it so much more real, given it so much more resistance to my combating common sense. It would have been so much harder to overcome, both for me and the people I told—I must keep it as shadowy as I could. Yes, I would save everybody else from having it, and I would save myself from being weakened by their knowing about it. I would husband all my strength against it.

As I foresaw, so it was. Back and forth I wrestled with it for six or seven years.

But still I always felt hopeful that it was all foolishness. Carl, for one thing, was so exactly the wrong kind of person to have a presentiment about. He lived in a clear daylight world, and was somehow too firm and dignified to submit to the onslaughts of imagination. I had already begun to stand in awe of Carl. He was so firmly reasonable, and he always knew so many things that I could just as well have known, or so it always seemed. When I read in the morning Psalm, "I am afraid of thy judgments," I often applied it to myself and him. My seniority was ceasing to be in any shape or form a superiority. Even when we wrestled, he now could almost put me down.

56

There was but one thing in which I still felt myself to be braver than Carl. When the gypsy wagons came through in the spring, he still used to slip unobtrusively into the house and stay there until they were well past the cemetery. Right up to twelve years old, he clung to the idea that the gypsies carried off children.

I went to the other extreme, and didn't believe that they even carried off hens. Far from being afraid of them, I found them, as I still find foreigners, unduly attractive, and I was rather silly about them.

In that same thirteenth-fourteenth year I underwent my greatest foolishness over a book. Now when I look at the very mild work of fiction which occasioned my transports, I am puzzled. Years before that I could discern goodness in stories well enough to warm immediately to Mary Wilkins, at the first glimpse of one of her beautiful plain tales which was in one of our juvenile magazines—a story, I remember well, of a little girl whose pocket, swinging outside of her dress, was eaten off by a cow. Why, therefore, I should erect a work entitled *Marjorie's Quest* into an idolized eminence, I can't form any guess. But in the midst of this subjugation, I found one month in *St. Nicholas* the first of a series of extracts from great novels. It was the childhood experiences of Maggie Tulliver which had been skilfully extracted and presented here for children to read. Fresh from the watery delights of *Marjorie,* I thus came full into the presence of the Tullivers, and all my natural delight in realism opened its big mouth and gulped down the beauty, fidelity and satisfying penetration of this family portrait. I now had the unforgettable experience of feeling, so far as my age was capable, the gulf between the pretty and the beautiful, the enticing and the compelling.

Experience with the reading of adolescent boys and girls of the present time has convinced me that by thirteen or fourteen they can appreciate great novels; and that if they are separated from the thin gruel of juvenile and semi-juvenile fiction, and let loose upon a shelf full of great novels, they will soon immerse themselves in

"——vintage that hath been
Cooled a long age in the deep-delved earth."

How well I remember Dorothy Costrell, at twelve years old, entranced with *Jean-Christophe,* and coming over from her corner in the school library to mine again and again to interrupt me with her pleasure in one of those remarks about human nature which make such a rich tapestry of that book! I must confess that much of my experience has been with Jewish young people, who possess, of course, the racial gusto for good literature and the high racial order of intelligence. But side by side with them were Gentile boys and girls of the same age; and where the Jews began to read and praise Tolstoi, Rolland and Bernard Shaw, the Nordics quickly followed. In the same school were a few Negro children, the sons and daughters of cultivated homes, and they, too, soon became enchanted by great writers. All three races readily left the juvenilia for the full-grown works, just as they all preferred to enact shortened scenes from Shakespeare to the undistinguished plays that are often proffered for young people. I particularly recall the absorbed interest which two boys took in *Growth of the Soil.* These were boys who, when they read aloud, halted, stumbled, bumped along repetitiously, and when they wrote or typed had infinite difficulties with spelling; boys, however, of action, independence, manhood and high, chivalrous pride. They were profound lovers of the earth, and of animals, and the farmer's calendar. They savored *Growth of the Soil* to the very marrow, and read it in a slow, intense, living fashion that Hamsun would certainly have loved.

I often think of what Lamb said—"Had I twenty girls, I would tumble them all early into a closet of good old English reading, and let them browse at will upon that fair and wholesome pasturage."

My education was about to receive a great advance by way of a horrible wound.

I always read *The Tribune* all the way home from the mail. One day I read something strange and fearful. It was an account of the

58

burning alive of a Negro by his white neighbors somewhere in the south. This ghastly thing, by far the most sickening event of my life up to that time, *The Tribune* had strangely put into an obscure and very tiny news item not over an inch long.

Up to that time I had regarded *The Tribune* with great respect. But that item, so ghastly and so small, shook and troubled my confidence in *The Tribune* and in America. How could the rest of the paper be so calm and so cheerful? Burning people alive was what Bloody Mary had done; and it was mentioned in the histories as an instance of the evil nature of Indians. It was what Nero had done to the Christians; what Joan of Arc had suffered, whose ashes, Dickens said, would rise against her murderers at the last day. Why was it considered unimportant that now—this week—a Negro had been burned alive by us—an American by Americans?

Of course those of us who did such a thing, and those who consented to it, thought this Negro was frightfully bad; and for some strange reason they thought that people who were good could perfectly well commit frightful atrocities against those who were bad. The more bad people suffered, the better; that seemed to be their idea. It was now that I felt my first overwhelming onset of wonder and rage that the sufferings of the wicked could be so calmly contemplated by the people who were supposed to be good. Good! Why, they were not good at all—they were cruel! What other crime was half as bad as cruelty?

Did they assume that wicked people suffered less when you were cruel to them than good ones? But it was exactly the other way around! A very small child could have told them that! As a matter of fact, pain was much worse if it was your own fault. Martyrs, on the contrary, were upheld by inward might and purity, and by the dazzling consciousness of infinity and glory close at hand. And I thought, as always, with wonder and joy of Latimer, my favorite martyr, even more my favorite than touching, human Cranmer; for in all the history I knew, there was nothing so comforting to my sharp realization of other creatures' pain, as the merriment of Latimer, leaping over the stiles and hedges on the way to be burned at the stake, cheering on Ridley and shouting;

"Be of good cheer, Master Ridley; we shall light a candle in England today that will never be put out!"

Mobs who burn alive or torture always seem to me far more wicked than their victim, no matter what he has done; for he has yielded to some fleshly passion, but they to the cold bitter desire to punish, the hateful malice of self-righteousness. I think the most blasphemous words I know are "make an example of him."

This was my painful graduation exercise from childhood.

I had another, a small, light, happy moment; one of those social landmarks that make a young creature realize with sudden, incredulous joy, "People no longer think me a child!" It was only a remark made at a boarding-house table in New York by a delightful young journalist, whose wife was a great friend of Aunt Jessie's. At dinner one day Mr. Kingsbury passed me the macaroons with these words, which I remember as perfectly as the Lord's Prayer,

"Miss Sally, will you partake of these excellent cakes?"

Though slow in the uptake about many things, I was fairly quick to feel courtesy and consideration in the human voice and manner, and for this bit of humorous delicacy, which at once gave me a foothold in adult conversation, I was glowingly grateful—nor at threescore have I ceased to appreciate it.

There was in Manchester, that rich and fortunate village, an old coeducational day and boarding school of noble traditions—Burr and Burton Seminary; a private school for farmers' sons and daughters, democratic to the last degree, and with a tuition too tiny to be believed. Its double name had come about in this way; old Mr. Burr, a bachelor merchant here in the early days—he died in the latter eighteen-twenties—had bequeathed a sum of money, large for that time and place, to found a school for young men desiring to enter the ministry. Here as elsewhere, once a good school for boys had been established, a few girls raised their heads and asked if they couldn't go too; and the indulgent trustees let in one Lucy Barrett, who throve on learning and spread the news among the other girls how agreeable it was. When Mr. Josiah Burton, another childless old burgher of Manchester, died, some twenty years after Mr. Burr, he bequeathed five thousand dollars for a school for girls. The stone fortress on Seminary Hill, built to stand there long after the wooden houses in the village at its feet shall all be gone, could perfectly accommodate more students than it had; and the trustees opened its doors to the girls of Vermont, took, very fairly, the five thousand dollars and added Mr. Burton's name to the school's.

For several Junes I had gone up with other children to the Commencements there and had been greatly impressed with the size and bearing of the students, who seemed to us in every respect grownup persons, as much so as Aunt Jessie's young men, or in fact as my aunts themselves. My young ideas, I now think, were nearer right than those of my elders on this matter. To be sure, the Seminary students grew rapidly younger in my estimation as soon as I became one of them; and for a few years after my graduation they dwindled almost into children; but now that I am getting old, and have seen the maturity of the present generation, I have reverted to my childhood estimate of age. I find in my own youth, as I extract it from my diaries, an appalling lack of realization how old I really was; I blush to think how childish and inadequate was the part I played in a world that needs the strength of all its healthy inhabitants. To this unduly youthful condition of will and initiative, I think, was attributable a large part of the bored or belittling occupation with unimportant matters which still cursed many girls in my young days.

Perhaps my convictions about this arise partly from an ingrained habit of thinking grownup people much more childlike than we usually think ourselves. At any rate, I do feel strongly that boys and girls of sixteen were meant to be, not big children as many of us assume, but youthful adults—a very different thing. I have seen them as young as twelve, under the responsible freedom of a community

61

school, considering its affairs with grown-up seriousness, a grown-up sense of proportion—not, of course, with the full weight of grown-up judgment. But at sixteen or so, the young adult is usually laboring under a sense, as I may call it, of non-achievement, and nature, I believe, is deeply dissatisfied that we should prefer feeling our benevolent power over the young to feeling satisfaction in *their* power and importance in the world.

Certainly in times of emergency adolescence leaps to the helm and is not found wanting.

It was in the autumn of our first year at the new house that Carl and I entered the Seminary—entered abreast, in spite of the two and a half years between us. Previously to this the only teachers outside of home whom I had studied with were Mrs. Martin the drawing teacher at the Seminary, a very Victorian one, with whom I drew grapes, oranges and mugs, and the delightful music teacher of the town, Mrs. Simonds, who had in me the densest and least musical one of her many pupils. Nevertheless I never received a discouraged word from that beaming, generous, well-beloved lady, nor even so much as a patient look; but only her rich ardors for great and noble music, which she poured out so abundantly on all our heads; the beginnings, too, of a long, warm friendship and a hundred gossips over books.

Emma Way, who entered the Seminary along with us, and whom I'd only known as an occasional acquaintance, became immediately with propinquity a close, warm friend and so remains at threescore. Emma was the first of my friends who loved poetry. She was gentle, soft, shy and romantic. She had billows of dark red hair, gentle eyes and the most virginal, delicate mouth. Walking, she looked like the illustrations in our Tennyson at home, to the "Idylls of the King."

It was about her and Vermont that I afterwards wrote "Emilia." *The Atlantic* took this, and it's also in *The Home Book of Verse.*

> Halfway up the Hemlock Valley turnpike,
>   In the bend of Silver Water's arm,

Where the deer come trooping down at even,
  Drink the cowslip pool, and fear no harm,
      Dwells Emilia,
  Flower of the fields of Camlet Farm.

Sitting, sewing at the western window,
  As the too brief mountain sunshine flies,
Hast thou seen a slender-shouldered figure
  With a chestnut braid, Minerva-wise,
      Round her temples
  Shadowing her gray, enchanted eyes?

When the freshets flood the silver water;
  When the swallow, flying northward, braves
Sleeting rains, that sweep the birchen foothills,
  Where the windflowers' pale plantation waves—
      Fairy gardens
  Springing from the dead leaves in their graves—

Falls forgotten, then, Emilia's needle;
  Ancient ballads, fleeting through her brain,
Sing the cuckoo and the English primrose,
  Outdoors calling with a quaint refrain;
      And a rainbow
  Seems to brighten through the gusty rain.

Forth she goes, in some old dress and faded,
  Fearless of the showery, shifting wind;
Kilted are her skirts to clear the mosses,
  And her bright braids in a kerchief pinned;
      Younger sister
  Of the damsel-errant Rosalind.

While she helps to serve the harvest supper
  In the lantern-lighted village hall,

Moonlight rises on the burning woodlands;
    Echoes dwindle from the distant Fall.
            Hark, Emilia!
    In her ears the airy voices call.

Hidden papers in the dusky garret
    Where her few and secret poems lie—
Thither flies her heart to join her treasure,
    While she serves with absent-musing eye
            Mighty tankards
    Foaming cider in the glasses high.

"Would she mingle with her young companions!"
    Vainly do her aunts and uncles say.
Ever, from the village sports and dances
    Early missed, Emilia slips away.
            Whither vanished?
    With what unimagined mates to play?

Did they seek her, wandering by the water,
    They should find her comrades shy and strange;
Queens and princesses and saints and fairies,
    Dimly moving in a cloud of change;
            Desdemona;
    Mariana of the moated grange.

Up this valley to the fair and market
    When young farmers from the southward ride,
Oft they linger at a sound of chanting
    In the meadows by the turnpike side;
            Long they listen,
    Deep in fancies of a fairy bride.


My second great friend at the Seminary was Halley Phillips, the
daughter of the beloved doctor of Arlington. She was a girl of high

spirits, good looks, a good mind and a conquering habit. "That Phillips girl," my observing brother said, "walks around there holding up her head as if she was the queen of the school!" My friendship with her was partly due to our mutual love for poetry. At one of the annual speaking contests she took a medal reciting "The High Tide on the Coast of Lincolnshire." It was a great event in my life—the first time I had ever conceived how enhanced poetry can be by the beauty and drama of the speaking voice. I had never even read the poem; and when Halley delivered it with simple and deep feeling, I could scarcely contain the keenness of my delight.

Many years after, when that very enjoyable fraternity, the Poetry Society of Southern Vermont, was flourishing, Halley Phillips (Gilchrist) was its moving spirit. And I still like hearing her read poetry better than hearing most other people.

I took part myself in that speaking contest where Halley won the first of her poetry honors. I'd chosen "The Battle of Ivry," but the principal toned me down to a descriptive piece about a sparrow; it was probably just within my powers, but I knew better than to think anybody would listen to it. On the same occasion, one of the Seminary boys presented that old favorite, "The Deathbed of Benedict Arnold." Following the current tradition, he threw maniacal fury into this piece; he staggered about the stage, wildly delirious, tortured by dreaming of the American flag, until even my hardy patriotism had received a surfeit of this worship and vengeance of the tribal god.

Whenever I see that old "Man Without a Country" on the required lists of school reading (the Regents of New York are still faithful to it, I believe) I am reminded of the horrible extravagance of "The Deathbed of Benedict Arnold."

In our second year Blanche Brownell came down from the north of the state and became a member of our class. She was something like her pretty name, a sort of Quakerish belle. Halley and I were both very much attracted to her, and we soon formed a sort of three-cornered friendship, to which Emma made a semi-detached fourth.

Like all the other girls of the seminaries of the United States when we were young, we got our chief daily education from adolescent talk. Our teachers, like other teachers in other seminaries, made no educational use of it at all—never brightened up the classroom with it. We sat on the wide window-seats in Halley's or Blanche's room and subjected practically all our thoughts and desires to each other's scrutiny; at least, I showed all mine except those social insurgencies which I never thought of showing anybody. And after our talks we tried to remodel our thoughts and desires to suit the consensus of our triple opinion.

In my last autumn at the Seminary—the September of the tornado, that uprooted so many trees and knocked over so many chimneys and tore off the belfry and half the Principal's roof—a new Principal had come, and brought with him two middle-aged teachers, sisters by the name of Snyder.

These two spinsters brought a great deal to Manchester. While the town lives, I suppose they will not be forgotten. The Seminary girls quickly warmed to them, no whit deceived by the economy and old-maidishness of their dress and appearance. They were women of wide cultivation and deep, wise humanity. They had the warmest notions of hospitality. In their sittingroom, full of photographs of great paintings, bits of Italian and French pottery, and a thousand homelike keepsakes of former pupils, the Seminary boys and girls were welcome for afternoon tea, and the tea itself was foreign and delicious. Miss Frances taught mathematics, the Bible and the history of painting; Miss Marcia taught English and literature: and once when our Zenophon class had no teacher, she took us over serenely, without any time to brush up.

Miss Marcia was my fourth great Seminary friend. She had a look in her gray eyes of being able to penetrate beyond phenomena: a look I wondered at and loved. At the Seminary I began almost to like mathematics again (on the humble plane of dexterity) for we had one of those sure, lucid teachers whom the pupil has only to trust and give attention to, and "all shall be better than well." What you

66

learned with her you could "bound," as Lincoln said "on the north and on the south and on the east and on the west." The meaning of number, to be sure, never peeped into our classroom; but all of us who wanted confidence acquired it. And this was all that any of us even dreamed of ever finding in number.

Emma and I took to Latin—and a little Greek—with pleasure. Every girl admired Mr. Mead's dark eyes and subdued voice; but we two were enough interested in the world of words to like Latin grammar itself and the delicate distinctions in Greek. What Emma and I disliked was the laboratory. The dreary, cluttered, artificial appearance of shelves and tables distressed us. And for me already a dark shadow of cruel fanaticism was creeping over the picture of science—the vivisection of animals justified itself to the world under that name.

Cruelties that stuck in lumps of blood to the pages of history had been justified to the world in bygone times under the name of religion, to be sure. But they were past. Methodists, however distrustful of Roman Catholics, had no desire, nowadays, to burn them alive. Roman Catholics would never have screwed the thumbs of Unitarians, in any part of the modern world. But just as these actions had been put aside by religion, here was science, which abhorred the cruelties of religion, carrying on its own Inquisition, and hesitating at nothing, not the implanting of abscesses in the eyes of rabbits, not the slow rotting away of the bones of dogs, not the actual killing of doves by pure intensity of pain.

Aunt Jessie had a certain old school-desk painted a cheerful red, in which she kept her "animal papers"—the monthly magazines of New York and Boston humane societies and the leaflets and cards they sent for distribution at our local S. P. C. A. Aunt Jessie was the founder and Secretary-Treasurer of our S. P. C. A. and anybody who knew of an overworked horse or homeless dog, unwatered cattle, hens packed too tightly in crates, or an unvisited string of the hellish steel traps which were then legal in all states, (and still are in most) complained to her. Her name, accordingly, soon got into the mailing list of the oldest of the anti-vivisection societies in the United States, the Philadelphia society, of which Miss Biddle was then the Secretary. I didn't, however, read these leaflets; like the overwhelming majority of my fellow-countryman to this day, I knew not one single detail of that "peculiar institution." Considering it in principle only, as they still do, innocent of all knowledge whatever of its methods, I came to the same conclusion that they ordinarily come to, the conclusion which supports and protects an ingenious collection of unrestricted tortures side by side with a code of highly humane laws; "It's all right for animals to be killed, even painfully and slowly, for the benefit of man."

I well remember saying this to Aunt Jessie one day as we walked home from Manchester Center. She mildly opposed me; but I was perfectly sure that she was wrong. I little knew what soiled, torn leaflet of the Philadelphia society was even then blowing about the barn floor, where I should find it when I next took out our bicycle.

I was about to receive another great shock—and education far beyond anything at the Seminary.

That one leaflet, describing one particular experiment in the language of the experimenter, changed my mind once for all. It was too dry and abstract, too circumstantial to sound fabricated. It gave chapter and verse, and had the dreadful calmness of truth. No action for libel, so far as I know, was ever brought against this society—or others—for publishing it and sorrowful hundreds more.

I experienced, that autumn afternoon, what Froude describes, when, in speaking of the Inquisition, he first admits that, given the premises which were then universally accepted, it was entirely logical and justifiable; and then adds something with which history overflows—

"But the heart must often correct the follies of the head."

It became to me, that afternoon, when I had realized the torments to which a few dogs had been subjected, a great wonder that I had ever said, "But it's right that *they* should suffer all this to cure *us*."

68

It was as great a wonder as it had been eight years before, in Minneapolis, to realize that I had stood in front of a fellow-being and cried, "You don't call him a gentleman!"

What I thought of vivisection at fifteen, after taking one intimate look at it, I think at fifty-nine after learning a thousand details. It is an incurable treachery—it is (in the light of evolution) exploiting our poor relations. It is the animal sacrifices of antiquity in a modern dress. It is as peculiar an institution, in this age of societies for the prevention of cruelty to animals, as slavery was under the Declaration that all men were free.

Much of it, I know, is not very cruel—not more than we ourselves, if courageous, might volunteer to bear in our own bodies. If its defenders would *relinquish the right to inflict the appalling cruelties they never mention*—if they would endorse a law for preventing, for example, the slow gradual malformations and sewings-together of living animals—the planting and developing of cancers, baking alive, running to death in treadmills, inserting coins and buttons into dogs' bodies to fester there—we could listen less sadly to their soothing talk about anæsthesia; it would begin to have some point when all painful experiments had, by law, to be short enough for anæsthesia to cover them.

And though I do believe the comforting doctrine that animals react less keenly to pain than we, yet from the same cause—the lesser development of their brains—I fear they have far fewer defenses and makeweights against severe pain than we, and so are more helpless inwardly as well as outwardly when we torture them. Their senses are keener than ours, and I sometimes fear the total effect of their pain may be.

Two or three years before his death, William James wrote a letter (which the New York *Evening Post* published) holding with an even hand the scales between the two sides in the vivisection controversy. He freely admitted, out of his familiarity with the inside of the practice, that tortures were inflicted, and sometimes wantonly; he recognized, on the other hand, that our side was ignorant and sometimes

69

untruthful and pigheaded; he acknowledged that there was untruth and provocativeness on the other side too, as is inevitable, he remarked, when any group of persons are under fire from the outside; and he concluded that our agitation, with all its faults, would have to go on in order to remind the vivisector that "there is a God in Israel to whom he owes account."

When he died, I endeavored to persuade one or another of the New York papers, where a good deal was being said in praise of him, to quote this letter; but none of them was willing to mention it.

As my other interests have widened, I've turned now and again to look at vivisection in its relation to them. It seems to me to serve the purpose of an unintentional red herring across the trail of what medical opinion might do (by corporate appeals through its great annual conventions, for example) for better housing, security in employment, a rise in unskilled labor's wages—in a word, for health on a large scale. If doctors can go before legislatures, as they do, to oppose restraints on vivisection, in the name of children's health, why can't they go to oppose child labor, or to support a better tenement law?

Since the war, my interest in pacifism and in vivisection have come together at one horrible point—I mean that impenetrably secret experimentation on animals which is now carried on by the War Department.

I wish more and more that health were studied half as much as disease is. Why, with all the endowment of research against cancer, is no study made of those who are free from cancer? Why not inquire what foods they eat, what habits of body and mind they cultivate? And why never study animals in health and natural surroundings? why always sickened and in an environment of strangeness and artificiality?

In this manner my views of the practice have been amplified during forty years.

Though my distaste for science, as its A B C was presented in that day to us, consisted in the most part of this revulsion from its cruel sanctions, I don't think myself capable of envisaging, then or now, for more than a moment at a time, the real splendors and heights of science. Scientific persons still appear to me, on the average, a little less livable-with than other persons; though they have a real and beautiful humility toward nature, yet they seem often arrogant and impatient toward the deeper spirit and inward nature of man; as if man were not worthy of science. Occasionally they also seem to me puritanic; they are so painfully self-denying toward the deep comforts of spiritual experience. Though I am aware that the best benefits of science to man don't consist in its countless riches of ameliorating inventions, but of spiritual values—the profound and searching candor, disinterestedness, and quiet, comradely devotion to great ends, of which science has given the world so many unsurpassable examples, my sense of proportion still balks at the exaltation of the impulse of curiosity. I cannot think the Bible statement "God is love," would be improved by reading "God is the disinterested thirst for knowledge." It was not the thirst for knowledge that took Father Damien to Molokai, or Thomas Mott Osborne to the punishment cells of Auburn—or, for that matter, Walter Reed to suffer yellow fever. And some such thoughts were present in the bouncing, awkward schoolgirl of fifteen, in whom they mingled with rather pessimistic wishes that one of the two young men teachers at the Seminary might somehow become a beau of hers.

My loves in poetry followed a usual pattern; Longfellow up to twelve, then Tennyson up to fifteen, then Keats, (and through Keats, the love of Greece); then Browning. It was not until the year I graduated that I saw, in our church paper, a review of poems by Kipling, in which the reviewer quoted the haunting and glittering lines,

> "Yes, the old lost stars wheel back, dear lass,
> That blaze in the velvet blue.
> They're all old friends on the old trail,
> our own trail, the out trail;
> They're God's own guides on the long trail,
> the trail that is always new."

These rich lines instantly took root in my mind, and planted there the name of Kipling; but we had then no such library in Manchester as we came to have a few years later; and our family were by no means rich enough to send offhand and buy a book, when it was neither Christmas nor a birthday.

Somewhere, at about this time, I read a reminiscence of a group of young Englishmen, in their college days, coming suddenly, and with great joy, upon Swinburne's *Laus Veneris;* and I derived from this account a strong anticipation of having the same experience when a new great poet should swim into my ken. But it was not to happen to me until long after college age, and Kipling was not the one to confer it.

That same year, however, Charles Eliot Norton wrote a widely read article on Kipling, concluding, as I remember, with saying,

"Kipling continues the royal line of English poets."

All I knew at that time about Walt Whitman was that he had written a book with a title I then thought as uninteresting as I now think it inspired, *Leaves of Grass.* My father, who sincerely liked Pope, and greatly admired Byron, had heard of Walt Whitman, and considered him grotesque to the point of derision. "Here's the way that man writes," he would say; "What do you think of this line? 'Oh, I am very sick and sorrowful!' " No children in my young days knew, as they all do now, "O Captain, my Captain." It was my father, however, who first introduced me to Walt Whitman, by giving me one Christmas an anthology called *Where Meadows Meet the Sea.* In this collection by Harrison Morris were several of Whitman's great sea passages, "Out of the Cradle Endlessly Rocking," "Proudly the Flood Comes In," "At the Last, Tenderly," etc. Swinburne too was nobly represented in this half-forgotten book, one of my favorite anthologies. I first read here Swinburne's

"Out of the golden remote wild west where the sea without shore is,
Full of the sunset, and sad, if at all, with the fullness of joy."

It was years later that I found the poem of all Whitman's that I best love, "This Compost," first printed under the title, "Poem of Wonder at the Resurrection of the Wheat."

Nobody at the Seminary wrote verses except me; and so mine never had any difficulty getting into the school magazine. I wrote on such subjects as "Venus" and "Fair Rosamond" and hidden sorrows. Lines on the deaths of Whittier and Tennyson, which came the same year, were printed in *The Troy Times*.

Mark Willing used to say, "Been writin' any poems lately? All about lovin' and dyin', I suppose?"

When Cousin Willie made her excellent pastel of Carl, the hereditary desire of the Cleghorns arose in me, to learn to draw. My aunts couldn't believe that a child whose father "understood pictures," whose grandfather had written a book on art, and whose mother had painted quite creditable copies, could help learning to draw. In spite, therefore, of the curious stiffness and oddity of everything I drew, Cousin Willie took me on as a pupil, and gave me our marble head of Psyche to copy. I slaved away, but it was hard, and I couldn't feel myself getting hold of it; and after a while I gave it up, convinced that drawing was beyond me. The worst of it was that Carl, who drew so much better than I, cared so much less about it.

For two or three years, now, he'd said he was going to be a doctor. Once he mixed up some nice-looking cough medicine when Papa had one of his obstinate bronchial colds, and was quite annoyed because he wouldn't take it.

Previously we'd always thought he would be either an artist or a naturalist. My father liked to think so. Occasionally my aunts romanced about his being a clergyman—a bishop, Aunt Fanny used to suggest, with shining eyes: and she would add, "Your mother would like to have you enter the church."

Carl went so far as to pass the plate in St. John's. Mark Willing and Molly Prentice, though Presbyterians, often came with us to five o'clock service at St. John's; and Mark passed the plate on one

73

side, Carl on the other. Mark Willing, a boy of endless jokes and explosive laughter, had in repose the most solemn face I ever saw. He was Carl's favorite boon companion. They had a long repertory of comic dialogues, and made me choke with floods of laughter when they enacted together the "Man with the Wooden Arm Reciting Horatius at the Bridge." They used to go to the three-days' autumn fair on a season ticket made out to "Mark Willing and Wife."

We usually dined with the other Hawleys on Thanksgiving Day, and they dined with us at Christmas. One Christmas Cousin Charlie let out the fact that he was engaged to Miss Lester of White Plains. The wedding was to be late in February—we should still be in New York—White Plains was very near—we'd all go and see Cousin Charlie married.

The day of the wedding began as a wild, drowning day of slush and rain; you could hardly cross the torrents that flooded the gutters. In the middle of the afternoon the wind shifted and it came off cold. The rain turned to snow and the floods in the streets froze. A friend coming with us, we took a five or six o'clock train to White Plains. The storm had become a blizzard; the snow was already thick and was drifting wildly. Carriages met the train to take the guests up the steep hill to the Lesters' home. The five of us entered one of them, and the struggling horses plunged into the snow. Half way up the hill, the carriage stuck fast in the drifts. Nothing to do but walk. Carl and I were enjoyably excited, but Mrs. Burton fainted away and men had to be found to carry her. The rest of us staggered through the drifts and arrived alive; and we all saw Cousin Charlie married with music and flowers and a rich, delicious supper. Carl, after bringing supper to all the women in our party, had no time for a bite of salad himself before somebody exclaimed, "It's time to go! We may miss our train!" Tugging on rubbers, leggings, coats and mufflers we were conveyed down the hill, made the train and got into warm beds before midnight.

A cold and cough that Carl developed caused none of us any

74

special anxiety; but one morning he was strangely drowsy; it was impossible to keep him awake through breakfast. Dr. Peterson came and said his temperature was a hundred and four. It was pneumonia.

Dr. Peterson sent a nurse, whom none of us will ever forget. She was a Miss Adams. Her hair was truly golden and she was as fair as a rose. She sat up with Carl all night, and all the morning hours; in the afternoon she took a few hours of rest, while Aunt Fanny and Aunt Jessie relieved her watch. She was angelically kind to all of us; and when I remember that I once intruded my anxiety upon her too short afternoon rest, going up to her room with a blind instinct to get some comfort out of her, I know it was the wickedest thing I ever did. The next case she took after Carl's was scarlet fever, and she caught it and died.

Papa had gone to Minneapolis after his usual winter visit, but now he was telegraphed for and came back. Carl was very sick indeed. Aunt Fanny's burning love and anxiety would not let her leave the house; Aunt Jessie, white and tender, would scarcely take a breath of air. I'd never known how sweet and compassionate strangers can be. An old, worn chambermaid was kindest of all.

I don't think I ever remembered my presentiment. Now that the shears were trembling over his thin-spun life, I thought of nothing but the daylight dangers we could all see; and the shadowy menace of years took itself off and was no more known.

Every morning the fever relaxed a little; every afternoon it came up again. I heard Aunt Fanny saying one afternoon, "They're going to give him (I think it was) phenacetin." A day or two after that the fever broke. He was frighteningly weak passing through the crisis. Dr. Peterson stayed with him all night.

I only remember that the joy of his recovery was beyond everything I'd ever supposed the human heart could feel. Up to that time, in my small experience, illness had never come into our family except to bring death. Now a thick cloud blew out of my conception of life: chance and fate were more benevolent than they'd ever seemed:

the being I loved best, my bright-starred brother, who had been my infant darling, was coming home to mortal youth and earthly happiness.

Physically we were all very much spent. Aunt Fanny, who had never left the house once, seemed the least worn. Immediately after Carl was out of danger, we all had fearful colds, and our eyes all looked like burnt holes in a blanket. It was a long, cold, muddy, coughing, sneezing spring, and a spring that was well worth living seventeen years for.

Two recollections had tormented me during Carl's illness; one was the selfish preference I'd often indulged for reading when a game of cards or halma hung on my taking a hand; the other was my insanely urging a boycott of rubbers and umbrellas on my brother just before he had developed that almost fatal cold.

Atonement sometimes works itself out in ways that continue to injure the original victim. So it was with my remorse about the campaign for roughing it, and the boycott of the rubbers and umbrellas.

Swinging too far in the opposite direction, I soon began to make life objectionable for my beloved brother. I was forever suggesting rubbers and an overcoat. When he was engaged in baseball, (he played on the Seminary team) I suffered agonies of apprehension if it began to sprinkle as an inning ended; I watched him with acute distress when he sat down on the wet grass all glowing and perspiring, to cool off, without even noticing the shower; and I couldn't always restrain myself from picking up his coat and laying it round his shoulders in an irritatingly humble and sneaking manner. Great balance and forbearance he must have had many a time to hold back from boxing my ears. I so often suggested to him that he might catch cold, it's a wonder he didn't. But in spite of me, he went on growing up quite healthy and good-natured.

That had been the winter of my first completely grown-up clothes. My first long dress was a green brocaded cloth. Miss Isabel Smith at Manchester Center, our friend and dressmaker for forty years, made

76

it and many another. It was just about the end of the bustle era. It seems to me that the bustle must have reigned altogether for six or eight years; for I can remember, toward the end of my child-hood, how all the children used to say that "If you could once climb up on it, you could ride all over town on Mrs. So-and-So's bustle." Bustles were hot things, almost as hot as corsets; and in warm weather, when I wasn't "going anywhere," I used to leave them both off. Of course one still had on one's undershirt, "corset cover," substantial drawers, and two starched petticoats, the short and the long, made of stout "Fruit of the Loom" cotton "cloth." I can remember Aunt Fanny, who never in her daytime life left off her corsets, and who wore, beside what everyone else did, a long chemise, a thing she had perpetuated from her youth—Aunt Fanny, I remember, panoplied in all these, called out to me one summer afternoon, "Sally, what on earth is the matter with you? You look perfectly awful! Oh, I see! You *haven't got your bustle on.*"

# 4

AUNT FANNY was a curious combination of loyal Victorian respectability with a lot of refreshingly irregular ideas of her own, which kept cropping out amongst all her devout observance of conventions. It was a savory combination. Her friends and neighbors enjoyed it very much, and so did Aunt Fanny enjoy herself. She had more than her share, anyway, of animal spirits and gusto for life. "My idea of a good life," she sometimes said, "is to clean house all day and go to a ball in the evening." Her notions of the relations of duty and pleasure were far ahead of her times—they were almost early Christian. "I never get any sense of virtue," she used to say, "from doing my duty, unless I enjoy doing it." For a quarter of a century this view seemed to me bottom-side-up.

Most of all the people I knew, Aunt Fanny liked to tell stories in which she had come out at the small end of the horn. I suppose she had at heart such appreciation of her successes and achievements that she could be genuinely tickled by her momentary downfalls. Having been a very pretty girl, with plenty of beaux, she could well afford, for instance, to tell us with much gusto how fearfully homely she had looked after having her hair shaved off in typhoid fever.

"The family all tried to comfort me," she would relate, "with telling me how becoming the little cap was that I had to wear over my bald head. One day, however, in a crowd, I overheard an old Irishwoman talking about a young relative of hers that had had typhoid fever and had her head shaved. 'Yes, she looks terrible, Katie does,' said this old woman; 'she looks just like that woman over there!' Pointing to me!"

78

Another of her pet anecdotes included my father. Aunt Fanny had seen an advertisement about soaking seeds in whiskey, which would make them sprout twice as fast as ordinary seeds. She immediately tried it. "John Cleghorn, when I wasn't looking, stuck some blades of grass in my flower pots, and when I came in and saw them, I was idiotic enough to say, 'Well, it's really so! Those seeds are coming up, and I only planted them this morning.' Your father was tickled to pieces, and every time my back was turned, he pulled the grasses a little higher in the pots; then I would come in and exclaim over them. Finally your grandmother couldn't stand having me fooled any longer; and she told me. Your father was quite disappointed. He said he'd intended to put a cabbage in each of my flower pots the next morning before I was up."

Aunt Fanny could ha-ha as loudly as she liked over this and other matters in which she had been fooled, such as the gun Bert Willard told her Mr. Kellogg had carried at the battle of Bunker Hill; for everybody knew she was not only a clever woman, but a woman of affairs, with plenty of public spirit—indeed she foresaw, long before most of the men in town, how advantageous it would be if the water could be piped through at public expense; but she wasn't allowed to speak about it in town meeting, and was only allowed to be present and hear the discussion on Aunt Jessie's word of honor that if she made a move to get up and talk, she should be pulled down again.

I recall every detail of how she looked forty years ago, setting out for the village on a summer morning, in one of her white lawn dresses freshly ironed, wearing her little black "English walking hat" slanting well down over the nice straight nose the Hawleys all had, and carrying a black parasol; Keturah, our little terrier, trotting at her heels. She would spend three quarters of an hour in Cone and Burton's famous old general store, under the big elm south of the Equinox House. Very little of this time, if any, she consumed in merchandising; it was all spent in conversation with Deacon Cone, Deacon Burton, or Mr. Theodore Swift (whom I admired most of all

79

the men of Manchester) about Biblical criticism. "Well," she would conclude, hoisting the black parasol and extricating Keturah from mouse-hunting around the rich black molasses barrels in the crypt of the old store, "I believe every word of the Bible. I believe Jonah swallowed the whale."

Carl and I felt sorry for her not saying it right, and only realized many years later that her malapropisms were one and all intentional.

From Cone and Burton's she would go over to the drug store, and spend another half hour talking over village affairs with Walter Hard's father, who she always said was a saint, and Mr. Towsley; and she would round out the hour by recrossing the street to the Equinox House office, and talking at length with Mr. Franklin Orvis, the king of Manchester, about the prospects of the Republican party. If it were a Presidential election year, he would promise to send a boy down, as soon as the result was known, to scream it out under her windows in the small hours of the morning. Last of all, she would stop at Mrs. Miner's, sure there of the shrewdest, spiciest and most variegated dish of talk to be had anywhere in southern Vermont.

If she did this on a Monday morning, she might spend Tuesday baking, preserving and jellying in the kitchen, with Carl or me to assemble her material, sift her flour three times, stone the cherries or raisins, weigh out the sugar on the old iron scales Grandfather had had in Troy, lick the cake batter out of the yellow bowl, and dip deep into the preserves. Mark Willing and Molly Prentice, whose mothers she had known in her own girlhood, and whose grands and great-grands had known ours in early Vermont, were free of the kitchen, and Mabel Cone or Lewis Hemenway might venture in once in a while; but not so my new Seminary friends Halley and Blanche, who were always on formal exile in the parlor.

And if on Tuesday she did this, by Wednesday she'd have three or four tables of ladies in, silent as nuns, playing duplicate whist; and by Saturday she'd think it was time for Carl and me to be having a party.

80

AUNT FANNY

Aunt Fanny had a very quick and only partially controlled temper, which she called "expressing my opinions," and which sometimes became "my private opinions publicly expressed." It never led her to slap or to punish, in any way or shape, Carl or me, any more than Aunt Jessie, whose temper was very gentle, would have done so; but she sometimes visited us with quite heavy remonstrances, though when we called this scolding, she was very much grieved, and would say, reproachfully, "Why, my dear child, I'm not *scolding!*" In these years we had as cook Mrs. Claudia Shorter, a young married colored woman, whose temper was even less under control than Aunt Fanny's, and who was just as much of a high stepper. Claude had a rich line of epithets, and to Carl's intense delight (he memorized them all) she would sometimes pour them all together in a breath on the head of her good-looking young husband, who received them with a quiet smile, for he knew that Claude loved the ground he walked on. In the second year that Claude lived with us, she brought her baby; he was baptized in our church, and was Carl's and my great darling.

It was in the very year of Carl's convalescence from pneumonia that Mary Büchler came to live with us. She was twelve years old; the daughter of a German widow, who in those days before mothers' pensions had been unable to keep her little family together, and had placed her daughters in a Home. From time to time children from this Home were placed in a private family; and one of the directors had suggested this particular little girl to my aunts.

How pretty, how clever and how dainty she was! Nothing in Aunt Fanny's notable cooking skill escaped Mary; bit by bit she acquired it all, and then began enlarging her borders beyond it; and beside cooking, she soon began to be extraordinarily skilful with her needle.

We all grew very fond of Mary, and she stayed with us for nine or ten years. When we went to New York in the winters, she would stay at the Hards' or the Reeds', or the Charles Hawleys', helping them about the house and always winning their friendship.

She was fond of pets, adopted a lame chicken of my brother's, and drew it around on her sled to amuse it; and much more than she missed any of the rest of us, she missed our little dog, Keturah. Her beautifully written weekly letters to us always ended

"Love to all. And Keturah."

One occasion, soon after she came, brought Mary and me into very warm relations. It was bedtime for us young ones, and Aunt Fanny, for some reason which I forget, had become mightily displeased with Mary. She gave her a severe scolding; and Mary, taken unawares, and having no habit built up like ours of discounting Aunt Fanny's fiery tongue, retired in heavy tears. I instantly sought her out and we expressed ourselves to each other in a long close embrace; such a one as we realized, even then, that a whole lifetime of crowded days and quiet nights, and many years apart, doesn't obliterate.

Though I could discount it pretty well, I knew what it was to be reduced to tears by Aunt Fanny's scolding. From Papa I inherited the whole of his absent-mindedness and helpless habit of losing things. Especially on Sunday mornings I was late—my leghorn hat was gone—vanished from the house. I'd looked in every possible place at least six times. "Hunt till you find it!" Aunt Fanny used to say, in tones that filled me with actual despair. As soon as she said this, I always wept, and tears prevented me from seeing as well as before. By the laws of association, I soon had the habit of weeping and despairing as soon as anything was mislaid. Strange that, remembering all this, I should ever, in my own care of children, make heavy, instead of light, of any child's failings!

Mary had by nature, or perhaps it was by grace, what I entirely lacked, a gracious manner. I was one of those who blurt out all sorts of things, especially opposing opinions. Aunt Fanny often commented on this, and recommended to me "a little suavity—don't be so brusque!" I knew I was brusque, and other people were courteous, but I couldn't any more see how people avoided being brusque, than where my leghorn hat lay, as big as life, in the bureau drawer. How they thought up what to say, and how they fixed their faces to smile, in that humorous, questioning way, or tilted their heads, or gentled their eyes with faint motions of the eyelids, or shook an affectionate finger in fun, I couldn't see, just because it was right in front of me all the time, and I was so accustomed to it, and so unobserving. Or if I did see a corner of the process here or there, I didn't dare try doing it, because of *mauvaise honte*.

"Thank him, Sally—" what a desperately hard suggestion that was to fulfil! I couldn't thank people, not even my father, for his loveliest Christmas presents. And yet all this adamant of an inhibition, that had covered my manners for years like a cast of bronze, melted off in one golden moment when Aunt Fanny suddenly praised the graciousness of my remarks to the expressman.

It was in the middle of dinner when the package came, and I went to the door, greeted Mr. Crawford, and gave instructions where to put the box. When I came back, Aunt Fanny said, "Why, Sally! how pleasantly you spoke—nothing could be nicer!"

When we remember how quickly a languishing plant can be set in the sun, and how much quicker children are than plants to profit by it, isn't it strange that we ever keep them in the shade? I so fast leaped ahead in my manners from that moment that before the week was over, I began to imagine myself speaking to my aunts as Milly Huff did to her mother, with a pat on the shoulder, and an "All right, dear!"

Aunt Fanny made an excursion, in the interests of her household, in a totally opposite direction from sweet little Mary, and acquired Willie Woodward, who was easily the most sparkling boy I ever knew. He lived alone with his grandmother, a very ancient looking woman, a few rods down the Valley Road. She went abroad wearing a long black cloak and a black hood with a long peak. She was devoted to Willie, a comely fair-haired boy with roving Bohemian habits—something of a Huckleberry Finn. She contrived for him—for they were very poor—a few cut-down and made-over clothes, which looked exactly as if they had been cut down and made over

83

by a loving but very dimsighted and amateur grandmother; but somehow they became Willie, as his wandering habits became him, and his good-natured, picturesque, disrespectful language, never twice alike, and always, in its random sparkle and wit, possessing a sort of inspirational flow.

To this youth Aunt Fanny made overtures, and he accepted a part-time position, for several summers, of handy boy at our house; and used to come up, for two or three hours a day, (when convenient to him).

Aunt Fanny had notions of moulding him into a kind of Buttons —she used to have him stand behind a screen back of her chair at dinner, and issue forth to pass the plates, etc. She would then fill a generous plate for his own dinner, and he would sometimes eventually wash the dishes. He was a good deal of a tease. He always pretended to an intense anxiety to keep the dishes down to a minimum; and so when Aunt Fanny began to stock his plate, he would rear his fair, rumpled head up over the top of the screen, and call out lustily, "Don't give me clean plate! Me want dirty plate!"

Village opinion disapproved of Willie, and coldly frowned on his Huckleberry ways. Aunt Fanny naturally felt that this must cause something in the nature of an inferiority complex in Willie; though I suspect that he sincerely prized his freedom above all things and pitied more hidebound boys. "Willie, you have a distinguished name," she used to say; "William Proctor Woodward. You know the Proctors are great people in Vermont—there are two towns named after them. Now, Willie, you are a handsome fellow, and I want you to save the money you earn here in vacation time, and buy yourself a new suit."

This latter idea was quite dear to her heart, and she eventually carried it out. In due time she displayed to us a new suit she had bought at Mr. Blackmer's for Willie, with shirt, tie, socks, all complete; and one Sunday afternoon she got him to put it on, unprotesting, and gave him a note to take up to Mrs. Hard, at the other end of town. "There!" she said, as Willie left the house with the note

84

in his pocket. "Now everybody along the streets of Manchester can see what a nice, respectable-looking boy he is! I really feel very well satisfied with myself." Looking out the window to feast her eyes on the rear view of his clothes, she exclaimed, "Why, where *is* he? Where *has* he gone? He's nowhere in sight!"

From our house you could see a quarter of a mile of marble sidewalk stretching up as far as Captain Wooster's, toward the village. Willie nowhere appeared against this snowy background.

Somebody suggested, "He's gone off somewhere. He'll tell you tomorrow that he couldn't deliver your note, because he had other fish to fry!"

Aunt Fanny was positive that the note would somehow be delivered. "Willie said he would."

Late in the afternoon Willie came down on a vertical path from the mountain. He had delivered the note and brought back an answer; but he had not passed through the village. "I knew they'd all laugh at my store clothes," he explained, "so I went up to the mountain and along the mountain as far as the Hards' and then I come down across country and left the note, and then I went back on the mountain and come home through the woods."

Willie had his own nomenclature both for man and beast. Aunt Fanny was "Old Miss Particular." I was "Miss Pigtail." Domestic animals he addressed only by a generic name; if he called Keturah, he merely said "Dog! Come here." He was, as Aunt Fanny used to say, "no respecter of persons." Being asked to sweep the piazza, he tipped my two young cousins, Kate and Jessie Hawley, off the piazza bench on which they were seated writing letters, with an unceremonious "H'ist!"

His complete absence of respect for age, wealth, distinction and authority had nothing impudent or provocative about it. It was an attitude of pure innocence and utter unconcern. Free, natural and simply human, he brought into life wherever it touched him a breath of freshness and wildness like the spring. He was incapable of making anybody angry—no, not quite.

85

Such a boy as Willie, though sometimes without shoes, overcoat, breakfast, or a dime, always has a gun. Willie sat one day on the loose-boarded tail of a wagon jolting down the Valley Road. A dog ran out and followed the wagon a little way, barking. Perhaps he snapped at Willie's bare, hanging feet. At all events, Willie discharged some small shot, and the dog, loudly yelping, ran home. His owner swore out a warrant for Willie. He was arrested.

The trembling, tender-hearted old grandmother put on her peaked hood and came up to see Aunt Fanny. "That dog ain't hurt very bad," she said, "for he's runnin' all over the meadow—and here's Willie arrested, and they'll put my boy in jail." She dropped her puckered, loving old face on the table. "Them shots never hit that dog nowheres unless they was one or two hit him in the tail."

Willie and the sheriff came down to our house. "He says you and your sister are the only folks he knows of that would bail him out," said Mr. Giddings. "His bail is fixed at fifteen dollars."

Aunt Fanny saw here a chance to develop Willie's sense of responsibility. "Why, of course we'll bail him out," said she. "Don't think of putting *Willie Woodward* in jail, Mr. Giddings. But look here, Willie—what have you got that you could give us as security that you will be at the courthouse the day of the trial?"

Willie thought and offered his bicycle.

"All right," said my aunt. "Mr. Giddings, will you let him go home and get his bicycle and bring it up here?" The sheriff consented, and he and my aunts sat talking as Willie started off.

He was gone a long time.

"Seems to me he ought to be back here by now, on that bicycle," said Mr. Giddings, uneasily. "I oughtn't to 've trusted him, I guess. Great temptation to that type of boy to go off and jump his bail, poor young one."

"Well, I think he'll be back," said Aunt Fanny, peering anxiously up the road.

At length he did come back, trudging along on foot and tenderly wheeling his broken bicycle, which was entirely useless, and had

86

been so for some time. But Aunt Fanny was highly pleased. "There now, this transaction is on a good business basis," she cried, beaming on Willie.

The case, in the end, was dismissed on a flaw in the warrant.

Aunt Fanny ought to have been married to a lovable, unsuccessful man, who endowed her with many children; so that while his faithful diligence supplied the roof and larder and underwear, her fierce loyalty and creative resourcefulness would have found a wide field in supplying home-made amenities and enrichments of all sorts; such, I decided, would have been her fullest and happiest fortune.

My aunts certainly possessed a talent for keeping children young and carefree. Here I was at an age when I might have been engaged to be married, and like my brother, I was childishly free from any practice in real responsibility. Instead, we had a rockbound sense of security and permanence, seldom invaded by an inkling of the grown-up possibilities of life; though, in my own case at any rate, when my tranquillity was thus invaded, it was invaded deep. Perhaps my aunts deliberately tried to keep us thus childishly secluded, out of an intense desire (since all our brothers and sisters had died) to preserve our splendid health and vigorously placid nerves. Life, as they ordered it, was pleasant, anyway, and we were cheerfully unaware how sheltered we were, for like all young people or healthy older ones, we would have hated like poison to think we were sheltered.

There was nothing singular in our ignorance of the economic pain and struggle of the world. The people we knew were all thus ignorant. The adults who protected the adolescents were themselves protected, by their lifelong shelter under the books and papers they read, the sermons and lectures they heard, and the talk they took part in. Over us all, like a huge, warm roof, hung the tacit assumption that poverty was, on the whole, voluntary. People were poor because they wouldn't make the "effort" and "sacrifices" required to "get ahead." This doctrine I heard expressed or assumed on every hand up to the year 1932, when it began fast to fall into silence.

Meanwhile, individual poor families were often kindly and generously helped by the very people who subscribed to these barbarous views; but these poor families were regarded as exceptions; they had had misfortunes, and strange to say, it wasn't their fault that they were obliged to ask for help.

Our church weekly, *The Churchman,* never mentioned (in those days) the unemployed, any more than it mentioned vivisection or lynching. I never heard a sermon that mentioned them though I faithfully heard my fifty-two sermons a year. There were no prayers in church for the families of the lynched, or the unemployed, and no collections were taken up for them. No social service commissions had been formed in the churches then.

In 1892, when I was sixteen, and had been reading the papers for six or seven years, I first began to do a little cogitating about labor troubles. It was the beginning of the great depression of the nineties. Aunt Fanny and Aunt Jessie had read *The Tribune* ever since Grandfather had renounced *The Times* because it was mugwump. Now, when the great Pullman strike came on, though I got from *The Tribune* the proper impression that strikes were entirely unnecessary commotions, created by Labor leaders just because they were hellbent on sticking their fingers into the contented relations of workers and owners; and though I felt a strong distaste for that violent, pigheaded Debs, still I began to wonder a little on my own account about strikes and Labor leaders, and even to feel a little pigheaded myself on their behalf. Perhaps it was just because everybody I knew and everything I read was down on them. Anyway, there gradually dawned on my mind at this time the idea that newspapers had attitudes on these questions—took sides.

There was a pleasant, middle-aged friend of my aunts' in town, a business man from Chicago, and they turned to him, one day when he was calling at our house, with feminine appeals to "tell them what to think" about these awful times in Chicago. I remember how gently he deplored the ignorance of the workers, whose welfare was being snatched out of the friendly hands of their employers, and sacrificed to crazy ideas by irresponsible and selfish Labor leaders like Samuel Gompers and Gene Debs. But both with the views of our Chicago friend and with *The Tribune* editorials I was becoming dissatisfied, and I said to myself, "There's more to it, I guess."

What more? I only knew there was revulsion rising in my heart against organized respectability. I felt a need to think; talking to myself on solitary walks, or in the night, I tried to know what I was feeling.

One recurring observation which I'd made in my own small experience threw, when I thought it over, a side-light on my unformulated questions. Many a time I'd heard some matron, calling on my aunts, say that her cook or waitress was ill, or had been obliged to leave because of some calamity at home. And usually in such cases the visitor, without even telling us whether the cook were better or worse, would hurry on,

"Just as I had company coming for lunch! It certainly was hard on"—(not Maggie or Katie, but) "—it certainly was hard on me."

Putting two and two together, I began to see that somewhere in the owner-worker relation, there was a Pale, such as I'd read of in Irish history; on the inside of it, certain courtesies and considerations were important; on the outside they were unnecessary, and in fact would have been ridiculous. It was a movable Pale, differing from one employer to another; some pushed it farther out; some pulled it farther in, but nobody ever took it down.

Going back to that early sore in my heart, I saw that there was such a Pale in race relations, which the abolition of slavery had by no means taken down—a Pale topped with barbed wire and broken glass. How different the publicity would have been, I now realized, if Negroes had burned a white man! Even to myself, at fifty-nine, having been, as I believed, without race prejudice these many years, it has, I confess with soreness and shame, a different sound.

Among animals, too, I saw, there was a high and very arbitrary Pale. Our own terrier, Gem, whose loved old body had been disinterred and brought, with the little evergreen tree that marked his grave, from Sans Souci to Fairview, and our new one, Keturah, were by common consent on the safe, warm, protected side of the Pale; and the trapped animals on our hillsides every fall, perishing from long-drawn pain, thirst, fever and terror, and the live material stored in laboratories for poisoning and infecting, were outside it. "I'll write an article some day," I thought, "on 'Pale Morality.' "

The only way I could make peace with the gathering tumult of resentment I felt was, naturally, by resolving to do something about it. The day would come! I was terrified to think what it would have to be. To do something about vivisection, I might have to offer myself to be vivisected. To do something about lynchings, I might have to beard the mob and share the victim's fate. Many times I imagined the headlines; "White Woman Killed Defending Negro From Mob"—"Revulsion of Feeling Against Lynching Sweeps the Country." I knew, of course, that I could never get up the courage to do anything even remotely approaching these acts; but just because they were so impossible, I felt that they must be necessary. Surely, if mere persistent *effort* to rescue these victims could have captured public opinion, it would long ago have been done! When I laid these fancies down, I realized why, and never tried to think, "Well, I would do it if it would do any good: but I know it wouldn't."

This part of my life was carried on in complete loneliness. Nothing was ever said about such matters by any of our friends and acquaintances, any more than they would have spoken at the dinner table about slaughter houses. Of the organized battling for the oppressed that went on outside their ken and mine, the industrial conflicts towering up into calamities that would be famous for centuries, I never heard a word. The only organized effort of a humanitarian sort that entered our house—and in that regard we were beyond our acquaintances—was the protection of animals.

Most of my adolescence took place during the depression of the nineties, yet I never heard or saw a reference to it that made it seem human. Banks and businesses failed, I knew; factories shut down. I had no idea that that meant people being turned out in the rain to sit among their bedclothes and frying pans on the sidewalk. The despair, the riots, the hunger-marching, the helpless resentment of the unemployed in the cities—I never heard them feelingly mentioned.

We all read of Coxey's Army, to be sure. It had no lack of publicity. The papers we saw were amused, tolerant, not at all worried. They had a sense of humor. They saw the funny side. They knew, of course, that the Army would peter out. There wasn't, you were led to feel, any necessity for such a gesture; of course the times were hard, we "had to *do without luxuries";* but everything would come out all right if people would only have patience. What in the world made them so hasty? No use in going off half-cocked, like poor Jacob Coxey. He meant well, of course; there was no real harm in him, beyond his evident liking for the free advertising he got out of his ludicrous Army.

The depression, the Pullman strike, the Haymarket tragedy, Coxey's Army; none of them was taken any notice of by either students or teachers at the Seminary. I don't say "so far as I remember." Because I would remember. If anything had been said about them, I wouldn't have forgotten. We had no current events classes. Our histories usually stopped a few years before the times we lived in. With such events as the Chartist agitation, Shays' Rebellion, etc., they dealt briefly and reprovingly. The only exception was the French Revolution. Here there was a light on the pages, an echo of human beings rising in their human strength.

My father had an insatiable love of the sea. Every year he took us off to the seashore for a week or two of his summer holiday. Carl swam much better than I did, but I loved the sea more than he did. The element of water is unspeakably delicious to my skin. I feel in it a heavenly lifegivingness. No wonder, I often think, that it revives the fainting! No wonder it is the very backbone of plant and tree! I feel the truth and significance of what William Beebe says about water and man's life in his book *Half Mile Down*—and more beside; much more! In late middle life I've tried to express it in my poem "The Life of Water," which appeared in *The World Tomorrow*.

It lives beside us and we often mingle,
The life of water and the life of man.
St. Francis called it "humble, serviceable,
Precious and clean"; he viewed it, as I think,
Too much—for once—utilitarianly.
I don't see how he can call water humble!
Yet water has a pleasant disposition;
It takes whatever shape you ask it to,
With frolicsome abandon to your wishes;
It never sulks, like fire or like wind.

The life of water runs a swifter cycle
Than ours, or fire's. I never any more
Walk down at Manumit to springtime breakfasts
Along the brook, but this comes home to me;
"The wheel of water is turning, over our head
And under our feet; from springs to river and sea,
Back to the clouds, and under the earth again.
And all this water has run this way before
And knows its way. Then how can Plato say
We never twice step into the same river?"

From thinking of the water so, I come
To thinking of the year and of the spring,
Thus; "Spring is present and spring is also past
And spring is future too; all three at once.
The wheel of spring is turning, over our head
And under our feet; the farther passing away
The nearer back it comes to flower again."
Such thoughts as these the spring at Manumit,

92

The shadow of death, the sun that makes all shadow,
The fluid fire of life, that cycles on,
Renewal—death—renewal, ever the same
(And never alone the same) bring home to one
Who looks on water in the calm of morning.

Or if you go to some remote great pasture
Like Munson's Falls in Manchester, Vermont,
Where there's a brook that leaps a dozen ledges—
A brook you know and have known a long time—
If you plunge in and rear your breast against it
And toss it back by handfuls as it runs
And wrestle with the current, does it seem
To share your pleasure? be companionable?
Is there perhaps some consciousness in water,
Unlike, indeed, the consciousness of man,
Yet loving freedom, action and companions?
Why call it too far-fetched if one should think so?
Isn't it arrogant of man to think
He has the only form of consciousness
And only language to express it in?

Though water can make nothing of our lingo
It may have some expression of its own,
Less cumbersome, less crabbed, and less poignant;
Perhaps more widely and more calmly true.

When we went to the sea, my father would begin to sniff, from
the train window, or the steamboat's deck, the (to him) pleasant
smell of fishy boats and nets; "Ah, children, I smell the sea!" He
was so thin that his knuckles soon turned blue in the water, and
with great reluctance he had to come out long before we did; his
teeth would chatter, he was shivering and wan, and his thin fair
hair stood up in a curly froth on his head. Then he would wade,

and gather shells, with a child's pure simple joy. I shared it. My inland life made every shell a rarity.

My bathing suit of dark blue merino, trimmed with white cotton tape, had been abbreviated from the ample proportions of a previous generation. It had consisted originally of Turkish trousers, covering the ankle, finished there by a neat frill (edged with the tapes), which spread protectingly over the foot (in its stocking and sandal); a full skirt, coming decently down half way between knee and ankle; and a high-necked and long-sleeved top, tied with the white tapes from chin to waist. My generation had become so immodest as to remove the sleeves, leaving only a puff, and cut the trousers to just below the knees; the skirt still came pretty well down. Girls ordinarily wore caps and stockings into the sea, but I couldn't keep them on, and after trying once, went in barefoot and bareheaded.

When in this costume I ran down from my bathhouse into the sea, so overwhelming was my pleasure that I could seldom refrain from shouts and roars of impassioned joy. I could scarcely swim at all, and I never got up the courage to dive. What I felt was the mere exaltation of great waters, chill and glittering, flowing over flesh. It was a taste of bodily paradise, and so at threescore it still remains,

"All a wonder and a wild desire."

Though the ocean gave me this intense bliss, yet my sense of beauty lived chiefly in the mountains. If I tried to express a thought in imagery, it was drawn from woods and hills.

It was while we were at the seashore that I once tried to tell my father, in these adolescent years, how sweet and promising life seemed to me. I said, "Life seems to me like the woods in spring—you are likely at any moment to come upon a crowd of flowers."

Did I believe, he asked, that it would be like that all along?

I said Yes, I really did.

He said no more.

Now at threescore I think the same as at seventeen, though the flowers vary much more widely than I then supposed, and are found in much stranger places.

94

We went to the World's Fair in 1893. Our week there was the one rainy week of the season and we never saw the glittering whiteness of it. What had interested me more than anything else was the Congress of Religions that had taken place earlier in the summer—I should have liked to see the Parsees and Swamis, to have heard their thoughts about life and nature. I don't suppose another meeting like that has ever taken place before or since—was there anything, I wonder, of such depth or breadth, at the Fair last year? There was perhaps some such assemblage of the powers and possibilities of light.

# 5

In moving from the schoolhouse end to the cemetery end of the long village of Manchester, I could never have supposed that the cemetery itself would have so great an attraction for me as it gradually came to have. To be sure, from the beginning we regarded it in a not too solemn light. I more than once went strawberrying there, and in winter a crowd of children skated on the upper of the two beautiful little ponds. It was a lovely place; more like an Italian garden than a village burying ground. It was laid out on both sides of a beautiful little ravine; it had clumps of beautiful, some of them rare, trees; and it was rich in ferns and wild flowers. At one point a flight of steps, cloaked in a double evergreen hedge, went down a steep hill toward a foot-bridge over the brook—a happy solitude in which to mould into stanzas the poems that you felt you must write.

I went over to the cemetery to write the class poem, the year Halley and Blanche and I graduated. I went over there also, and sat close to the sound of falling water, to write my graduating essay on "The Brownings' Italy." I wanted them to be beautiful, and that meant to me that there should be nothing raw, stark or uncompromising about them. I really loved beauty, but I understood it even less than I do now. I suspected, perhaps, but certainly didn't know, that between beauty and prettiness, beauty and sentimentality, beauty and softness, there are great gulfs fixed.

My class poem was written in the echoes of Tennyson's murmuring lines. However, I had begun to read and to love Matthew Arnold, whose poems my father had given me. In them I recognized with joy the spirit of candor, the sense of purity and sincerity in emotion. I felt in Arnold as never before, what depths of implication poetry can reach. I can never, I fear, express the power which poetry has had over my life. I am innocent of ever having read it for anything but the joy it gives. I've never read it to be well-informed, to fulfil an obligation, etc.

I've read it when ill and begun to feel health springing up within. I've read it in sorrow, and a light arose in the darkness. Above all, I've read it in the midst of my tawdriest interests, and they fell from my heart like unsanitary rags.

What vigor, tranquillity, vitality, what clearing of the spirit, what deep looks into nature, expansion of consciousness—what confidence in life, death and mystery, poetry can give! "I would go through much more than life has dealt me," Hazlitt said to his son, "to have read the books I read in my youth."

In the spring of 1895, while having the dress made which was to serve both for my graduation and my cousin Julia's Easter wedding, I espied in a fashion paper an account of Radcliffe College, and conceived a desire to go there for a year. My father's slender means could do no more, and I only wanted the one year. Unwittingly I'd set my heart on a college where special students were plentiful and welcome; about half the little student body of three hundred-odd were specials. All unknown to me, too, when I'd seen the article in the fashion magazine, Radcliffe was especially rich in English courses. I obtained the catalogue and did the simple required reading, and in August Papa and I went to Cambridge and with the Secretary made out my list; Modern Prose and Modern Poetry, English Composition 22 (both these with Mr. Gates); Shakespeare with Professor Kittredge, and a beginner's course in Philosophy, which in the second half year would be conducted by Dr. Santayana.

Radcliffe's outfit then consisted of little more than Fay House. The Library was at the top, above the principal classrooms, which already were crowded. The auditorium was on the ground floor, running out toward Shepard Memorial Church. All the student dances, club meetings, plays and receptions were held there; the ices and cake were served from the little anteroom. Through the windows could be seen the substantial fragment that still remained of the Washington Elm. On the ground floor too, behind the Secretary's office, were the President's and Dean's reception rooms.

Mrs. Agassiz was the President. She was getting to be an old lady, and was not very often seen by the students. In the evenings, and often in the afternoons, she was accompanied by her sister, Miss Sally Cary. I embarrassed myself more than once by jumping up when Mrs. Agassiz called out in her clear, brisk voice, "Come, come, Sally!" I possess, in my autograph collection, a whole letter from Agassiz which she gave me; it was in French, and had been written about forty years before.

The Dean was Miss Agnes Irwin. When I went to Radcliffe, she had only been there a year, and was still exceedingly unpopular with the girls, partly because she had previously been not a college faculty member but the Headmistress of a school; but chiefly because the students' wishes had been completely disregarded in her appointment over the beloved head of Miss Coes, the college Secretary. The girls greatly loved Miss Coes; I couldn't at first understand why. She was a very brisk, forthright, humorous, unsentimental woman. Within a week or two I began to feel her quiet wisdom and unadorned humanity attracting me also, and quickly came to feel happy and at home with her.

A few years later, to the universal joy of students and graduates, "Cosy" became Dean. The best memorial tablet I ever saw (to an adult) is the one in Fay House to her memory. It glows with truth.

Miss Irwin was always kind to me, and not least so when, early in the year, she had occasion to let me know that the Instructor in the Philosophy course was embarrassed by my talking so much to him during his classes. She did this very well, and not in the least like my idea of a Headmistress. Students told me this friendliness was purely because I was an Episcopalian.

Nothing Miss Irwin ever did or said was felt to be more outrageous and ridiculous than her forbidding the girls to wear men's

98

clothing in their plays. Those were the days when the 47 Workshop was rising into fame—I heard a great deal about it from the students; and interest in plays was very strong at Radcliffe. In vain it was pointed out to Miss Irwin that at the Idler Club plays, at any rate, there were never any gentlemen present—Mr. Arthur Gilman might have been the sole exception. Were the girls then to give no plays with male characters? or how should they dress the parts? Miss Irwin indicated that gymnasium bloomers would be permitted. Immediately the Idler Club put on a play in which there was but one female character; its one act consisted of a young lady receiving evening calls from six or seven young men, who were all on the stage at once. These young men all wore evening coats and waistcoats, with proper shirt fronts; but their legs were billowingly clad in gymnasium bloomers. Miss Irwin's prohibition could hardly survive this. In the course of the year it slowly faded out of memory. By spring Beulah Dix could appear in the right costume as hero of her lively swashbuckling plays, seat herself with one foot resting on the other knee, and rap out her odds-bodikins speeches.

The President of the Special Students for the previous year was one Marguerite Fiske. I looked on with delight in her grace and amenity as she delivered up her office to the new President. She was also the head of the Cercle Français and an outstanding lover and student of Italian; and yet by spring I had really, to my incredulous pleasure, come to know her quite well.

Marguerite's uncle, Francis J. Child, the famous ballad collector, was still the head of the English Department at Harvard. I once during the year heard him read aloud—one of the last possible of such occasions it must have been, for he died the following year. There must be something in heredity, for Marguerite, when she became a singer after four years of language and other study at Radcliffe, sang nothing more delightfully than old ballads. There is something arch and quaint and simple and delicate and lively in her ballad singing, of which in many years one cannot have enough. I was so much in love with her singing in this kind that I once wrote a poem called "Margarita Singing Ballads," which appeared in the *Atlantic Monthly*.

Ruth Delano was also at Radcliffe when I was there.

Julia Ward Howe, already an old lady, with age's look of strength and peace, gave a lecture before the Emmanuel or Idler Club. Her subject was woman suffrage, and she was very vigorous. I noted with mirthful appreciation of her thrift how every sheet of her lecture was written on the back of some note of invitation or the like; from where I sat I could have read several of these. At the conclusion of her address she was asked to say "The Battle Hymn of the Republic"; and with calm simplicity she folded her hands over her stomach and repeated it.

Of my four courses the one I thought the most of was English 22. Its high point was a continued theme in six parts. For this I took Willie Woodward. I succeeded in giving a pale, diluted account of him, rearranging it to the detriment of the original material. His wit, insouciance and wildwood charm slipped through my fingers— but not all; a thin reflection remained.

Anybody at Radcliffe (or Harvard) was considered lucky to have courses with Mr. Gates. Though contemptuous of the arts which are supposed to make one so, he was exceedingly popular. He was fair, slight, pale, nervous and weary-looking; cool and critical in manner, extremely impersonal, with quiet literary ardors, which his students came to share, and an obstinate, scrutinizing sincerity which I think was the basis of his fixed hold on the young.

Very different was the expansive, hair-trigger nature of Charles Townsend Copeland, who, though still a young man when I was at Radcliffe, was already celebrated as a reader. At Sanders' Theatre, when he read poetry, every seat was taken, and in the aisles young men sat cross-legged on the floor. His beautiful, unerring tones gave a fresh realization of poetry. Hearing him read Keats, in particular, I felt that I'd never fully known that fruity, honeyed loveliness before. Well as I'd loved the "Ode to a Nightingale" ever since my

100

aunts had given me Keats on a bygone Christmas, the verse about the magic casements reminds me still of Mr. Copeland, after all these years.

Dr. Santayana's glowing and serene young face is what I best remember about the one semester when he conducted our little course in philosophy. Now when I read his celestial prose, and try, for love of it, to think its thoughts, I wish indeed that I could remember much instead of little of what he said to us over the pages of Josiah Royce. That course itself I remember very well. It must be that I remember Dr. Santayana so little as a teacher because he was able so entirely to immerse his comments in the philosophies themselves into which he conducted us as far as we were able to be taken. The longest light along my life which anything at Radcliffe cast came from his course. I felt the homelike deep wisdom of William James and the intense power of Spinoza. Without understanding Spinoza's thought, I perhaps understood the spirit of it. The kings of thought took hold strongly of one's mind and spirit.

My delightful but not very memorable year at Radcliffe, I now realize, was almost purely a literary experience—a year of acquisitive pleasures, which titillated and sparkled more than they glowed and warmed. Owing I am sure to my own immaturity, I was under a mild enchantment there much more than I was under the influence of beauty and greatness. Nothing caught me up for long at a time into any power that could obliterate my small self-congratulatory enjoyments. To be sure I felt the clearness and poignancy of Clough's poems, which I'd never read before, and the passionate sweetness of *Richard Feverel*.

No more than at the Seminary was there student discussion at Radcliffe, in any of my courses, at any rate. We listened, imbibed, endeavored to remember; occasionally, in our talk on the staircases, disputing the lecturer's conclusions. But not often. That we had anything to contribute to each other's education was an idea entertained by nobody, so far as my experience and hearsay went. What we did receive was sufficiently interesting and appetizing; the efforts of a set of fine and thoughtful minds helping us to understand the great figures of the past.

As for social challenges to the *status quo,* I never heard of them any more at Radcliffe than at the Seminary. Our reading courses made no mention of *Progress and Poverty* or the *Communist Manifesto.* We were not even assigned to read *The Dream of John Ball* or *Looking Backward.* The early Victorian lyrics we read included none of Ebenezer Elliott's—but would they have been included in any other college?

Something Mr. Gates told us one day about Jenny Lind has some applicability, I guess, to my own case. She said Sir Walter Scott "did her soul no good." Mr. Gates with dudgeon remarked "Let her take her soul somewhere else." If at this late date I realize that most of my Radcliffe courses, with which I was so highly elated at the time, did my soul no particular good, perhaps I deserve no greater sympathy.

Two among the handful of Harvard students whom I'd known during the year put me in touch, by way of a joke, with a young man whom I was not soon to forget. They were seniors and he was one of the initiates in their fraternity. For part of his initiation exercises, they assigned him to call upon me and discourse for seven minutes on the disadvantages of higher education for women. It was the middle of the spring when we thus met, and we soon saw each other very frequently. Nothing I had ever imagined compared in sweetness with the experience of hearing the beautiful voice of this youth beside me on a summer evening. I came home to Vermont with a glowing dream, and asked nothing better from life than to feel it take complete possession of my whole self.

Poetry, in such a case as mine, is implacable. I could not feel that the poetry I had loved and believed in so long described merely so soft and mild a spring moonlight love as this. Those mighty lines referred, unmistakably, to a blaze of full noonday power. I knew from deeper inside, too, even if poetry had not refused to credit me,

102

that love in its full strength was infinitely deeper, richer and more burning than the sweetness I felt for him, and he for me. Yet it lasted, for us both, a rather long time. How many boys and girls must have tried thus to let a Mayday happiness mature into something more than it can possibly contain!

Perhaps, in the world of sleep and dreams, where we spend a daily third of life, we receive at need some foretaste of what love in its fullness is like; and perhaps this foretaste, be it only for an instant, decides us for the whole of life. Sleep is a form of consciousness so released from time and space, perhaps the future flashes through it at the desire of the present for a longer view.

The young man for whom I conceived this youthful love was himself a lover of poetry, and he quoted to me, on a spring afternoon, this line from Lowell,

"And beauty's law of plainness and content."

It came to have, for me, many layers of meaning, some of which I may have imported into it as years went on—I received it permanently into my life, at all events, and it was the chief of his gifts to me.

# 6

A FAMILY of delightful girls from Columbus, Ohio, by the name of Neil, used to come in summer to the Equinox House in Manchester. They were great bicyclists; we used to see them riding three abreast down the village street with arms on each other's shoulders, steering without hands on handle bars. They could keep score like reporters at baseball games. Withal they were unassuming and unself-conscious and well educated and nice, and everybody liked them.

In Columbus they lived near Dr. James H. Canfield, then Chancellor of the University of Ohio, and knew his daughter Dorothy. And whenever I mentioned to Fay or Julia Neil the Manchester Canfields (admired friends of ours, and cousins of the Columbus ones) they always replied with wonder,

"But you don't know Dorothy Canfield? You ought to know Dorothy."

One day when Julia Neil said this, she added,

"Dorothy's in Arlington now. I'm going to take a horse and buggy and drive you down to see her."

The next morning we drove the long pleasant eight miles to Arlington along the Battenkill, and stopped at the Frank Canfield house. Canfield was an even more familiar name in Arlington than in Manchester. They had been early Vermonters, and branches of them had settled all up and down our valley. They were people who liked to read, but they were no dreamers. Active, shrewd, and public-spirited, they were distinguished for their plentiful endowment of common sense and understanding of human nature as much as they

104

DOROTHY CANFIELD AT NINETEEN

were for their learning. They were never much interested or particularly successful in making money, but fairly adequate to anything else.

Into the pleasant parlor of the Frank Canfield house, as we sat there talking to Lena and Nell, came a small figure of a sixteen-year-old girl, in a blue percale dress, and wearing her hair in a pigtail. She came up to us with the naturalest sweet frank pleasure I'd ever seen, and from her entrance I never took my eyes off her, or ceased to drink in the singular delightfulness of her presence. "No wonder," I thought, "that Julia Neil talks about Dorothy Canfield!" I soon began to talk about her myself.

But I didn't see very much of her until after her graduation from Ohio State University, when her father became Librarian of Columbia, and the Canfields came to New York. Dorothy was working for her Ph.D. on Racine and Corneille. I saw her, whenever we were in New York, as often as I could without being under foot too much; like Booth Tarkington's young man, I would have liked to say, "You don't mind, do you, if I wait in front of your door until it's time to call again?"

And it was in New York, when I'd begun genuinely to know her, that I made the fundamental discovery that she really meant it. All those gracious, welcoming ways, that lighted-up look when you came in, weren't forms of politeness at all. They were Vermontishly honest and real. After I went out, she had the same look of liking for me on her face that she had when I went in.

How does one find out a thing like that? It's very simple. I saw her meet other people, welcome them, and when they had gone, retain the same kind of look for them, as she told me about them in the same cordial voice. Then I saw that these were fast colors, all wool and a yard wide. She felt that way.

She felt that way about old and new friends, bashful strangers, Arlington neighbors, children in the elevator, old gentlemen who had known her great-grandfather. It was as straight from nature as the rich sweetness of maple sugar.

Her cleverness and learning were only the spices, I thought, that enriched the sweet juices of her nature. Many years later, I read in *Tertium Organum* the doctrine that unselfishness literally clarifies the intelligence. As soon as I read this, I thought "It's true! My own mind is much the clearest and quickest when my heart is clear and free." And I thought "Intelligence is an endowment, while loving kindness is a voluntary attitude, a turning and 'Friend, come hither' of the will."

Carl's pneumonia had cost a year of his education. He graduated from the Seminary the year I met Dorothy, and went to Princeton in the fall. His choice of a college had been as instantaneous as mine. At the seashore the previous year we had known a young Princeton man so near in all respects to a schoolboy's best ideals that my brother immediately wanted to go to the same college.

After he went away, I went on reading Spinoza's *Ethics,* which I'd been slowly worming my way through all summer. The desert parts were redeemed for me by an occasional monumental saying; "Saint Paul's faith is the full assent of the soul"; the illuminating analysis of pleasure and pain, and that immortal cry, "Not rejoicing because we have quelled our lusts, but contrariwise, because we rejoice, quelling our lusts!" When I came to that, I received it with an inward shout that has never died away. Now I began to understand what Aunt Fanny had meant by her strange theory about pleasure as a requisite for virtue. I began to understand better what I had always felt about those unexpected strawberries. As in a microscope, or telescope, or both at once, I seemed to see far into the nature of humanity, and was transported by the brightness I discerned in it. I faintly began to realize what the *New Testament* must mean by the word "grace."

I also went on, during that autumn, writing endless variations of openings for what I hoped would be short stories. Eventually one of these minute stories really got finished, in a manner which I hoped suggested Stephen Crane. It appeared in Elbert Hubbard's *Philistine.* "But we pay nothing!" remarked Mr. Hubbard, gayly. I placed some verses in the *Harvard Monthly* and *Advocate*. The next year I got a check for one of my stories. It was forty dollars, from *The Glass of Fashion*, a Butterick magazine. I felt that I was well started now toward a distinguished and lucrative literary career.

Manchester summers, when Carl was home, were sweet and exhilarating. Dewy summer mornings, with the brief fair-weather mist rolling up along the river somewhere between our orchard and the Green Mountains, the sun sucking up a dew almost as thick and white as frost—such a view was at my elbow as I woke up; and at night from the same window you could see the whole Milky Way and that constellation, Orion, I think, that looks like some ancient stringed instrument, such as I imagine a dulcimer or psaltery to be. In Vermont, wherever you turn, you drink up beauty like rich milk, and feel its wholesome strength seep into your sinews. Even when, as in my case, you scarcely use a twentieth of the power it gives, you undeservedly share its sweet nights' rests. In the night I sometimes lay awake from pure excess of vital pleasure and joyful confidence. Often in such nights I said to myself "Life is running strong in me tonight!"

On other nights, when I lay awake burning up with pity and rage to think of man and beast bearing unbearable pain, I always thought the while "But I will do something! I'll attack it!" In the absence of some definite plan, the old sacrificial idea came back again and again. It seemed to me that I must die a martyr to light up and burn away some of the monstrous wrongs that life was unfolding to me more and more. Fear blew coldly over me all the while, and I knew that I could never do it—(while remaining merely myself).

I suppose we are all born with an ascetic thread or two, and it has to be educated out of us by the simple realization that it isn't the point at all whether we live or die, suffer or enjoy, in doing something useful, but only whether we do it. Sometimes I feel now that the blood of the martyrs, far from being the seed of the church, was an actual drawback to the church's usefulness; for by calling too

107

much attention to these tragic sufferings, it distracted people from simple devotion to the cause the martyrs had loved better than either their lives or their martyrdom.

The glory that martyrdom sheds has not been confined to good causes either, I began to realize, but has gilded a great many Juggernauts and Molochs, wars and Inquisitions, which had nothing but martyrs to recommend them.

Yet martyrdom does shed a glory! Late in life, however, I began to see how the martyrs must have felt toward their own deaths; how, knowing that all mankind must die, and seeing how slowly their efforts attained their hopes, as age came on, and vigor slackened, they must have realized with sudden joy, "Why, my death itself can lend a hand! Let my death also make itself useful!"

With all my midnight resolves, what I found courage and wit to do for man and beast was very tiny, fragmentary, costing more effort than it was worth, I suppose. I spoke up for the Negro and for Labor, as well as I could, among our friends, taking to heart Stevenson's admonition, "When you are ashamed to speak, speak up at once." I expected our conservative friends to be angry, but they listened in a friendly spirit, and I surmised that they probably didn't take me seriously enough to be annoyed by what I blurted out in ungainly fashion, my ears reddening with embarrassment. While the Audubon societies were trying to get the egret outlawed, I made a practice of handing strangers who wore them a slip of paper asking them to join in the crusade. I did the same thing, sometimes, to people in trains and subways who wore fur. Getting gradually bolder, hardened by practice, I took an unfair advantage one day of an acquaintance, a woman, a young doctor associated with the Rockefeller Institute, with whom I was discussing the ethics of vivisection as we traveled together on a street-car. Glancing about her, and seeing a man who continued to expectorate on the floor of the streetcar, she advised me to give up my puny efforts against vivisection, and devote my attention to stopping the practice of public expectoration. "But I already do!" I exclaimed. "I often speak to them. Let's go together and ask him to stop, or else speak to the conductor." But she declined to accompany me, declaring that it wouldn't do any good. What she had meant me to do about it was something else —I forget what—something more ambitious and less direct.

Whenever I wanted to engage in some small practical effort at my elbow, there was no use in mentioning it to anybody else, because they were almost certain to throw cold water; and I usually had had to get warm after throwing cold water on myself. But I did find at this time or soon after, a somewhat longer and stronger string to my bow; it was writing a letter to the papers. Say what people would about those old bores, Vox Populi and Constant Reader, who were always writing to the editor letters which "nobody read," I found my attention always caught by that column on the editorial page above all others. Whatever I left unread, I glanced over the letters to the editor. *There* was something which hadn't been ordered for the paper, something somebody had cared enough about to spend a stamp and a few minutes. Furthermore, I found my letters were usually printed, and once or twice they were replied to editorially.

It seemed to me a modest assumption that five hundred persons would read my letters in *The New York Times*. That allowed for the immense majority to pass them by. "Well," I said to myself, "if I had a chance to speak about this matter before an audience of five hundred people, wouldn't I be a ninny to refuse? And here I can do it at my leisure, and the hall already hired."

If I had had any doubt about the usefulness of writing letters to the papers, it would have been dispelled by an experience I had in a strike headquarters in New York a few years later. Stepping in there to see how the strike was going, I was asked my name, and found it was already familiar to the secretary. "Oh, you're the woman," she said, "that wrote a letter in *The Tribune* asking readers to contribute to the strikers, and giving this address. Do you know I've had contributions amounting to two hundred dollars from people who'd read your letter?"

And indeed I often wonder why this method is not oftener used to secure help from that host of unknown sympathizers who are not on any available mailing list. Such persons would often contribute if they knew the address to which to send their dollar or dime.

Why should we be afraid of flooding the offices of newspapers with our letters? Only a few, to be sure, can be printed; but these will very likely be the best of them, with of course a sprinkling of the oddest, since variety and sensation are in demand. Let us remember that when a quantity of letters on any matter come into a newspaper office, then a real pulse of public feeling is being felt there, and some heed will surely be paid to it. Let us remember how much, after all, has sometimes been accomplished by a bold assumption on the part of a few innovators that it is possible for them to accomplish something. The abolition of the slaughter of the egret is a case in point. These struggling Friends of Birds, Friends of Freedom for Ireland, Freedom for India, Leagues of Mutual Aid, War Resisters and Civil Liberties—penniless organizations making appeals without a rag of profit to recommend them—how they do leaven the lumps of government, and that in our own day, not for our grandchildren! When the egret trade went down before the law, I hitched my belt tighter and went on writing letters.

If I wasn't learning anything else in these years, I was learning more about the nature of a newspaper. Reading the papers as I'd done all my life, I was still very slow in the uptake—was only beginning to see that a paper not only took sides, as I'd long ago discovered, but took sides formally and once for all; became a frame, and would always pull the news to fit the frame if possible. I now at last noticed that the arrangement of the news, the proportion of publicity, the captions, were all nearly as interpretive and moralizing as the editorials. I also began to realize that a newspaper is never wrong, and never changes its mind, repents or apologizes. The only one, at least, that I ever knew to do it was the old (Villard) *Evening Post*, which made an amende honorable to anti-vivisectionists for falsely calling one of their statements false.

To be sure, I only saw the one kind of paper. Under twenty-five, I don't think I ever saw a Labor paper or a Socialist leaflet, to get an idea how far one could go in the opposite direction with these same tactics. I often (but without knowing what they meant) heard the words "Single Tax," for Mr. Bolton Hall's wife was an old friend of Aunt Jessie's. But I usually heard Mr. Hall identified, when my aunts mentioned him to strangers, as "Bolton Hall, you know, the Single Taxer—*a son of Dr. John Hall*." It would have surprised them indeed to hear anyone say "Dr. John Hall—the father of Bolton Hall."

Five or six years later I did read that great fire of a book, *Progress and Poverty,* and saw what a passionate Franciscanism had given it birth.

Aunt Fanny and I went to Bermuda in 1898 to spend six weeks visiting an English cousin who was in command at St. George's; and shortly before coming home we went to a state dinner at Government House. It was there that we heard—from sympathetic Englishmen—of the blowing up of the *Maine.*

Of course working up what little war propaganda was needed for the Spanish War was very much easier than for the World War, because, unlike the Germans, the Spaniards were already firmly in the black books of the provincial American mind, such as mine, and had been there from our school days. Thousands of us had learned from our first school histories to look with a hold-over of Elizabethan suspicion on the Spanish; they were very cruel, they had (unlike other nations) a lust for gold, and they were incapable of colonizing. We thought of them more or less in the words of Tennyson's poem "The Revenge"—

"—These Inquisition dogs, and these devildoms of Spain."

On top of this we now knew of the dreadful suffering in the concentration camps in Cuba. Young men—among them Macy King, a boy we'd played tag with in Gramercy Park—had run away to fight with the Cubans for independence, and brought back machetes. People embroidered soft pillows with the Cuban flag and "Viva Cuba

Libre!" All the while we were in Bermuda, Captain Meyer, an old German-American veteran of the Civil War, a great character there, beloved by the English officers, was believed to be sheltering the young Americans who were running away to fight with the Cubans.

The particular form of propaganda I remember hearing oftenest at that time was, "A Spaniard, you know, would offer you a glass of wine, and while you were drinking it, would knife you in the back." I remember good Captain Meyer telling me this, in his patriotic ardor. It's strange and sad to think what the benign old German, who sent his sons to a Quaker college, would have thought of the fierce anti-German propaganda of the World War.

Nothing, as I near threescore, troubles me more than the readiness with which I myself, and so I suppose many others, have believed such obvious lies as that knife-in-the-back one. And though I've now read many a noble incident in which some Spaniard played a splendid part, from Las Casas defending the Indians from slavery, to the Jesuit fathers establishing what's sometimes called the first Soviet state, in Paraguay, still my first reaction, even yet, to the name Spaniard is a defensive one, a fear of treachery. Sometimes I remember parenthetically that the regular adjective for England throughout Europe at one time was "perfidious Albion." It's no comfort to see how readily two or more can play this game of scandal.

All my life I'd felt a noble enthusiasm for the Union soldiers in the Civil War. That any of them could have been intoxicated, thieving, bestial, cruel, in Sherman's march, of which I loved to shout the chorus—that the march itself was a horrid measure of destruction— I could never, in my young years, have believed. It wouldn't have been possible for me or any of my friends in those days to think the Civil War could have been avoided. To the bottom of my heart I was convinced that every drop of blood drawn by the lash had had to be avenged by a drop drawn by the sword. Company E of the Fifth Vermont had been assembled from our own village. Their relatives to the third generation bore in mind how they had been annihilated at the little battle of Savage's Station; how one of the Burton boys had written home that night,

"I am in command of the seven of us that are left."

It would have made the hair rise on my head as well as our neighbors', to suggest that those boys needn't have died.

Accordingly I entered the summer of the Spanish War with wholehearted partisanship, listening with complacency to the popular jingle,

"Remember the *Maine!*
To hell with Spain!"

Embalmed beef scandals didn't seem any real part of the war, but only an exceptional piece of individual villainy. I didn't suppose such scandals had ever befouled any other war. Any possibility for people like me to learn anything about war at that time was prevented by the shortness of this one. Then there was the chivalrous rescue of Admiral Cervera and his men, and the magnanimous glow we felt about that. It was very favorable to my rosy, genial views about war.

I was perplexed, though, by our keeping the captured islands, and by the fighting that went on in the Philippines so long after the formal war was over. The veiled accounts of cruelties by our soldiers against the natives were rather sickening. I got a faint idea of the "water cure." And the capture of Aguinaldo seemed to me a repulsive piece of treachery; though I met nobody who expressed such an opinion and I didn't see it in print anywhere, either.

Aunt Fanny, in the last year of the century, had one or two very severe short illnesses, and once or twice fell into a profound strange silence of a whole day's duration. Outside of these interludes, she was as enterprising as ever.

We all went down to see Carl graduate in 1900, attending that thrilling ball game, the third of the series with Yale, when Princeton entered its ninth inning without a run to its credit, while Yale had finished its ninth inning with four. In that miraculous last inning

113

Princeton won five runs straight with but one man out—the inning was never finished, for as the fifth man ran home, all Princeton swarmed over the field in a dance of triumph, and late that night the streets were still full of tramping feet, and voices chanting

"Yale, Yale, they can't play ball:
What the hell do we care?"

## 7

LATE in the summer of 1901, two young girls made a special point of inviting Aunt Fanny to a german they were giving at the Ekwanok Club House. Gratified by their insistence on her coming, she went and had a particularly good time. It was the last of her many parties. The illness that had been casting preliminary shadows over her for a year or two took hold of her now with dreadful fits of pain and great prostration. All through that autumn of the assassination, apparent recovery, relapse and death of President McKinley, she too was several times apparently recovering, and then was thrown back again into bed and into pain. Time has not softened, I am sorry to say, my memory of her pain.

Carl had already had one year at the College of Physicians and Surgeons in New York, and in September he returned for his second year. He was the apple of Aunt Fanny's eye. He looked much more like her than like either of his parents, and she thrilled to hear occasional strangers say "How much your son looks like you!" It seemed to all of us that we could never let her struggle on week by week against this illness without the joy of often seeing him; but motherlike, she was eager for his education, and wouldn't allow him to lose a recitation in order to come home and see her.

Aunt Jessie, Mary and I realized that she knew, for some time before a veil of unconsciousness gathered over her mind, that she was dying; and it was clear that she confronted the knowledge without a tremor. She was only sixty-one, and of a vigorous constitution. She lived until the end of the autumn.

I am one of those in whom the certainty of sorrow pierces deeply once, and can never again probe in so far. In smaller matters it had always been so—when my father left us, for example, after his visits. On the night before he went I was accustomed to suffer a long time with painful, desolate and longing tenderness; but on the following night, when he had gone, I was only a little sad.

I walked up to the village for the mail on the afternoon when my last hope for Aunt Fanny's recovery was flickering out. As I started on the way home, the realization that she would die flooded my heart full. I was passing the old Pierpont house, where two elderly ladies belonging to the Roe and Wickham families were living. Overwhelmed, just at their door, by a tide of sickening grief, I went in and sat down with them and told them I couldn't go home. Without trying to console me, they gave me that sort of sober, gradual easement which the veteran in life knows how to give the novice. After a little while I went home. The sick revulsion was already beginning to turn into the solemn wonder and the unexpected fortitude. I could comfort Aunt Jessie's tender weeping in the night, and Mary's inarticulate sorrow.

Carl came instantly hurrying home, but it was during his journey from New York that Aunt Fanny passed into coma. Her unseeing eyes and uncomprehending silence when he came in seemed to me impossible to endure. I called on the doctors to rouse her at all costs. "Hush," said the strange doctor, drawing me into the next room, "don't distress her rest. It's very possible that she knows everything about her, though she lies so still."

Later she recognized Carl with great joy and talked to him.

A few weeks after Aunt Fanny's death, I had the first dream to which I attached special significance. Like other memorable dreams, it will scarcely bear telling. It slips through words and is always something different from what one has described. The motive of it was that familiar wounding compunction which covers us at the first knowledge of irretrievability—the universal wish that we had known enough, been loving enough, to crowd all possible kindness into the present that was to have no future. What the dream conveyed to me

116

from her was some wordless consolation, of a sort which I suppose is frequent in such cases—I hope it is; for when I woke up, my regrets were all blown away by some sense of perfect understanding as sweet and pleasant as a summer wind.

Thirty years after this, during a time of long and severe household strain, I used so often to see Aunt Fanny's face whenever I closed my eyes, that I thought something telepathic might be taking place among the unexplored areas of life.

Aunt Fanny's death brought Aunt Jessie out of the status of younger sister, in which she had always contentedly lived. "I was the fifth child," she always said, "and the fifth wheel to the coach." Now she was the front wheel. The activities with which she'd filled her life, the care of the church which she'd inherited when Mrs. Miner grew too old, the rather adventurous humane work, etc., continued and she took over Aunt Fanny's cares beside. She was almost fifty when Aunt Fanny died. She had always assumed, as her world had done, that Aunt Fanny was the competent, clever sister, and that she had been assigned by nature to play a second fiddle. Unobservant and self-absorbed as youth is, I couldn't help observing this; but with youth's usual acceptance of the personalities of their elders as fixed quantities, I'd never conceived of a change. I now began and for thirty years have been trying more or less energetically (and more or less in vain) to alter this state of my aunt's mind—fortified, as I was, by the opinions of a number of discerning people.

My younger aunt's abilities were of an unobtrusive kind. She had a noticeable ability for getting along with other people. In her relations with colleagues and subordinates there was none of those ructions with which Aunt Fanny occasionally enlivened us. Whereas Aunt Fanny would have said to the butcher, with sparkling eyes, and half, but only half, in fun, "Don't you bring me any of that tough meat again—I'll go right up in the air if you do," Aunt Jessie said, "I don't know a thing about cuts of beef—I shall have to rely on your goodwill to send me good ones." Aunt Fanny might say to a maid, "I want the halls swept the first thing in the morning, please."

Aunt Jessie would say, "What do you think's the best time to sweep the hall? right after breakfast?" But she undervalued her talents because they'd never been featured in the family, just as Uncle James's unerring talent for modest and gentle goodness had been regarded by the family with lefthanded and deprecatory acknowledgment rather than with frank and envious admiration.

Aunt Jessie was our family musician. It was she who played for our pleasant hymn-singing on Sunday nights, an hour which Mary and I grew up loving and continued to love. Standing a kerosene lamp on each end of the keyboard, Aunt Jessie played the hymns we called for, the rest of the family singing at a pleasant pitch, while I drowned them out by my loud, unmodulated, exultant voice, not consenting to having a single stanza cut out. But music wasn't Aunt Jessie's real art. She should have been a house architect. Everything about building fascinated her. She loved as much as I hated to be shown over a half-built house. She was fond of making imaginary changes, additions, to all the houses she knew. Changes and additions to our house she planned very cleverly. When builders couldn't think how to do what she wanted done, she woke up early in the morning and figured out some ingenious way; and when she submitted this to the builder, he would say "Oh? Yes! I can do that, sure enough." The porches, cupboards, etc., that she put on (or took off) our old house always seemed to make it look more natural—and older.

Aunt Jessie always took time by the forelock. It has been wonderful spiritual discipline for her to live with me, for I am always late; and her torments, as she, hatted and coated, with the lamps turned down and the catch ready sprung on the front door, waited for me to begin to get ready, while the clock went from twenty minutes to (the time we'd said we would start) to fifteen, twelve and even seven minutes to—these silent agonies of hers were perfectly apparent to me, though I was very callous to them, hurried and absorbed in the letter that had to get off in that night's mail. I suppose it was this habitual cruelty of mine that drove her to seize time's forelock ever closer and closer to the scalp until, in recent years, she has begun to

118

take down the curtains and roll up the rugs six weeks before the autumn closing of our house.

Though in older years she has developed a few peremptory ways of talking, Aunt Jessie has seldom hurt anybody's feelings. When greatly annoyed, she always used to hum a tune. Her peaceable humming didn't fail to indicate her resentment—it was as transparent as gossamer; but it did no more than indicate—it aroused no return fire; and in a little while she had managed, with her unobtrusive melody, to restore peace.

Yet of all the people I ever knew, I most dreaded her resentments, precisely because she never expressed them. They had all the fearfulness of mystery. "Have I hurt your feelings, my dear, by denouncing the House of Bishops (or *The Tribune,* or the Republican Party) the way I did this morning?" "Oh, no—not at all—don't know what you mean, hurt my feelings," she would reply, in an unnatural, chilly tone, that left you high and dry, wondering how permanently you'd estranged her. Aunt Fanny had been accustomed, and truthfully, to boast, "The sun never goes down on my wrath." Aunt Jessie mildly admitted, "I don't know that I'll ever get over it. Let's talk of something pleasant."

There breathes from half a dozen of Aunt Jessie's old photographs a most lovely, heart-free joy of living. In her talk and laughter among old friends there is always a provocative, delicious note of pure spontaneous frolic. At parties Aunt Jessie was out for fun, while Aunt Fanny cherished in herself a streak of worldly-mindedness and social ambition, which she threw over whenever she liked, like a child its rattle and blocks. The maxims of both of them were cautious, prudent, and always attributed, with religious respect, to Grandfather. In practice, however, they were accustomed to let generous impulses have their way without ceremony, justifying them afterwards by some rationalizing as if to prevent them from becoming a legal precedent or an example the younger generation might follow too recklessly.

Unlike Aunt Fanny, Aunt Jessie had never been engaged. In my childhood I knew her various young men well, and in later years I knew two or three older men who had been her early admirers, and who still in grandfatherhood or settled old bachelordom cherished sweet little tintypes, or locks of her hair. Curiously enough, every one of these men was of a debonair, enjoying nature. I could have done with any of them for an uncle, and two or three were really winsome. Aunt Fanny would always tell us about her love affairs; Aunt Jessie even at fourscore won't unseal her lips, and I don't know yet whom, among two or three, she cared for. But perhaps none of them found her at home. She's always had a virginally expectant attitude toward life. Apparently it hasn't yet reached high noon. I feel a good deal older woman than Aunt Jessie.

I made the following small water-color sketch of her at about this time.

## PORTRAIT OF A LADY

Her eyes are sunlit hazel;
  Soft shadows round them play.
Her dark hair, smoothly ordered,
  Is faintly touched with gray.
Full of a pleasant kindness
  Her looks and language are—
A mirth that's never wounding,
  A laugh that leaves no scar.

With store of friends foregathered
  Before a cheerful blaze,
She loves good ranging converse
  Of past and future days.
Her best delight (too seldom)
  From early friends to hear
How fares that small old city
  She left this many a year.

AUNT JESSIE

GAZING AT MY FIRST NEPHEW

There is a narrower converse,
  A cosier council still,
When, all these friends departed,
  Close comrades talk their fill.
Beside our smouldering fire
  We muse and ponder late,
Commingling household gossip
  With talk of gods and fate.

All seemly ways of living,
  Proportion, comeliness,
Authority and order
  Her lips and life profess.
Then with what happy fingers
  She spreads the linen fair
In that great Church of Bishops
  That is her darling care!

And yet I dare to forecast
  What her "new name" will be,
Writ in the golden volume
  Beside the crystal sea.
Instead of "true believer,"
  The mighty Quill hath penned
"Of the poor beasts that perish,
  The brave and gentle friend."
              —*Scribner's Magazine*

Carl took his M.D. degree at the College of Physicians and Surgeons in 1904, after a triple onset of examinations; those of "P. and
S." itself, those of the State of New York, and those individually set
up by the hospitals before engaging the young graduates as internes.
It was Saint Francis Hospital, then still down town, where my
brother succeeded in becoming an interne. He spent a rather happy

year there, on terms of warm friendship with the Sisters, whom he found, with all their self-denial, a rather merry lot. I recollect his telling us how Sister Josephine, who had charge of the medical supplies, used to appeal sometimes to another nun, "Pray to Saint Anthony, Sister Margaret! I've lost the key to the medicine chest!" and how he sometimes took the liberty of replying "Just look again in your habit pocket, Sister Josephine, before you take St. Anthony's time."

The Sisters for several years remembered my brother at Christmas.

Aymar Embury, Carl's Princeton room-mate, had two younger sisters. During his year at St. Francis, Carl became engaged to one of them. Susan was a tall, pretty girl—at first one noticed little more about her, except that she was fun-loving. But as a matter of fact, she was full of knowledge. Though only twenty-one, she knew a great deal about housekeeping, and (from her care of her two younger brothers) a great deal about children; she had assumed responsibility, and learned to meet emergencies. And from the very letter that she wrote in reply to my welcoming one, I began to feel the bright warmth of her energetic generosity, a quality that catches you up and draws you along, half unconsenting as you are. It's required my being her sister-in-law for a quarter of a century to make me understand it to the full—and do I fully understand it yet? for even more than in her expenditures of time and trouble, it shows in her ready sharing of her rights, honors and affections; and the opportunities for it seem endless.

I was a bridesmaid. It was a day of joy, which I remember with a full and happy heart—I began to say, with a light one. Old as I am, I take all my original delight in going to a wedding. What must it be, one often wonders, to be married for love when the marriages that surround a single life so much enlarge and enhance it?

My father was now well over threescore. Liking all the fattening foods, and indulging freely in them, he grew steadily thinner—but he remained boyishly vigorous. Every summer he and I went to the sea, both delighting as much as ever in the lifegiving onset of salt water. This winter after Carl's marriage, Aunt Jessie went with us to the beautiful town of Daytona, Florida, whose shaded streets would have been noticed even among New England's lovely villages, and whose beaches were delightful beyond the dreams of Cleghorns. We were in Daytona when Dalton, Carl and Sue's first child, was born. A grandson meant more to my father than to most men. He had a peculiarly keen joy in racial and family continuance, and strongly felt that individual death was practically nullified by the succession of the generations.

Then, too, this little boy of Carl and Sue's was the only one at that time to carry on the Cleghorn name. And yet my father had been one of four brothers, and Uncle George, the eldest, had a patriarchal family, seven sons and four daughters. All those sons were living. But all were Tancreds. Uncle George had inherited a property in Yorkshire, called Arden Hall, on condition of changing his name. And of my other uncles, Uncle Tom had died at sea, young and unmarried, coming home to Scotland from China. Of Uncle James Cleghorn's six children, five were girls, and the only son was then unmarried. He has since married and died, leaving only two daughters.

I was a quarter of a century old when Aunt Fanny died. It seems to me now incredible that I could have been so immature, so quiet, so often busied with small ladylike affairs as my journal reflects—so unavailing to the working world. I don't know why I have more patience with my frittering and unfruitful present, for there's not half so much excuse!

I genuinely wanted to be useful. I thought it strange that the church had no real work for young women like me. Hadn't it even as much for me to do as the Historical Society, whose Journalist I was, keeping records week by week of births, deaths and marriages, unusual weather, interesting doings, village changes, etc.? But perhaps the church did have a job for me. I'd never inquired. When we went to New York the winter after Aunt Fanny died, I called on Mr. Seagle, the rector of St. Stephen's Church on West Sixty-Ninth Street near Columbus Avenue—the neighborhood in which we had an apartment. Could he find any work for me to do? Well—I might help the Altar Guild with the flowers. My heart went down. Wasn't there something more active—something with a human side? Perhaps so. Would I like to teach in the sewing school?

I landed, the next Saturday morning, in a crowd of little Italian girls, of whom I was assigned to teach the hemming class. Each of my little girls had a square of unbleached muslin to hem. Their sewing was huge, painful, soiled and often decorated with drops of blood. Often they sewed their little aprons into the square. Their warm young tightly clothed bodies leaned sweetly against mine to have the needle re-threaded or the knot twitched out; they looked at me and across me in every direction with rich, gleeful, gentle eyes. They were merry, loud, quarrelsome and loving; they showed off, had tantrums, gabbled and slapped each other; they called and murmured to me; their soiled, perspiring fingers fondled my hands. I felt a wonderful sense of home among them. Their collective presence was like honey.

There seemed to be no good reason why I couldn't find means to enjoy their company at other times than the bare two hours on Saturday mornings. We soon made up expeditions to the Museums on Saturday and Sunday afternoons. At the Natural History Museum they liked the monkeys, the whale, the blue butterflies, the Indians, the Chinese toys and tiny shoes, and the elevator. At the Metropolitan they cared little for the pictures, but liked the Italian laces and above all the mummies, all shouting musically "Let's go and see the dead!" I loved to go down West Sixty-Ninth Street among masses of them, clustering finally so thick that I couldn't proceed any farther; to go in and see Mary or Teresa, and meet their courteous and hospitable elders, and drink sweet cordial with them in liqueur glasses.

After our Museum trips, some of the children preferred a flower to an ice-cream cone. I thought "How easily I can send them flowers from Vermont in summer! A big responsible girl like Mary Schemoni to take charge of them, and I can label the individual bunches."

124

Picked at evening, in water over night, firm flowers like daisies could be tied in bunches, each bunch with a lump of moss to hold the water in the stems, nosegayed in newspaper, and packed fairly close together without harm. A box of moderate size held substantial bunches for two or three dozen children.

I had letters, too, from Orazin Palumbo and Mary Fiordalisi and many others, most of all from Teresa, until they began getting married, or moving away up to West Farms, and other places where they could get flowers for themselves.

If sewing class in New York, why not one in Manchester? I soon had five or six little girls coming down on Saturdays, sitting on the grass making aprons and pincushions, and before they went home, singing, while Aunt Jessie played for them, "Rig a jig jig," and "Here's to good old Yale, drink her down." When we began meeting round at the children's houses, the little brothers came in and didn't see why they, too, couldn't belong. We had picnics, brothers and all, at Munson's Falls and Orvis Pond, and this band (and its picnics) coalesced with the local Band of Mercy, the children's Humane Society, of which I was the brood-mother also, and whose summer fairs became a juvenile landmark of the year.

All this time I still entertained the idea of being a successful writer. I was selling only an occasional short story, but fifteen or twenty pieces of verse a year, earning two or three hundred dollars. My verses had a much better market than my stories. They were almost all verses of the old-timey kind which I call sun-bonnets. They portrayed characters in pinafore and pantalette, curtseying and going to singing school, kissing daguerreotypes goodnight. Olden times had long had for me a strong enchantment. I read everything Mrs. Alice Morse Earle wrote, and all the old documents and diaries I could find. My head was full of the idiom and manners and the modes of thought which have been preserved to us in print or seem to peer at us from the wooden surfaces of old rustic portraits. Laying these impressions against the Vermont background, I made a set of old figures and a gallery of old landscapes, all marked by the same stiff gentleness, mild

125

rumination, faded sweetness and wild, remote northern backgrounds; they had more than a spice of Miss and Mr. Kellogg, (whose golden-vined Sunday waistcoat figured in two or three of them) a daredevil dash of Mrs. Miner, a corner of Mrs. Baldwin's garden and many a like remembrance.

## NOCTES AMBROSIANAE

From Windward Mountain's barren crest
The roaring gale flies down the west
And drifts the snow on Redmount's breast
    In hollows dark with pine.

Full in its path from hill to hill
There stands, beside a ruined mill,
A lonely house, above whose sill
    A brace of candles shine.

And there a lonely bachelor
And maiden sister, full threescore,
Sit all forgetful of the roar
    Of wind and mountain stream;

Forgot the wind, forgot the snow,
What magic airs about them blow?
They read in wondering voices low
    The *Midsummer Night's Dream*.

And reading, past their frozen hill
In charmed woods they range at will,
And hear the horns of Oberon shrill
    Above the plunging Tam:

Yea, long beyond the cock's first crow,
In dreams they walk where Mayflowers blow:

Late do they read, and liker grow
To Charles and Mary Lamb.

Few of the magazines I ever tried them on but accepted my sun-bonnets. But I always felt that *The Atlantic* was really my best and most discriminating customer, and when I was writing verses which I liked very much myself, I always thought of them in *The Atlantic,* (where "Noctes Ambrosianae" appeared) even when it was the turn to send them somewhere else first.

The motive of the behavior of the characters in my verses was generally the same, something of the good Samaritan. The upshot of them always was— Human creatures, be kind! They said it not challengingly but mildly and wistfully. Within I felt a furious fire burning, but when I tried to write with a hot pen, everything burnt away without a coherent word. Of what I felt powerfully and angrily I couldn't write, but only of what sweetly enchanted and beguiled me; informing it, at best, with a Franciscan character and a memory of the strawberries.

When I tried a novel, its burden and its setting and what mild charm it could muster up were all the same. *The Turnpike Lady* was a kind of daguerreotype in print. Henry Holt and Company—or perhaps it would be truer to say Mr. Henry Holt—published it; I say this because I had a letter from him saying "If that dear little book of yours sells, I shall be much surprised."

There was one emotion that did overflow into poems which weren't sun-bonnets: it was the unbridled and uncontainable joy of life. One of my attempts to express this was called "Hesperides"; it appeared in *Harper's.*

> Legacy of golden days,
> Whence falls such sunlight on my ways?
> What holy magic, what white art
> Delights my body and my heart,
> Looking, on a summer morn,

On falling fields of shining corn,
Of hearing, storm-bound in the wood,
Roar of cataracts in flood?
When many masts of shipping meet
In vistas of a crosstown street,
Or when the sound of trestled trains,
Heard half drowsing, looms and wanes;
When old ballads, bravely read,
Ring out like cymbals in my head—
When I hear the noble vaunt,
Radical and militant
Chivalry of bold young men—
Whence have I such pleasure then?
The lovely fruit of Eden's tree,
The fairy garland, whence to me?

My delight is not made of
Young years, or requited love,
Nor comes it from brave days well spent,
And honor porcelain-innocent.
I cannot think the mystic art
Springs from an ever-loyal heart.
The silver bough, the golden rose
Surely in some far garden grows,
Brought hither by a silent ship,
Whose oars the liquid ether dip
Unheard, unseen by mortal sight
In the dead of night.
So lucid, thrilling, sweet it is,
To taste it would not come amiss
To the saved souls; they would but think
Suddenly sweeter grew their drink;
The angels and the archangels
Might pour it in their sapphire shells.

JOHN AND DOROTHY FISHER'S HOUSE

ZEPHINE HUMPHREY (FAHNESTOCK)

It was the next spring after Carl and Susan were married that Dorothy Canfield's marriage took place to John Redwood Fisher. They went to live in a very old, very small farmhouse in the township of Arlington, well out of the village, well off the main road and actually on the side of Red Mountain. The house and land were a wedding present from Dorothy's aunt and great-aunt, "Miss Mattie and Miss Ann." There were a few acres to begin with, which Christmas and anniversary presents of a field or a piece of woods gradually broadened; "John's field," etc., they used to be called; and on the north side was a lovely wild ravine filled with splendid old pines. They've never moved away from this first home, but have reforested some of their hills, planting fifty thousand pines in which, and in the other woods above, are a hundred rambling paths, with footbridges, and outlooks to the valley below.

My delight was to bicycle down to Dorothy's, spend a day with her, walk in the pine ravine, sit down on a log, show her the verses I'd been writing, and hear her last short story in rough draft. She reads aloud in a clear light voice, in a matter-of-fact manner, never stressing a point, never putting in a footnote, always leaving her narrative to stand alone. At the end of the afternoon or evening, her husband would read aloud, often George Meredith's poems; or Dorothy would read Blake's.

The attraction I felt in Dorothy was only an intenser degree of what everybody seemed to feel. But it was steadily intensifying, drawing more and more into itself, year by year, the few and simple currents of my nature. She fulfilled my two great hungers; my passion for inclusiveness, for downing all pales, and my intense desire to see life lived with amenity, with grace, in every direction. To her every creature seemed an object of respect, of concern, and of a pleasure to behold. And then, beside this double sense of fulfilment, her hopes and conceptions were endlessly enlarging to mine. There was a perpetual enkindling between us, which I can only describe by the exclamation of Montagne, the final word in all friendships, I suppose,

"And why did I love Étienne de la Boëtie? Because it was he! Because it was I!"

Dorothy already had a deep repugnance, deeper than mine was in those days, for arbitrary authority, for children who jumped the moment they were spoken to—the unqualified obedience of soldiers and monks. And she had, already in her twenties, a working technique of the opposite kind; that sympathetic and creative searching out of another's deepest wish and will, which issues in such extraordinary success in all sorts of human relationships, so that the successes of the authoritarian methods seem very shallow and transient by comparison. She is essentially a great educator—the complete antithesis of one who trains, imparts, instructs, corrects and exacts, contact with whom is "a discipline." If she, who so reveres life and human nature, had founded a school of creative education, it would have drawn students from every country on earth. Perhaps her novels have done more, because they have carried into family life those ideals of unfailing mutual respect and flexible understanding which are also in partial practice in a few vision-following schools.

In the first year of her marriage her first novel, *Gunhild,* came out. It was published by Henry Holt, who in the same year took my *Turnpike Lady*. Indeed it had been Dorothy who suggested my trying the Holts.

*Gunhild* was a love story, laid in Norway. It sold, I remember, six hundred copies, and my book sold three hundred. We were to have received royalties of ten per cent on all copies sold over fifteen hundred. Of the various reviews we pored over together I only remember what the *Sun* said of each of us. Gunhild, it declared, was an unconscionably long time hanging over the waterfall in her hypnotic absorption before she was rescued. My little book it recommended—as a soporific.

In the same year with ours, Henry Holt brought out a third young woman's book, which a number of readers liked and told their friends about, and so a modest success began for it, which, thirty years afterward, is still quietly going on. It was Zephine Humphrey's *Over Against Green Peak,* the first of those delicately written, cordially intimate, unobtrusively profound and touching books of hers, which bring, year after year, a scattering of congenial strangers to her door on pilgrimages from all parts of the country. There seem to be in every community two or three readers who are enchanted by just her blend of humor, simplicity and profundity. Never selling in large numbers, her books are always sure of this small discriminating audience; and none of them more sure than *Green Peak,* old as it is.

I already knew Zephine before *Green Peak* was published. Her village, Dorset, is distant the same eight miles from ours on the north that Dorothy's town, Arlington, is distant on the south. I remember well my first meeting with Zephine, and our standing together before a bookcase in the square old historical house which the Humphreys lived in. I was thinking the while, "I must soon see you again, calm and comprehending stranger."

Zephine has blue eyes of somewhat the same quality as those of Robert Frost, candid, open, calm—penetrating beyond appearances. Both have surroundings of eyelid and lashes which moderate with humor the boldness of thought. Zephine's are somewhat softer, less challenging, less intense.

I couldn't see her very often because of distance—yes, eight miles was still distant to those who had no cars. But there were two or three chances every summer between her friends and mine, and none of them was missed.

Dorothy and she had never met, when Mr. Henry Holt, greatly tickled with the quiet advance *Green Peak* was making—crowing over his professional readers about it—and interested in all of us, invited the Fishers, Zephine and me for a "round up of Vermont authors," over a week end, at his place near Burlington.

It was in June, 1908. We had a pleasant time indeed, being shown his woodland vistas of Lake Champlain and all Burlington's high lights by Mr. Holt driving four-in-hand; he had the party photographed thus, and when we went home, he exclaimed in the station, "I don't see why I shouldn't kiss you goodbye all round!" "Why don't you?" replied Dorothy.

I brought away with me an affectionate memory of Mrs. Holt, so graceful and so gracious, permanently tired, we'd all thought, by being the mistress of three or four large houses and entertaining, all the year round, for a hospitable husband and children and stepchildren of varying ages. Mr. Holt had long been a pillar of the Simplified Spelling Board, whose recommendations he faithfully carried out in all his own letters, spelling "have" and "give" "hav" and "giv," etc. Mrs. Holt told us that during their engagement (she was a Miss Taber of Boston) an elderly relation of hers accidentally picked up one of Mr. Holt's letters and was found soon afterward in tears, exclaiming "Florence is going to marry a man who can't even spell!"

From the time of our Fairholt visit, Zephine, Dorothy and I have seen a great deal of each other, and done a great many pleasant things together. Especially have we shared with each other whatever we might be writing, or even projecting; and in this way all Dorothy's novels, back to and including *The Squirrel Cage,* have been familiar to Zephine and me long before the publisher saw them. Weighting down her three or four chapters with apples to keep them from blowing away, as we sat on the grass in Zephine's orchard, Dorothy would read us, in her rapid, lucid, easy manner, an early draft, perhaps a little angular, with events not mellowed yet by detail nor fully shaded with sidelights and shadows—not deepened by reflection; and the next month she would read us the same chapters in second, third or seventh draft, coming out now in rich complexities of deed, thought and character.

It's always illuminating to see Dorothy in process of stabilizing all she writes by her constant re-pinning of it fast to the common lot, to generic human experience. Her greatest achievement, to my way of thinking, lies in her power to stand firmly on this realistic ground while at the same time she pulls a possible future right through the present. It's a thing teachers sometimes do, but they seldom know how they do it, and I'm fairly sure Dorothy doesn't know how she does it. Teachers do it for individual children, whom they know fairly well; Dorothy does it for an unknown multitude. In her public speaking there's the same double reflection of the audience—a picture soberly true, yet expanding under its own eyes, in full daylight, into a whole category of its possibilities.

"The future does not come to meet us; it streams from behind us over our heads."

Nobody could single out the influences strongly affecting American life for the first quarter of this century without including Dorothy's novels. They seize the reader by an intimate hand and take him at once on an incursion and an excursion. Readers have learned to expect that her next novel will take them a little farther still into their possible selves.

# 8

A SHADOW now occasionally crossed my simple, sanguine and life-enjoying mind, a notion that I was never really going to accomplish those powerful literary works which would blow a noble trumpet of social generosity and *noblesse oblige* before the world. What? should I find myself always planning and never achieving a solid Bookful? a richly complicated and yet firmly unified novel? No! No! my workwoman's conscience replied; I wasn't afraid of work—I wasn't a procrastinator! Like Strafford, "I was for Thorough." Why was it, then, that in spite of cherishing this hope above most others, I seldom wrote anything but short poems? Was it the human interests, all so small, but each so appealing, that thronged in every day, asking for some little, urgent, immediate help? Partly it was these. They often took two of my three possible writing hours. It was sending up to the Pittsford Sanatorium somebody from our town; it meant writing half a dozen notes to summer people who might help with the expense; rather carefully written notes they ought to be, putting the case's best foot forward. Half a dozen posters needed to be printed by hand for the children's little Fair, and thumbtacked up in the postoffice, Equinox House, etc. It was time to send that box of daisies to the little Italian girls in West Sixty-Ninth Street.

Yes, it was partly these things. But I wasn't the only one who had these strings to her bow. Other people had them, and sometimes they cared just as sharply as I did about them. Dorothy had more of them, even in those early days, than I had. Yet she wrote; she found solid time every day for writing. So did Zephine, whose heart was also vulnerable.

I don't know why I didn't realize better, by that time, what other

134

difficulties I had, inside ones; that my mind had only a lyrical short span of creative impulse, just enough to labor joyfully at short sets of verses, some of which were really poems, though many of them were written only under the playtime sense of enchantment, not the all-powerful sense of beauty. And beside this, I think there's always been something over-speeded and elliptical in my prose thinking. Getting up in the morning, walking up for the mail, I was overwhelmed by troops of strong arguments, trampling one after another through my mind. One or more article seemed as good as written every day. Mounted on analogies, they galloped after each other too fast for more than one in a hundred to be written out in comfortable fashion for readers to follow.

Perhaps this short-circuiting of thought, this swiftness like the elliptical speed of dreams, is common to most immature writers, and gives them their greatest difficulty? Perhaps it's the reason for the halting and trivial utterances of adolescents, whose intensity of feeling is all the while beating at their throats for expression. At all events I made slow headway against it; progressing not year by year, but only "if" as Hazlitt said, "I count my life by lusters." I did succeed in writing a few coherent articles, such as "The Case Against Vivisection" for *The Forum* and such tiny, trig ones as fitted "The Contributors' Club" in *The Atlantic;* sometimes managing to tuck into these articlettes a small stab of live human concern. But I couldn't release into verse or prose any real sample of the angry pity which always boiled just under the crust of every other feeling. Why couldn't I open the valves to that? Whenever I tried, it always cracked the dish. What Wordsworth said must be so; poetry had to be made out of emotion remembered in tranquillity. And my red-headed pity showed no signs of growing tranquil.

My disquiet was increased by a note I had, in the course of time, from Mr. Bliss Perry, editor at that time of *The Atlantic.* Though accepting another of my pieces of verse, he nevertheless shrewdly inquired whether I wasn't ever going to open another vein beside this narrow one of country places in the olden time?

It was ceasing to be a great comfort to me to remember Hazlitt's remark, "For many years I was dumb and a changeling."

This failure to let the principal fire of my life into my poems troubled something much hotter than conscience—fellow-feeling. I more and more felt that I was withholding my little bank account of power and publicity from my sisters and brothers in extremis.

In my prayers I often remembered this.

Praying was still a vital resource of life. My confident prayers at five years old or so had not yet become outmoded. Of course with maturity—and long before strong grief—I felt the slow widening, deepening of inward life. There grew up among my petitions a core of contemplation, a taste of orison inexpressibly deep and calm.

Zephine talked of the mystics. Eventually she lent me one of Evelyn Underhill's books about them. As soon as I began to read it, I found myself in the presence of a new kind of beauty. I realized that I had already come some way toward mysticism without having known anything about it (except from the inside).

Religion, as St. James said, consisted in being beautifully useful and kind. That was all there was of it, fundamentally. Of course, it could never be beautiful or useful to befriend one creature at the expense of maltreating another. In religion there could be no Pale, no failures or waste material, and no preferred souls.

Bringing along this unshaken conviction of what it is to be religious, I came into the outer courts of mystic thought. There I found a far better conception of God than any other which I knew. Instead of conceptions of God as lawgiver, king, captain, champion, etc., a God who took sides and had enemies, and, what was worse and more unGodlike, punished them, the God I found among the mystics was an infinite life, flowing through all forms like illumination, and readily reached at any time by any fragment of finite life, which it instantly lighted with divinity. Here was a God who was really different from man, though wonderfully and realistically inclusive of him.

136

Though this conception left unsolved, or rather unreconciled, as I think all reasoning does, the problem of evil; and though it left unsolved the question What is circumstance? yet I found by this conception, slowly unveiling within, a deeper form of prayer, and instead of my childhood habit of petitioning in detail for "the relief and benefit of the estate of man" (and beast) I began to pray to the divine love,

"Enter my heart; be my life."

A part of this gradual discovery (or so it seems to me) was a very concrete experience with a friend, which finally, long afterward, in a very roundabout way, released my convictions into my poems, all hot as they lived.

There was among my correspondents a lonely woman with whom I had sought acquaintance through a "Sunshine" society. She was a woman of about my own age, delicate and depressed, living from hand to mouth in New York, as people did who could play a little, draw a little, teach a little. Sooner or later it dawned upon all her friends that she was heavily encumbered by a weight of self-pity which she never succeeded in throwing off. Whenever she secured a job, her natural desire to make good in it and win recognition was soon swallowed up in her incessant hunger for the pity and compassion of everybody about her. She needed to fail, to be defeated, to win this necessary pity.

She also greatly discouraged and perplexed those who could only help her by an occasional lift. When she had asked urgently for winter underwear, and when it had been furnished, her next letter showed no relief on that score, but was entirely occupied with anxiety about the care of her teeth. And when some kind dentist arranged about the teeth, the next letter was filled from end to end with fresh anxiety about goloshes, and only in a postscript remembered, as if by the bye, that "Dr. Smith has fixed my teeth."

I was subject myself to self-pity. I had plenty of it on tap, and could spray it all over any little ail that clouded the blue sky of my health.

It was clear how, in my poor friend's case, the malignant bacillus had had plenty of misfortunes to feed on, in the cellarlike loneliness of her life.

How to help her in this regard? There was freshly beginning in New York at that time a branch of the Emmanuel Movement which Dr. Worcester had been carrying on for ten years or more in Boston. This "Episcopalian form of Christian Science" was an attempt to revive the apostolic art of healing on a modern foundation of psychology, and with the advice and help of distinguished doctors. Starting with a memorable clinic at the Emmanuel Church parish house, the movement had widened out like a river, and everybody who was interested in health and happiness on a large scale had read *Religion and Medicine*. Dr. Batten, then the rector of St. Mark's Church in the Bowery, was the chief practitioner of it in New York. There were also two or three young clergymen engaged in it.

Freshly touched by those new, penetrating thoughts of the mystics about our nearness to the divine springs of life, I heard with joy of these efforts to widen a pathway toward them for the sick and discouraged. It seemed to me that my unlucky friend Amy might perhaps find here the very help she needed.

But how to suggest it to her, and not, by the very idea, turn her sensitive habit of grief and defeat against it? Nothing, in those days, was more offensive to persons who clung to trouble than to suggest that they consult a Christian Scientist, or try the Emmanuel Movement. Plenty of other people as well as Amy would be indignant at the first word.

My best chance of persuading her, I thought, would be to take it up first in my own behalf; and I had at hand the very thing to invoke it for; namely, my chronic sneezes, a sinus ail for which I'd had a number of small operations. To be sure, I was scarcely in sufficient discomfort to crowd in among Dr. Worcester's beneficiaries. Still, I should like a better nose. Having begun inquiries on my own account, I asked Amy if she didn't want to try it too. I would if she would.

138

Amy went to one of the young practitioners in New York and became interested in what he told her. My hopes were rising for her when her adviser left New York for a parish in the west. This cut off one beginning, and she never fairly made another. Delicate and discouraged people, I now better understand, find it all but impossible to persevere. It takes vitality they haven't got, and habits they've never had the physical capital to acquire. Their best chance seems—to have a persevering friend at hand who has time and goodwill enough to keep pulling them along. Amy had no such luck. The partial and intermittent help her friends could give never went half far enough.

Her last years were spent in a County Home—and perhaps they were, after all, the serenest. It was a humane and comfortable one.

I often think how much perseverance we expect from the poor, and how little perseverance we ourselves display, fat and comfortable as we are, in helping them. We give them up after a few setbacks, saying (just as they do) "Oh, it's no use trying any more!" And we dwell quite as often, I fear, on their faults and failings as they dwell on the faults and failings of their situation in life; showing as little hardihood in making the best of their drooping courage as they themselves show in making the best of an underpaid job, or a nightly backache. Our example, in short, is quite contrary to our precepts, so cheerfully proffered to them; and "What we do (or don't do) is too loud in their ears for them to hear what we say."

In this matter of appealing to the Emmanuel Movement, as in every other circumstance, I was infinitely more fortunate than my poor friend. On Dr. Worcester's advice, I'd bought two small books, one of which was *The Mystic Will,* by C. G. Leland, (the Harvard professor who made himself much more famous by writing the song of "The Lone Fish-Ball"). In Leland's book I found a short formula for self-suggestion which brought down to earth, for the first time, those useless vague generalities some of my friends were so free with, "Take your mind off your nose," "Think you're going to be better and you will be," "Forget it and remember the *Maine,*" etc.

I had a spectacular success with my nose the first time I used the formula from Leland's book; one that I cannot verify, but it resembled this—

"I steadfastly will, and calmly believe, that I shall rest and be refreshed by the night, and go through tomorrow with confidence, health, pleasure and success. Fears and apprehensions, blow away . . . blow far away . . . over the edge of the world! Be lost there, lost and forgotten."

One to whom words are so living as they naturally are to me takes such a form of them into the imagination, dwells intensely on every vital word, repeating the whole, with full leisure, until it is realized into the marrow of the bones. Whenever fears intruded, I repeated the latter part, no matter how often they returned. (Indeed, this part of the formula seems never—for me—to wear out; I have used it for many years, and I still occasionally banish fidgety fears by means of it.) The process was soothing, fortifying and enjoyable. As Leland or Dr. Worcester had advised, I went to sleep while suggesting—an easy thing to do, for the process relaxes nerve and brain, releasing the whole of being from that exaggerated anxious carefulness and sense of responsibility in minute details which often keep people awake.

For some time it had been my unfortunate habit to wake up sneezing in the middle of the night, and to keep on sneezing until I was too irritated to go to sleep for hours. Now in spite of planting the formula firmly in mind, I woke up at the usual time and awaited the opening sneeze. When I didn't sneeze, I began to get excited and to wonder incredulously whether the effort I'd made could really work so promptly. For about fifteen minutes I hesitated to move. At last my confidence began to rise. The formula had worked. I turned over and still didn't sneeze. Unless one has endured a small chronic ailment it's impossible to believe how liberated one can feel at even a momentary escape. I was too elated to go to sleep, but it was a calm sort of elation. I felt the whole experience pouring like fresh life through my veins. Here was a power in my own hands, which I could readily learn how to use; a possibility like radio, taking from the natural air about us an unsuspected current, and turning it, with a bit of simple machinery, to great use and benefit.

Those violent night sneezes never returned.

This open window toward the sun, the cultivation of health by acts of thought, faith in life and energetic goodwill, gave me as it gives everybody an unexpected sense of power, as delicious and substantial as the sense of youth. It gave me a wide and sunny view of human possibilities, a view in a quite new direction,—inward. With little premeditation I found myself writing poems about it, such as "The Deep Spring in the Evergreen Forest—"

> Who will turn and enter the green forest?
> Who will seek and taste the fabled spring?—

and "The Soul and Body."

> Body and soul are married lovers;
>     God was their witness when they wed
> Beside the Tree of Life in Eden;
>     "These twain shall be one flesh," He said.
>
> But man has put them oft asunder;
>     And not alone by fire and sword,
> But duped by lying metaphysic,
>     He oft denies, in deed and word,
>
> This marriage between earth and heaven;
>     While ever, to the steadfast skies,
> The prayers of these old constant lovers
>     In patient iteration rise;
>
> "O priest, my little love remember!
>     My patient love, the body, see!
> What thou canst do to ease her burdens
>     Shall greatly lift and strengthen me!"

"O wise physician, now no longer
  Neglect my lord and love, the soul!
While he lies sick with pain and fever
  No drug can make the body whole!"

These and other such poems Dorothy and I afterward gathered up in our little joint book on self-suggestion, *Fellow Captains.*

The dozens of operations on my nose and head which had probably saved me from the fearful headaches of sinus sufferers had been done by Dr. Lewis Coffin, chief of staff at Manhattan Ear, Throat and Nose Hospital in New York. Dr. Coffin had done so many things to the inside of my head that he used to say he'd tried all his collection of scissors, "snares," and other implements on me and there were few landmarks left there to guide him about. I had a cloudless confidence in him. He used to say, of the various mental and spiritual forces of health, "Far be it from me to laugh at them!" and this he said sincerely, though soon after saying it he was sure to laugh. But now when, after my first summer of intermittent but cumulative success with self-suggestion, I reported to him in the fall, he said "What have you done? The *architecture* of your nose is improved."

I've had in my life so little pain that I seldom encountered a chance to try self-suggestion for that. I have, however, once or twice in my life, had an ulcerated tooth; and though it was evidently a pale example of the appalling pain I'd expected, I did mind it enough to make the effort to take my consciousness off it, as one would lift and lug away a lump of rock. I succeeded thus in giving myself complete, though temporary, relief. And once having a double boil in the middle ear, which became sufficiently inflamed to clamp my jaws together for a day or two, I made a strong effort, when wearied with the pain, to pry my consciousness loose from it. I thus succeeded in obtaining a couple of hours of very refreshing sleep, free, to all intents and purposes, from any pain at all.

Though I told Amy of my experiences, and urged her somewhat, she couldn't muster up energy enough to renew her efforts. My conservative aunt, however, was impressed. Sure that nothing operating under the aegis of the Episcopal Church could be far amiss, she herself began to use suggestion. We found that we could benefit each other. I could sometimes quiet her nervous headaches; and when, a few years later, I fell into the dreadful habit known as common asthma, she could ease my panting distress by murmuring over and over, in her voice full of loving persistence,

"Easier breathing; quieter breathing; calmer . . . slower . . . comfortable breathing."

Eventually I got rid of this asthma in a manner so simple that I believe it might be used widely. My difficulty with trying to use self-suggestion for it had been the panic dread which even between bouts with it lay heavy on my imagination. A time came when I was suffering from it in a boarding-house where my helpless loud coughing and panting from one to three every night must have been intolerable to the occupants of neighboring rooms, though they were too good-natured to protest. My aunt several times protested in their behalf; couldn't I choke back those horrible coughs which bothered me and everybody else?

Like others in such a case, I was indignant. Did she think I coughed for the fun of it? Nobody could have persuaded me—and certainly no member of my own family—that I was hanging on to my misery. But one day, the local doctor's remedies being of no avail as usual, I became so weary and exasperated that I made up my mind to take her advice and choke back my cough even at the risk of bursting a blood vessel. I was alone in my own room, and I could struggle and fight the infernal tickle as I pleased. Squeezing both hands savagely tight over my mouth, I forced myself not to cough, though I tumbled about the floor like those characters in the Bible who were released with violent struggles from the devils that possessed them. Extraordinarily soon, however, all inclination to cough disappeared. On succeeding days I went through the same struggles a few times, and then my asthma disappeared.

Asthma, I knew, is accustomed to disappear abruptly and for a long

143

time. I had it again once or twice. But in the end these cave-man methods banished the habit, and with it all those coughs which usually accompany colds. Perhaps if the fear of asthma goes, the asthma goes too. I think I acquired it from a too vivid description of it which Mrs. Miner once gave me; it stayed in my memory all too clear, and perhaps took root there and began to put forth branches. After a time without bouts of asthma I found that the first faint preliminaries—the squeaky breathing, and the meek little cough that had formerly made my heart sink—could be ousted by a very mild method. I choked back two coughs and let the third have its head; this, with a difficult but effective relaxing of the chest, would clear the whole horizon. Pillow your face (face-downward) high enough to leave a shallow interval between your chest and the bed; then relentlessly make your chest relax until it sinks down and rests on the bed. Of course asthma—I speak only of the common, not of the cardiac, variety, of which I know nothing—seems to vanish when the chest muscles are relaxed. By this means, plentiful encouragement, a little extra rest and plenty of drinking water or lemonade, I believe I have cured several children of asthma in the school where I taught.

But the difference I experienced between the cure of my sneezes and the cure of my asthma was a significant one. It was the difference between a mechanical device and a growing plant. When the asthma was cured it was ended, and that was all; the ashcart had come and carried it away, and if it came again, it could be carted off again in the same manner.

But when the sneezes were gone, there was an accession of vital power that remained. Out of the ashheap was rising a plant; something energizing, nourishing; it would bear fruit season after season. And as one releasing experience unfolded out of another, the fountains of my anger and pity would yet be unsealed by this power, and I should be able to write my "burning" poems.

This happened in Rome, when Dorothy, Zephine and I, with our respective families, were there in 1912. Strange—and how self-centered!—that better than the eternal monuments of Rome, I should remember that I began to write my burning poems there. It was at just about the moment when I was having my first delighted sight of an Italian garden—it was Villa Medici, on a clearing December afternoon that felt like May in Vermont. Just as we passed beneath the green arch of the gateway, the sun came out on the dark, shining ilex, and a form of beauty never imagined before laid its rich finger on my eyes. How many times I'd thought, "Why do people go on so about Italian gardens? A garden's just a garden." At this delightful moment I surely wasn't consciously remembering that on two or three previous afternoons, in quiet half hours, I'd been suggesting to myself that I should find—now! the longed-for power to write socially rebellious verse.

Yet in the midst of seeing this and other great Roman gardens, taking whole-hearted pleasure, even enchantment, in them, it gave me still sharper pleasure to find that I could write, at last, such poems as "The Jail," "Salem Hills to Ellis Island" and

## LAST SUNDAY

Threading the rusty pools and the inky rivers
That fill the dismal courts of the iron foundry,
By that blind endless alley whereof the children
Creep with their sweated work to the crowded doorways,
Giving and taking pestilence from the sunshine
That swarms with flies from the steaming heaps of refuse—
I passed the bright saloon whence young men issue,
Leering with mouths still sensitive, still aspiring,
At the pallid girls leaning out of the dingy windows
With eyes—O holy marvel!—still sweet and tender.

Thence turning sharply into a square of gardens
I came to a church of chaste and glorious Gothic,
Whereof the clustered pillars were bronze and marble,
The apse embossed with many reliefs of angels;

There was the tall rood-screen of fretted ivory,
The altar porcelain overlaid with crystal,
The holy Cup of rubies sunken in silver,
The Cross above it gemmed with the pearls of India;

And as I entered through these shadowy arches
Lighted with beams cerulean, Tyrian, amber,
The organ melted into a trembling silence,
And from his Book the priest began to utter
*"He that hath ears to hear, O let him hearken,*
*O let him hear what the Spirit saith to the churches."*

I think this was the first burning poem I wrote, and the first of
mine of that kind that *The American Magazine* printed. In those
days *The American* was almost the organ of the insurgents in Congress and in American life. In its brilliant band of editors Ida Tarbell
was one, and Ray Stannard Baker was another. The chief editor was
John S. Phillips. It was a chivalric magazine, bold and gentle as a
Quaker, and from a literary point of view, unusually creative and
symbolic; we have nothing like it now, for with all else it made a
popular appeal. It published, about 1912, and Macmillan republished
in book form, a daring pacifist story, called "The Impeachment of
President Israels." This utopian narrative was so veracious-sounding
that a good many people began looking through histories to see when
Israels was President. It related how this pacifist president met a
provocative international situation without bloodshed; and by a
curious chance, the nation with whom, in the story, we were in
danger of going to war, was Germany.

I always felt pride when my poems, and especially my burning
ones, appeared in *The American.*

Suggestion, then, had done for me two very substantial things
(among others). Later I came to think about suggestion in regard
to a need that's much more urgent. I am anxious to see the day when
pain—almost as a whole!—will fall under its benevolent power. For

it seems certain to me that the next fifty years or so will see a great development in the western world of the art of controlling the consciousness. If it is true that most healthy-minded adults and practically all children under fourteen are amenable to hypnotism, why have we not in all hospitals a reliable hypnotist, to relieve their pain? Since we are able, why don't we relieve the great bulk of the pain that is suffered on all sides? Why not also have a clinic, where patients can be taught the simple rudiments of relieving themselves, without drugs, of pain? Perhaps this would do more than repressive laws, to control drug habits.

I wonder if people really believe very much in the shadowy "dangers" of hypnotism? As a schoolgirl, I wouldn't let anybody hypnotize me—I was afraid they'd "weaken my will." Now I believe this was superstition. Of course human beings continually influence each other, and often in evil directions. That hypnotism increases this power, I scarcely believe. When I was young, there was a good deal of actual fear that by hypnotism being brought into public notice, some criminal would be able to suggest a crime to some upright citizen, who would be obliged forthwith to commit robbery or murder. It was also feared that the plea would be frequently made by criminals that they'd been hypnotized. This revival of witchcraft ideas soon evaporated, but it may have had something to do with the present neglect of the hypnotic power to relieve pain, and invigorate the mind. Not a hospital, so far as I know, has thought of adding to its staff of anæsthetists a qualified and upright hypnotist.

F. W. H. Myers, who knew Charcot and most other famous psychologists of his day, was able to state that it was the consensus of opinion among them that nobody under hypnotism could be made to do anything at which his moral sense revolted. It was their conviction, I believe, that what the hypnotist can do is only to reach and reinforce the subject's own innermost will. This seems to fit the experience of those who, like Dr. Worcester, use suggestion for the relief of humanity.

Most people seem to think that some of their acquaintances, at

147

some time or other, have worried themselves into some ailment or other, which overclouds life for them and for their families. They will commonly say of these acquaintances, "I wish she'd go to a Christian Scientist—that's just the kind of thing they cure." But many such observers never go farther than this. They don't go on to wonder, as they well might, whether, if the imagination can start a symptom of disease, and keep it going, it might not start a symptom of health, and keep that going, too.

In the middle of the summer of 1909, Dorothy's daughter Sally was born. When I heard her name, and that I was to be her godmother, I felt an extraordinary sensation—I was drenched with thrilling and incredulous vainglory. And not for a moment only, but every time I thought of it for years. It's one of the great and lasting elations of my life.

While Sally was a baby, I wrote the first of my many persevering attempts to portray her beloved mother.

## DOROTHEA

Young she is, and slight to view
    In her homemade cambric dresses;
Are her sweet eyes gray or blue?
    Shade of twilight are her tresses.
Fairy-fine at first she seems;
    But a longer look confesses
She's more wholesome stuff than dreams.

Yet I mind an April moon
    Shining down an orchard alley—
From one book, companions boon,
    There we read *Love in the Valley.*
And I saw bright phantoms race,
    Thousand phantoms fleet and rally
All across her lighted face.

Once, within the ancient ground
  Where her fathers all lie sleeping,
She, beside a recent mound,
  Still and tender, but not weeping,
Stood; that picture on my heart
  Fain am I forever keeping;
With that look I will not part.

O but in her maiden days
  How she led the children trooping
Through the old familiar plays!
  Up her sash and flounces looping,
If the tiniest lost his cue,
  To his side she ran, and stooping,
Caught his hand and danced him through.

Met you her in Hemlock Wood
  In the white midwinter weather,
When the pine's a tufted hood
  And the fern's a crystal feather?
Heard you then her yodel sweet
  And a far reply, together
Float in echo where they meet?

Ariel voice, from range to range
  Lightly tossed and sweetly flying!
All her notes to murmurs change
  When the winter light is dying.
All in magic murmurs she
  Laps and lulls the wee one lying,
Pearl of twilight, on her knee.
                —*The American Magazine*

My father was now well past seventy. I don't know how I can
have grown up without ever contemplating the obvious idea of going

out west and keeping house for him. Mrs. Miner, in her accepted rôle of our adopted grandmother, had once told me, in a burst of frankness, that everybody in town thought I ought to go. I received this information with pure and unmixed amazement. I still remember how utterly impractical the idea then appeared to me, so that I only wondered how anybody with any sense could entertain it; and in my innocence, extraordinary as it now seems, I supposed my father had never thought of it.

How could I have been so unthinking all my young life—how grown up with such a blind side to my immense affection for him? Was it that I had an exaggerated habit of relegating all initiative of this kind to my elders? Was it that I was too besottedly rooted and embedded in the beloved town of Manchester? Or was my imagination, which I thought so warm and alive, really sluggish, that I never dreamed my father might like his daughter by him in a home of his own? Has everybody some such mysterious stretches of conduct in his own life, to wonder at forever?

Mrs. Miner's words sank slowly into my mind, and kept on sinking deeper for years. Too late I saw that I ought to have gone long before, while my aunts were both living, and Carl unmarried. Now I should have left Aunt Jessie alone; she would have sold her home, and entered that boarding existence from which my father could only be released at her expense.

Meantime the academic fact that my father was growing older had no realistic side that any of us could see. His spare, limber frame moved as fast and as springily as ever, in that English walk that seems to say, with every bend of the knees, "How I enjoy this!" His pleasure in the sea, his modest skill in swimming, were exactly the same. He walked up the mountain with Mark and Carl, and chopped a tree down the next day. He took as fresh an enjoyment as ever in new inventions, and in camping and tramping with younger men. Among children he was as fun-loving as ever. With all his old bounce he made a bet with two Minneapolis schoolboys that Sir Thomas Lipton would "lift" the Cup; and when the boys rushed in to tell him that

Lipton had lost once more, he said in sepulchral tones, "Boys, I'll take me breakfast in bed tomorrow morning." Aunt Cecilia, in Scotland, his elder sister, had lost her memory. He had letters from Uncle George telling how she took her brother for her father, and her son for her brother; and my always forgetful father began to say to me "Sally, d'ye know I think me memory is going? like poor Cecilia's." But it was easy to laugh at him—indeed one couldn't help it. His memory was the same absent-minded thing it had always been. There may have been a touch of growing older in the great reliance he now placed on everything Carl said. It was so, to be sure, with all of us; we had a fixed respect for Carl's proved judgment and accuracy; seldom, indeed, would any of our family go counter to Carl's advice, in any important thing. I remember one quaint instance of my father's leaning upon Carl's judgment, remember it with a smile that is only half amusement—half of it is pleasure. We'd all three been at the seashore together over Sunday, and he and I were going to Manchester next day, while Carl went home to Garden City, leaving with us a memorandum of the rather complicated trip to Vermont, and admonishing us thus, "You've got three changes to make, and if you don't look out, you two absent-minded people will take the wrong train. Here's a list of the places and hours—just follow this, and you'll make it all right." Keeping this precious paper in his pocket, my father consulted it at all points of change. Once however, he glanced at a railroad time-table, in one of the stations where we waited. "What do you think!" he exclaimed; "this time-table is wrong! It says the train leaves at 3:15, whereas Carl, here, says it leaves at 3:10."

He was a high favorite with Susan, my brother's wife. She and Carl asked him to lay down business and come and live with them at Garden City. A pleasant life the Cleghorns led in that cheerful town, where Carl was the only doctor, and where everybody gathered at the Community Club. And my father was indeed thinking of giving up business. He even played with the seductive idea of a Florida orange grove. But we wanted him to come to Vermont, and the plan we all finally accepted was for him to spend the summers with Aunt Jessie and me, and for us to join him, in return, for the winters in Minneapolis. Meantime we'd been going south together for parts of several winters while we discussed these plans.

Many years before, he had wanted very much to revisit Scotland, taking Carl and me. By careful computings he had come to believe he could finance it. For two or three reasons (one of them was a momentary delicacy in health, and a desperate adolescent homesickness of mine) he gave it up. The chance never recurred. It's a grief to me that he never went back to Scotland, but I am glad he never gave up business, or left Minneapolis. He'd grown very fond of them both in a quarter of a century. And then he had come to be recognized as a competent judge of land and property in relation to banks. In our winter holidays he was very happy for a while, and then we could see him wearying a little for the office and the company of men busy with affairs, and the week-end trips into the Dakota wilds.

He went ahead of us one winter to Raleigh, North Carolina, to engage rooms for all three of us. One of his bad bronchial colds suddenly grew worse. Carl and I were telegraphed for. Carl got the message first and caught an earlier train. The trip with its gray waits at junctions and its unfamiliar stations creeping by seemed greatly longer than its nineteen hours, as I was slowly carried down alone. At first my father could talk, with all his natural objectiveness, of Wilbur and Orville Wright, whose flying filled the papers at the moment; he could laugh at my account of how my borrowed suit-case with a defective catch had burst open on the elevated train in New York as I started to leave at the station, and how my clean cotton underwear had strewn the aisle, and been picked up by half a dozen friendly passengers. But it was only a day or two before he was too weak for any of that. Without becoming pneumonia, his cold had grown too heavy for him to throw off. He rested away, after speaking a little of my mother.

"As soon as your father's better, bring him out here to recuperate," Dr. and Mrs. Hunter, of St. Augustine's School, had said. New acquaintances of the previous summer, they were the only friends we had in Raleigh. A sister and brother couldn't have been kinder to us, in all our strangeness and anxiety, than these every-moment-occupied executives of a great school. Twenty-five years have in no wise dimmed the memory of such warmth and goodness.

That being so delightful, gentle, droll, whose hand I'd never outgrown taking hold of when we walked together, whose company was always best and gayest in his own family, whose capacity for fun and pleasure were as wide and deep as his retentiveness for love and sorrow—and that was wide and deep—drifted into the profound sleep as softly as Aunt Fanny had done, as softly as most of us, the doctors tell us, will drift away when our time comes. As he died, I whispered love and forecasts of joy into his ear. Even at the moment of his death we rejoiced that his occasional fears couldn't now be fulfilled of long illness, pain or mental helplessness. He was a lifelong believer in euthanasia and so am I. I had often wondered—if he were to be confronted with the long pain he dreaded, could I, knowing his fixed wish, have courage to put his body to sleep? Death had been kind to him instead.

But when we started on the long journey back to Garden City, I felt suddenly wounded and weakened by sharp sadness as if from loss of blood. I felt sadness piercing all over me, and began to wonder "Who is there that I can bear to meet?" I thought of one and another, and rejected images the dearest and warmest. "Isn't there one?" I thought. "What shall I do if no one can speak to me without giving me pain?" The image of Dalton, my brother's little boy, came smiling into my heart. To play with four-year-old Dalton and hear his glee—there'd be no wound in that, but honey and balm. I thus discovered that little children's inviolable merriment is the perfect cure for the sad heart. My father's never-failing joy in children lent the discovery an extra sweetness.

# 9

How close together in time, and perhaps in significance, could we but comprehend it, is the coming and going of lives! My father died in January, and in May Carl and Sue's Fannie was born. She looked like a sprig of arbutus lying on the big bed in our guest room when they brought her up to Vermont in August. She had the same fair hair and brown eyes that my sister had had, and the same lively, confident spirit that Aunt Fanny had been so free with all her life.

My father's death had brought my age home to me. Half way to seventy!

Carl and I inherited from him a few thousand dollars, of which the income amounted to five or six hundred a year apiece. I was accustomed to earn two or three hundred dollars by writing, and sometimes I tutored children in summer. Now a thought came over me with startling suddenness which had never come into my head before; to receive interest on money was a heavy responsibility.

At first I only thought—what earned this interest? I didn't want profits from liquor, or steel traps, or child labor, or foreclosed mortgages. Gradually I came also to wonder—who earned this interest?

I certainly didn't earn it. I idly received it, while all my strength and time were free to earn money as I could in other ways. Somebody's time and energy were occupied in earning this money—who was it, and why didn't he receive the fruits of his labor? This was the realization that turned my thoughts toward Socialism.

The word, about which I had only the vaguest notions, had long sounded attractive to me. Passing through the purlieus that railroad trains usually entered cities by, or going down crowded West Side

Streets, it had been the only comfort I had against my inward nausea and anger at the harsh and sordid backgrounds where many a Mary Lilyflower lived, to murmur "Socialism" to myself. Vague as my understanding was, it was sound. Socialism was about the only energetic protest there was in the world against this huge, grimy, sickly, hateful tumor of poverty.

Everything else, and particularly the churches and the Salvation Army, only tried to soothe its inmates. Socialism resented it and attacked it.

Grateful therefore to Socialism before I knew any more than that about it, I began to read. I assembled what books I could find in its favor, and what I could find against it; fifteen or sixteen in all.

I had no *Capital* among my armful of books on Socialism, and only read it five or six years later; but I was already familiar, as so many are, with the unforgettable early part of it, the oft-quoted description of the horrors of life among the British workers in the early days of modern capitalism. I'd come across this description in what might seem to some Socialists an odd connection. As Jane Addams has pointed out, one avenue of protest always runs into another; and I had read the fiery words of Karl Marx in a book about vivisection. Among the few doctors who departed from group opinion in this matter, the outstanding American was Albert Leffingwell; and I was a frequent reader of his *magnum opus*. The most eloquent chapter of this book consists of a string of vivid historical parallels for the present-day indifference to the cruelties of vivisection; reminding us how Queen Elizabeth was a partner in the slave trade, and how bishops and members of Parliament were contented to have little girls working naked in the coal pits, and little boys bruised and suffocated in the chimneys; how those who opposed such barbarities were regarded as sentimental nuisances, just as we are now who want protection for animals in laboratories.

Meantime Anna Rochester, of the Child Labor Board, was spending her summers in Dorset, and Zephine introduced me to her. Anna was a Socialist. I told her what troubled me about Socialism—the bitter doctrine of the class struggle. Anna, bending upon me her unflinching gray eyes, threw a bucket of cold water in my face. "We don't want anybody in the party who isn't convinced of the reality of the class struggle," she exclaimed. "It isn't something we're trying to bring about! We're trying to get away from it. It's ten feet deep all over us."

From that moment I felt for her a great liking, and complete confidence. Her mind is analytical, accurate and orderly beyond any other I know. She keeps her facts in scrupulous array and proportion. She can safely play with them, and indulge her clever wits, for she is never tempted (apparently) to forget inconvenient ones in favor of a theory she loves, or in any other way to play them false. Everything in her life is the servant of fellow-feeling, and thus she had already, before I met her, given up the further study of her noble piano-playing, to work for children.

In the summer of 1913 I entered the Socialist Party. I received a welcoming letter from John Spargo of Bennington.

I was both happy and at home. The two hungers in the marrow of my bones were now richly satisfied; I was enrolled in the real Church Militant of all those who embraced a universal hope for this earth, a demand for full and boundless brotherhood.

In East Orange, where we now spent several winters, I met regularly on Sunday mornings with the little Socialist group there, a branch of the Newark Local. The word "comrade," with which we greeted each other, was to me inexpressibly eloquent. It has taken twenty years to begin, even, to dull it in my ears; and even yet, though a little fainter, it's a strain of music.

I was naïvely contented, at first, with what I had done in joining the party. I felt that I had concluded, rather than begun, a chapter. I remember how startled I was in my first call on Maud Thompson, a leader among the New Jersey Socialists, when she showed no particular interest in hearing what I'd expected to tell her in detail—how I'd come into the party; but asked me in brisk and breezy fashion, as soon as I sat down, what I was going to do for Socialism?

156

In the spring after I became a Socialist, there was rising very high a wave of war propaganda which was soon forgotten, but at the time nearly carried us into formal war with Mexico. The causes, according to the Hearst newspapers, which earnestly fanned the smoke, were many shocking outrages on Americans in Mexico. According to the Socialist papers, the outrages preponderated on the other side. The Mexican Ambassador in Washington was said to have submitted a list of forty or fifty Mexicans who had been murdered by Americans. Socialist papers said that the causes for possible war were oil wells owned and leased by Americans and legislation by Mexico unfavorable to their interests. After some "watchful waiting," Mr. Wilson yielded to pressure as he was to do at a more momentous time, and ordered troops to Vera Cruz.

It was then that I realized that I was a pacifist. Reading Socialist books, of course, soon turns one against war. Such books were seldom seen elsewhere, in those days; certainly not by me. It was very different from the present time, when everybody has read and heard something against war. To me the knowledge of Socialism's organized, impudent, pugnacious opposition to war came as its most unexpected element, but from the beginning I joyfully agreed with it.

I particularly remember Kirkpatrick's book, *War, What For?* which circulated widely among us in paper covers at twenty-five cents a copy. It was redheaded, defiant and concise. I think it was the first book I ever admired which had nothing wellbred about it.

I saw war now quite naked. Its Mexican mask was childishly transparent. Not the Mexicans, now or in the eighteen-forties, not the British, in 1776 or 1812, not the Sioux or Cherokees had ever been our enemies, but war itself. War was the enemy of all of us at once.

I saw its "necessity" exactly like the "necessity," three hundred years ago, to burn Protestants and rack Catholics in order to defend their respective religions. I saw it just as I saw the "necessity" to fight duels, the "necessity" to kidnap slaves, the "necessity" to hunt out witches, the "necessity" to flog children.

I saw its foundation in shameful and ridiculous timidities. It

157

throve on scaring people into murder; scaring them of foreigners as they had once been scared of witches, scared of Catholics, of Protestants, of Jews, of their own poor little naughty children going to hell.

I saw war as the great Pharisee of the world, causing every nation to thank God that he was so good, while his neighbor was so bad, that it was his duty to be the stern executioner.

I saw it as the apotheosis of the old superstition of punishment, that we can force human nature to be good by frightening and disgracing it and making it unhappy. And I began to have for war, as for poverty, race prejudice and all other cruelties, the kind of loathing that most Americans have for legalized prostitution.

I was, in short, a very thorough pacifist.

Burning with anxiety to do my little best against the war then threatening, I wrote some lofty, facile verses about it, which no one, I think, printed; and at about the same time I poured the burning joy of my new-found Socialism into my poem "Comrade Jesus."

It was the middle of Lent when I wrote this and sent it to *The Masses*. I think the editor then was Max Eastman. At any rate, I remember the note of acceptance which I received. In substance it said, "We fear we've printed too much of late about Jesus, but still we're taking your poem." The reason for this, as I remember, was that at Christmas *The Masses* had published a poem describing the nativity of Jesus as the birth of a natural child to a young unmarried girl, who was nevertheless a passionately loving and deeply enraptured mother, and who remembered her unsanctioned ecstasy with her lover as indeed the visit of an angel to earth. I recall it as a poem full of tenderness, beautifully reverent toward nature; but it shocked, of course, a good many persons who could not conceive of the Bible narrative under any such interpretation.

None of my poems has ever been so dramatically presented as "Comrade Jesus" in *The Masses*. The April number came out in Holy Week, I think on Good Friday. "Comrade Jesus" was in a box in the middle of the large page, and on all sides of it were

158

excerpts from supposed daily papers of Jerusalem, with the names of the New York papers turned into Latin—*Tribuna, Tempora,* etc. These accounts of the arrest, conviction and execution of Jesus were by Henry Alsberg, and wonderfully well done. They embodied that mixture of respectable stolidity and sober satisfaction with which the execution of an I. W. W. agitator might have been commented on in our generation.

Long afterward I heard that the rector of a church in New York read my poem in his evening service that Good Friday. For many years I preserved the page of *The Masses* on which it had been so wonderfully framed. At last the fabric fell to pieces; though even then it was not more worn than another copy which I once saw. After an evening of my poems in which I had read "Comrade Jesus," Mr. Darwin Meserole took a worn copy from his pocket and said that he habitually carried it about with him.

The last time I used it in a reading, however, I was struck with how much I'd emphasized the death of Jesus. I feel grateful to Mr. Halford Luccock, who quotes it in his recent book, *Contemporary American Literature and Religion,* for leaving out some of the later stanzas, though I wish he had had room for the final one.

### COMRADE JESUS

Thanks to Saint Matthew, who had been
At mass meetings in Palestine,
We know whose side was spoken for
When Comrade Jesus had the floor.

"Where sore they toil and hard they lie,
Among the great unwashed, dwell I.
The tramp, the convict, I am he;
Cold-shoulder him, cold-shoulder me."

By Dives' door, with thoughtful eye,
He did tomorrow prophesy.

"The kingdom's gate is low and small;
The rich can scarce wedge through at all."

"A dangerous man," said Caiaphas,
"An ignorant demagogue, alas.
Friend of low women, it is he
Slanders the upright Pharisee."

For law and order, it was plain,
For holy church, he must be slain.
The troops were there to awe the crowd
And "violence" was not allowed.

Their clumsy force with force to foil
His strong, clean hands he would not soil.
He saw their childishness quite plain
Between the lightnings of his pain.

Between the twilights of his end
He made his fellow-felon friend;
With swollen tongue and blinding eyes
Invited him to paradise.

Ah, let no local him refuse!
Comrade Jesus has paid his dues.
Whatever other be debarred,
Comrade Jesus has his red card.

I think more than ever at threescore that we ought to beware how we doom and darken goodness by featuring bodily pain and violent death before the eyes of the young.

It was in the same year with this that I wrote my four lines about children in the cotton mills. Aunt Jessie had had pneumonia, and on that account we went south the following winter. In the town where

WEENS HOUSE

we stayed were several cotton mills; one of them, visible from my window, ran day and night on two shifts only. I went through one of the mills with the mill-village school teacher. I remember how the fearful humidity in one of the rooms rained down the inside of the windows as if buckets of water had been thrown against them. My quatrain was literally true. The mill I wrote it about actually stood in the midst of a golf course. But my rhyme about it was such a bald little statement that I hesitated for some time about sending it to F. P. A.'s column in *The Tribune*. I'd hoped to do something better, and didn't realize that such a juxtaposition of facts as these would only be spoiled by any poetical effort. The four lines, since then, have floated about on the lips of many speakers and been many times illustrated; and F. P. A. remarked in his column last year the twentieth anniversary of their appearance there.*

In the same year in which I had joined the Socialist Party, Aunt Jessie and I had gone abroad again to make a spring visit to Scotland. Our Italian winter with Dorothy and Zephine was to have ended with a Scotch spring and visits to my father's old home and all the Cleghorn families; but an illness of Aunt Jessie's had prevented, and we had come home and waited a year.

The summer between our coming back from Italy and our going over to Scotland had been the Bull Moose summer, when so many people, (my brother among them) were caught up into the exaltation of the great Progressive platform, so human that it was almost Socialist. Most of us have forgotten now how good and neighborly it was. Man, woman and child figured on its planks as live human beings, as sensitive and deserving as our own relations, as worth while to succor and pay out good money for. Some people laughed at the platform because its planks were green and didn't fit together neatly, but they were all sound, sweet-smelling timber.

* The golf links lie so near the mill
    That almost every day
  The laboring children can look out
    And see the men at play.

Theodore Roosevelt made a whirlwind tour of Vermont. He came up through our valley, and took lunch at the Equinox House. We came out by hundreds to see and hear him; some having miniature mooses in our button-holes, some declaring that we had "only come to see his teeth."

The Equinox guests came out too, and filled the long piazza and sidewalk. Mr. Roosevelt stood up in his automobile, in a flapping raincoat, and waved his arms inclusively over the summer people and the rest of us, as he shouted;

"Don't say 'WE can't trust the rabble! WE can't trust the mob!' Why, YOU'RE the rabble! YOU'RE the mob!"

When we started for Scotland, we made straight for Weens House, the old home. Though my father couldn't come with me now, it meant a great deal to see Uncle George, his eldest brother, and to hear stories of his boyhood, and see the old postmistress who remembered him, the beechwoods he'd talked of, the garden "shaped like a pear," the little river Rule, and the churchyards of Jedburgh and Hawick, where my grandparents respectively lay, separated from each other, but not from their churches.

Uncle George and Aunt Mary had recently celebrated their golden wedding, and all their seven six-foot sons had come home for it with wives and children; we'd had a photograph sent us at the time, showing the great family gathering. Now there were only the two daughters at home. Three sons were in Australia, one in China, one in India, and two on the high seas.

Aunt Mary, so lovable and serene, was blind. She still wrote letters to all her sons, and sometimes even to me, her firm Scotch handwriting running its neat lines uphill and down into each other. She had been a great Aberdeen beauty, a Lumsden, the sister of so many brothers that the eldest and youngest never saw each other but once in their lives, and that was for an hour at a railroad station. One of her brothers, Sir Harry Lumsden, was the founder of the "Guides" of India.

Uncle George was eighty-one. He was fearfully stiff, and had to be let down into and helped up out of his chair by his tall daughter; but once standing, he could walk about quite well; and in every other respect he was the youngest old man I ever saw; for his color was fresh, his skin smooth, his brown eyes clear and kindling, and his teeth as white and even as a child's. Looking at him, I was constantly reminded of Stevenson's lines

"In the highlands, in the country places
Where the old plain men have rosy faces."

One of his daughters came in to breakfast one morning while we were at Weens, dressed for traveling.

"Where are you going, Fanny?"

"I'm off to Edinburgh to the dentist."

"I advise you to keep away from the dentists," said my uncle, with a sparkling look. "I haven't been to a dentist for fifty years."

We supposed this to be humorous extravagance. It wasn't, however—it was actually true.

My old uncle was a great antiquarian. He had brought out a book a few years before—his letters to my father had frequently mentioned it—called *Rulewater and its People*. Aunt Mary had also written to my father, "Dear Johnny—I don't think your brother George will ever finish his book. He's always coming in in a glow with something more to put into it." But he had finished it. A big book, printed closely, and consisting of all the family histories, famous parish characters, and miscellaneous lore of the valley, it was so delightfully amusing, and written in such a good forthright unliterary fashion, that the edition instantly sold out, and the reviewers gave it a rousing welcome.

My Yankee aunt was soon quite thick with my Scotch uncle. She was about twenty-five years younger than he, and therefore when some people were at Weens for lunch, he introduced her as "me aunt from Amerrica."

I was one day telling him how the portrait of George the Third hangs on the wall in Washington in such a position that he gazes forever at the Declaration of Independence. "You say they have him hanging on the wall?" inquired my uncle, carefully screwing his six-foot bulk around in his chair so that he could fix a shrewd look on me. "What! have they got a rope around his neck?"

Weens House has one famous characteristic—the bees under the roof. So far back as Cleghorns had lived there (it wasn't considered long in Scotland; two hundred years) it had been a bee sanctuary. From miles around, swarms of bees escape their owners and flee to Weens. My uncle had seen, more than once, two swarms arrive at once from opposite directions, meeting over the chimneys—pursued in vain by breathless bee-keepers. With strong Scotch superstition, our forbears would never molest the bees. Uncle George resolved to rifle away their honey. He went up into their fastness armed like a diver, but the bees settled so thick over his breathing holes that they choked him down again. Experienced bee men said they would beard the bees and relinquish all the honey to my uncle if they could keep the wax; but they also fled before the wild bees of Weens. Tempting patent boxes and hives have never lured them down.

The Cleghorns, or rather Tancreds, are no longer at Weens. Like the estate in Yorkshire for which Uncle George changed his name, it has been sold. But this wasn't during the lifetime of my aunt and uncle. They both died within a year and a half of the time when we were there; they went out with the era that closed with the World War.

I never saw old people so securely and completely fulfilled as they were, so natural, cheerful, satisfied with life and contented to die.

We made a visit, too, at my cousin James Dalton's near Ripon. Cousin Jim was a retired officer, who in younger days had visited us two or three times in Vermont; the son of my father's eldest sister. It was with him Aunt Fanny and I had spent a winter in Bermuda. He had gone there an old bachelor of almost fifty and married the Governor's daughter; indeed he had been courting her while we stayed with him at St. George's. They now had four lively children, the youngers, Joan and John, still at home with a govern-

164

ess. I had a happy time playing with them. True English children, they required no equipment for play but the inventive English playfulness, spirit and fire. "I'll be a suffragette," exclaimed John, flashing about an imaginary axe, "and smash everything to flinders." Spirited as he was, his sister was still more so; her brown hair streamed in the wind as she ran, and where she hid, nobody could find her.

> Her boyish locks all backward drawn
> And beech-brown eyes shot through with fawn.

I have several pictures of the four bonny Dalton children at play, and in every one Joan looks the boldest and gayest. She died at fourteen, fading away with a strange glandular disease, free from all pain, and with a clear childish expectation of immortality.

Going to see another of the Daltons, who lived in London, I had an odd encounter, the only one I ever had with the forbidding kind of Englishman or woman who figures so often in anecdote. We were spending a preliminary week in a London boarding house, and were one afternoon expecting a call from Cousin Isabella Dalton, whom we'd never seen. When therefore the maid came up and said "Mrs. Dalton was in the drawingroom," I rushed down expecting to meet a stranger who would promptly give me an affectionate welcome; but the lady seated there forbore to rise, nor did she extend a hand to receive mine.

"I'm Sally Cleghorn!" I exclaimed with a beaming smile.

"I know no such person," she replied.

"Oh, I'm sorry—I thought you were Mrs. Dalton."

"I am Mrs. Dalton."

"Well, then—aren't you Cousin Isabella?"

"Not at all."

Realizing at last that there must be two Mrs. Daltons calling there that afternoon, I explained how natural my mistake had been, but neither her features relaxed, nor did a note of compassion or amusement creep into her voice. When my cousin came, half an hour or so later, she explained her predecessor to me in a word.

"That Mrs. Dalton you describe is the wife of a former tutor of the Prince of Wales."

Cousin Isabella was indeed quite the contrary of the court lady; for she was warmhearted and childlikely compassionate; with a child's quaint lack, too, of the sense of measure. I was walking with her one day when an unemployed man accosted her, asking politely for alms. After a little conversation, she gave him fourpence; enough of course, in London then, to get him a cup of tea and a muffin; but as we passed on, she continued for some time to wonder anxiously whether she had done him any moral harm or disturbed his habits of thrift by her largesse.

There were a good many unemployed in London that spring. When we drove to the Daltons' in our "fourwheeler" a man ran beside us all the way to secure the shilling job, (we found out on arriving) of carrying in our trunks. My cousins had already provided somebody; it was an old sailor with but one arm; he wouldn't let the runner assist him, but agreed with us that the run had earned a full compensation. Our trunks, while not Saratogas, were solid American ones such as required two men apiece to carry upstairs in New York; and how one man, and he one-armed, could carry them up was as much a miracle after we'd seen him do it as before. "Sailors' tricks!" he exclaimed as he came running down, not even out of breath.

I was shamed out of my heavy trunk forever that year, when I saw the light cases Europeans carried.

It was in my father's old home that I'd first read Masefield's masterpiece, *The Dauber*. It had been published whole in *The English Review*. Late one night Frances Tancred gave me the sky-blue magazine, and I read the poem in one great plunge before breakfast the next morning.

I thus fulfilled my childhood's magnificent ambition, to come suddenly on a great poet in the beginning of his fame.

I have heard the story that Harrison Ainsworth, the editor of *The English Review,* had been going to refuse *The Dauber* and that friends and admirers of Masefield persuaded him, by their vehemence, not to "disgrace *The English Review,* and make it a laughing-stock for posterity!"

As soon as we got home, I obtained *The Everlasting Mercy* and *The Widow in the Bye Street.* I read them, I remember, going up to Dorset on that diminutive car with six or eight seats, which used to be attached for passengers to the dawdling "marble train"—my usual means, at that time, of getting up to see Zephine. I burst in upon her tranquillity with the excitement of what I had been read-ing, and the altogether new conception of narrative poetry which Masefield had given me. His manner of writing his three great tales was to all intents and purposes a new poetic form. All nar-rative poetry I'd previously known had been anathema to me. I never had been able to read even *Paradise Lost.* The interminable, complicated sentences, the prolonged, unnecessary analogies, the endless speeches which filled whole pages—how totally different they were from the impassioned lyrics I loved and lived on! Nar-rative poetry had always reminded me of those interminable Te Deums which defaced the church services of my childhood. But here were narratives as swift and thrilling as lyrics. Their analogies were cut to a hot word or two, coming in naturally; the characters con-versed not by long decorative paragraphs, but in quick realistic fashion, "like men of this world."

"This is my field!" "This is my wire!"

But the joy I took in the realistic swiftness of these narratives was nothing to the joy, as deep as my soul itself, which I took in the substance of them. Here were my hungers satisfied indeed. Here were no

"—princes and prelates with periwigged charioteers
Riding triumphantly laurelled to lap the fat of the years,"

but the underdogs in their bone-pinching necessities, their sick, forgotten pain, their appalling multitudes,

"The lame and the halt and the blind, in the rain and the cold,"

but each handled with the hot, unflinching tenderness that has been my lifelong dream of all that's good.

I am glad I didn't come upon Masefield as most people nowadays do, through his short lyrics. It's better to be born lucky than handsome, and I think it one of the best of my fortunes, that I plunged head on into his three mighty epics before I read anything else.

I thought for a long time that *The Everlasting Mercy* was Masefield's masterpiece. Sometimes of course the magnificence of *The Dauber,* its billowing, glittering stanzas, sustained through pages on end, and its intense account of the numbness, sickness and despairing fear of a sailor's novitiate, would persuade me that *The Dauber* stood above it. Then the mystic passages in *The Everlasting Mercy*—the faces glimmering through the belfry windows, etc.,—beckoned away and exerted a superior power. Now I am sure *The Dauber* is the best of Masefield's poems and the greatest English poem of the sea.

His great elegy, "August, 1914" I first saw in a newspaper. I think it will be remembered as the noblest of war poems in the English tongue. How poignantly tender it is in its penetration of the thoughts of the older men who are cut down along with the young, for cannon fodder, and what a line for generations to remember,

"And that dumb loving of the Berkshire loam."

To my mind his sonnets also belong among the greatest. They surely go beyond the ordinary limits of language, and excel in showing intensities of thought. And that conception of beauty almost as tenderness, obscurely, wildly and compassionately glimmering through life and the world, does indeed show us

"—a sense
of life so lovely, so intense,"

it may well "linger when we wander hence."

168

I've only seen Masefield once. It was at the Poetry Society's luncheon, given to him on his 1916 visit to this country. Owing probably to a sonnet of mine, "John Masefield," which had appeared a year or two previously in *The Atlantic,* and which I was to repeat at this luncheon, I sat at the same table with him. I thus had a near view of his serious, deep face and quiet bearing, and heard very well his wonderfully unaffected voice. It was a memorable occasion indeed to me, and no instant of it will ever be forgotten. Except Gene Debs, I don't know what other man, whom I could possibly have seen, I could have been so satisfied with seeing.

This is my sonnet about him—

Democracy's best pen, with passion vowed
  "To maimed and halt and blind, in rain and cold,"
  Three mighty epics of the poor hath told;
The Dauber, freezing in his sleeted shroud;
The Widow, kneeling in the gallows crowd;
  And that great idyl of the windy wold,
  The drunkard, walking where the dawn unrolled
And with changed eyes beholding one who ploughed.

Again, immortal! yoke that share divine,
And fix our eyes "forever on that sign";
Plough deep our souls, that can with mirth endure
Ease to ourselves and burdens to the poor;
Convert us wastrels, O undying pen!
Harrow our hearts, that we may "flower to men."

# 10

ABOUT a year before the war began, I stopped eating meat. I'd long wanted to do this, but had a nebulous idea that to be a vegetarian you had to study dietetics and balance a diet in some special sense, which meat eaters, generally speaking, needn't trouble themselves about. However, one summer day, I decided offhand to begin.

I was fond of milk and knew I ought to keep eggs in view. I wasn't interested in boycotting animal foods as such, but only those which required that animals should be perpetually dying to keep us alive. My great mistake was expecting to miss the flavor of meat, which had always been agreeable to me; I was extremely surprised to find that I didn't miss it at all. After a year or two, I began to realize how much more I now enjoyed the flavor of vegetables, no longer requiring that they should be so much "fixed up" as before with sauces and condiments. The delicate flavors of a briefly steamed, still green cabbage, with a bit of butter dissolving a dash of salt in the midst of it, and a couple of boiled new potatoes, eaten on a July noon after a busy morning, made the best dinner I can remember that I ever had.

What seemed to take place was that these tender vegetable aromas, no longer having to compete with the heavy, powerful taste of meat, began to show their charm to the awakened palate. At all events, if my experience was normal, vegetables taste much more delicious to the vegetarian; so that instead of becoming tired of them after he abandons meat, he finds them now for the first time fully appreciated.

It also dawned on me, after being a vegetarian for two or three years, that I no longer felt a particular kind of irritation with which I had been familiar before. The absent-minded man or woman hates—

even more than another!—to be interrupted in the midst of something he's concentrating upon. I used to be peculiarly aggravated when remarks were sprinkled over me when I was trying to read. Behind my aunt's *Tribune,* (frequently before she'd had a look at it herself) I used to breathe, softly and unheard, "Oh, do shut up, Oh, please shut up!" This sense of exasperation seemed gradually to lose itself and be dissipated away after I became a vegetarian. "Where's that old irritability I used to feel?" I one day suddenly asked myself. As years went on, it became evident that it had departed permanently. And though pernicious anemia came upon me after nearly twenty years of successful and vigorous vegetarianism (to which no doctor I've had has attributed it) and in consequence I've been forced back into meat eating, the habit the vegetables bequeathed me, of not being easily irritated, is left behind as a legacy.

The third thing I noticed as a result, apparently, of vegetarianism was freedom from fatigue. This I thought the less of while I lived at home; but when I entered upon an extra busy life as a teacher in a community school, I saw with wonder how quickly the meat-eating teachers tired out. At our faculty meetings, which often ran late into the evening, four or five much younger than I would often be fast asleep while Margery (my fellow-vegetarian) and I, as early up and as busy all day as they were, felt fresh and rested. But perhaps part of this was constitutional. Perhaps, on my part, it was inherited; for both my parents "had no nerves." Perhaps it was because of my kind and easy rural youth, in a calmer time in American history than these young teachers had had.

However, the vegetarian and near-vegetarian races like the Japanese seem able to perform manual labor and wrestling feats that are beyond the beef-fed western world. I note in the *Journals* of Audubon that he took pleasure in Gargantuan walks on his usual diet of practically all vegetables. The southern Italians living on macaroni and cheese carry pianos uphill on their backs. The Roman legions who conquered the world were apparently vegetarians.

Dr. Leffingwell, in his book *American Meat* makes a very interesting suggestion about a carnivorous origin for cancer. I wish the national cancer society would ascertain the percentage of cancer among vegetarians.

All these years, so crowded for me with feeling and thought, I'd almost never seen that little early playmate of ours, Molly Prentice. Her marriage at nineteen had closed for ten or fifteen years the succession of her Vermont summers. Now when she came back, her unreconciled absence had intensified the Vermont strain in her blood. Manchester's marble sidewalks seemed as storied to her as the Roman Forum. She must drive again with John Stockwell, behind horses, not in a car; her children must climb trees and steal apples in the same orchards where we, as children, had stolen them. They must go to the Battenkill Valley Fair, ride the merry-go-round and watch the mountain quadrilles in the dancing pavilion.

The house she bought and lived in was the one to which Carl and I had gone for pails of spring water every morning when we lived at Sans Souci. Now it had to have again its old picket fence, which had been the last one removed in the village. The Coys' old lily-of-the-valley bed had to be replanted all along the shadow of the fence, and waft lemony fragrance to the noses of passers-by. And when any of us spent an evening at Molly's bright fire in that old house, we did indeed revive our childhood, and scour bright with reminiscences the days of a quarter of a century before.

She brought back with her two possessions I hadn't been aware of in her childhood and young damselhood. I found them very endearing and deepening to our affection for each other. One was her love and veneration for the things of the mind, especially a widening love for books; the other, peculiarly her own, was a loving, reckless generosity, commanding and secret, on the scale and swiftness of an old Florentine.

And all these things together—I don't know which the most—brought it about that Aunt Jessie and she became great cronies. My aunt took great delight besides in Molly's beauty and grace, and in a warm sweet deference Molly has for older people. Tenderness deepened between them—the one found a niece, the other an aunt.

This bright experience of renewed and enlarging friendship came about in the years shortly before the war, and as I look back on them, they have that dramatic air of sunshine just before a storm, which seems to show how nature loves a contrast. There was another bright flash of sunshine in my experience just before the war thundered up dark in the sky. It was my first taste of Robert Frost's poetry. Spending a summer evening at Dorothy's, early in 1914, I listened while she read one poem after another from *North of Boston;* beginning, I well remember, with "Mending Wall." What first delighted me was their cool, heart-refreshing naturalness. Soon I saw the depths of meaning dawning beneath them. After Dorothy had ceased to read each one, I began to feel its unforced intensity of feeling rising round me in the silence.

I never before had seen a body of poetry at once so faithfully plain and so delicately, thoughtfully beautiful. They reminded me of Lowell's line, "Beauty's law of plainness." They reminded me of the few seventeenth century poems I knew well; but these sounded cooler, fresher, more natural and out-of-doors than those; closer, too, to the common lot, and the "marvelous hearts of simple men." And here I found my early ambition fulfilled a second time—again I heard and loved great poems at the beginning of their fame.

Many times in later years hearing Robert Frost himself read them, (for he settled in our valley soon afterwards) I concluded to my own satisfaction that the loveliest of his very short poems is "Spring Pools," and that its next-to-last line is the most beautiful single line in his poetry.

"These flowery waters and these watery flowers."

Next to Walt Whitman, I think him our best American poet. I think his deepest humanity is in "The Self-Seeker" and "The Death of the Hired Man," and the best thought about the universe in "West-Running Brook."

The beginning of the war stole almost softly upon people like me, who had no idea that it would endure very long, or cost a hundred-thousandth part of what it did. I never had any sudden awakening to it, either, but for three of the four years only a perpetually delayed expectation that it would shortly be brought to an end. I hadn't ever been able to see any reason why it began, and I never could see any reason why it continued. Every hope of mediation seemed to me much more substantial than the cobweb causes—whatever they were—that started it and kept it going.

In the beginning I thought that surely someone in office would pay some attention to the earnest, widespread distress that was felt about the American munitions that were feeding the war. Americans in Germany had protested in a body against the munitions trade. Friends of the long-deferred Russian revolution, remembering all the history they'd read, feared that a victory for the Allies would rivet the old regime, floggings, secret police, Siberian exile, tighter than ever on the Russian workers. I remember my amazement at the view John Spargo, then still a Socialist, took about this. He, who with his fellow-Welshman, Lloyd George, had had cabbages thrown at him all over England when in their youth they traveled about opposing the Boer War, was already a complete pro-Ally supporter of the war. Reasoning in some of those ingenious ways which sound all right as long as one is listening to them, he told Dorothy and me that a victory for the Allies would help the Russian workers in their struggle.

All that first year of the war our clever cousin who had done Carl's portrait was prostrate and slowly dying. Before I got into bed every night for another of those touch-the-pillow-and-don't-wake-up-till-morning nights that have shed such sweetness over my threescore years, I had to realize my vague awareness of natural immortality for her sake. I thought thus nightly of individual mortal life in the old, old image of a house or a room, and of the breadth and freedom of our universal immortality as a mighty pine forest that surrounded this brief, tiny dwelling. I thought of the possibility of our leaving the shelter and burden of mortal cares behind us, and camping out in that forest from time to time, even now in mortal life. I hoped my meditations might be dynamic enough, by thought's "direct action," to blow in at my sick cousin's window and help reinvigorate her brave and weary heart.

I wrote *The Spinster* that year—one-third fiction and two-thirds a slightly arranged autobiography. Beginning with our Vermont childhood, it carried me (much more dramatically than I went) into Socialism. I wrote it very fast, on a sudden impulse. Henry Holt and Company, who'd published my *Turnpike Lady,* published this too. It did a good deal better. I reaped several hundred dollars in royalties from it; it went through one small edition and into (I don't know how far into) another. An acquaintance sent, unknown to me, a copy to Mr. Howells, who wrote me a warm, understanding letter about it, which underwent a great many rereadings; and a few months later he discussed *The Spinster* in an article "Intensive Fiction," in *The North American Review.*

Mr. Howells has always seemed to me a very different figure from the timid, complaisant, follow-my-leader creature some present-day critics find him. He was, I think, the first Socialist among his literary associates. He was the literary godfather of the first recognized Negro poet. No man, surely, was ever more modest, cordial and fraternal with young writers—more socially-minded and simple-hearted, a more honest American. He could very sincerely make one of his heroines say, "I'd rather be queer in Europe than queer in Tuskingum."

It seemed to me that every other verse-writer in the United States had published a volume but me. Holt and Company, I found, were willing to bring my verses out, and soon after *The Spinster* they did so, in the only volume of poems I've ever achieved, unless I count the small typewritten collections I sometimes make for our village bookstore. It was called *Portraits and Protests.* By Protests were meant my burning poems. This book included also the best of my sun-bonnets, under the division "Of Country Places and the Simple Heart"; and a group of poems "Of Life and Immortality." The volume looked nice, though thin, in crimson sides. The publishers probably lost a little money on it—anyhow I never gained anything by its tiny sale. I was to have one other book appear, in 1917, and then nothing more for about twenty years.

When the war went into its second year, I wrote "The Poltroon," and sent it to F. P. A.'s column in *The Tribune* (it wasn't yet *The Herald-Tribune*).

> His country cowered under the mailed fist
> Of the great soldier-nation of his day;
> But did he volunteer? Not he; instead
> He talked in ill-timed, ill-judged platitudes
> Urging a most unpatriotic peace.
> People who had been once slapped in the face
> Ought to stand still, he thought, till slapped again;
> And if we were insulted, we should watch
> For chances to return it with a favor.
> I will say for him, milksop as he was,
> He was consistent; for he let himself
> Be knocked about the streets and spit upon
> And never had the manhood to hit back.
> Of course he had no sense at all of honor,
> Either his country's honor or his own,
> Contemptible poltroon! His name was Jesus.

F. P. A. printed this in the "Conning Tower," and a few days later wrote me a letter in his usual vivid green ink, saying that he was threatened with being "shot at sunrise" for printing it. He enclosed a thick packet of letters which he'd received about it; some approving, but many violently objecting to it, either as being a blasphemous insult to the Prince of Peace, or as being a libel on the military hero who drove the money-changers out of the temple.

I received, too, a letter in the beautiful minute hand of Kathleen Norris, commending "The Poltroon" and saying that we must meet. When we next went to New York, my aunt and I did meet Mrs. Norris and the F. P. Adamses too, for she asked us to have tea together.

Her vigor, warmth and liveliness, sense and sweetness, made a captivating recollection for us. I don't think I'd then read any of her books; if I had, it was *Julia Page,* perhaps her best up to that time; for it was years ahead that she was to write that American *Vanity Fair, Certain People of Importance.*

In that second year of the war the first outpouring of opposition to the American munitions trade was gradually losing its little strength. How prophetic it seems, looking back now, that the first grappling effort Americans ever made for peace was their early concentration on the "hell of a business," "steel against peace," the "merchants of death"! It was a feeble grappling, and it seemed more or less answered, after a bewildering fashion, when we were cynically told the very fact about the munitions trade which now we most recoil from —"Why, we're perfectly neutral! The Germans can come over here and buy all the munitions they want, if the British navy'll let 'em!"

Zephine became a complete pacifist that year. But her books just before and during the war, novels like *Grail Fire* and *The Homestead,* were animated by (the reader felt) a cult of self-sacrifice. They seemed to say, with great amenity, that mortal life at best was a denial even of normal joys, for the sake of the supernormal. After the war, she released into her books far more of the tranquil current of her own life, and the flavor of her personality; they were the matured, enriched successors of *Green Peak* and it's they that are the favorites of her public. In 1914 she had been married to Wallace Fahnestock, the painter—I almost said, the painter of Vermont, he so well understands the radiance and color of our mountains and their winter and summer lights. The years of the war were therefore—how lovely a compensation!—the early years of Zephine's married life, the years in which life was proving to her, with gentle obstinacy, (I thought) that it's more fruitful to be happy than to be sad.

But Zephine received her own special wound from the war. To her the church had long been the core of beauty and wisdom. When her mother died, she had found in an "Anglican Catholic" Church, her best understanding of sorrow. When we had all been together in

Rome, several of us had rather expected her to become a Roman Catholic. Her articles in *The Atlantic* at about that time were full of heartfelt comprehension of the rich symbolism of that Church. Processions, incense, vestments, ancient forms of prayer, the high-erected Mass, the language of humility and adoration, and the art, which she so well knew how to practice, of contemplation—all this, to Zephine, had an inward glow which neither Dorothy nor I could find there. But now, when the cross was actually followed, brushed against, by the flag in order to incite us to kill one another, her heart revolted with sick horror, and she felt a rending apart of loyalties from which her love for the church has never recovered, and I think never can.

Dorothy, too, was inwardly torn; in her case, by the conflict between her natural, reasoned pacifism, long since accepted, and her perplexed wonder "what else the Belgians and French could do but fight?" This conflict never ceased in her heart from the first gun of the war until the armistice—and I don't know how long after, or whether it is even now resolved. Her letters and talk during the war expressed it over and over. She felt, what neither Zephine nor I ever felt, a humane kind of sympathy with the governments; actually a pity for them, as fatally caught between two millstones. Here's a letter I had from her after she and Mr. Fisher had been one year in France.

"Oh, well, what is the use of writing or even thinking about it. . . . I wonder if you realize how faint-hearted and sick I am most of the time, even with the feeling not wavering that there was nothing for the French and Belgians to do but to defend their countries? . . . I have the feeling that our generation is pretty well done for, stunned and stupefied with the bludgeon of the war, and that it is only from the children that the future will draw enough vitality to stagger along. . . . Last night, as I sat at my desk writing, Emilie came in to call. She said, 'Oh, don't let me interrupt you—go on writing.'

"I said, 'What do you suppose I am writing? I am setting down for my own benefit the reasons why I am not a thorough-going non-resistant pacifist.'" And her letter went on to describe a perpetual recoil from what she was seeing, the actualities of war, yet how she was held back all the time by a sense that in spite of everything war was a means of righting present wrongs, and preserving humanity's faith in justice and in the future. She felt that my wholesouled revolt against this and every war must be more despairing than her bare toleration of this one; but I felt that without the inward rejection of this ghastly thing I could not have endured life at all.*

All this and much more of her wartime thinking, Dorothy eventually poured into the pages of *The Deepening Stream*. That novel, of a richer texture than any of her others except *Bonfire* and *The Brimming Cup,* seems to be her best loved book. But for ten years after the war was over, she was not yet ready to write about it. And of the writing she did after the war began and before she went to France, nothing was concerned in any way with the war.

She wrote in those years *The Montessori Mother* and that capital, charming book, first done in a hurry for *Today's Magazine, Mothers and Children.* The chapter titles of this book are in themselves epigrams; "A Sliding Scale for Obedience," "The Tarnishing Eye of Relations"! For years *Mothers and Children* remained my favorite of all Dorothy's books whatever, (and yet that was before I began to teach). I like it much better than *The Montessori Mother,* in which, after all, she was explaining another's ideas, fitting her own experience and these ideas together. Whereas in *Mothers and Children* we have the rich top cream of that warm understanding of human nature which accompanies all her shrewd observation of it; her genius for making it grow and mature.

*The Bent Twig* came out in 1915, three years after *The Squirrel Cage.* It became at once the favorite it still is. The stream of letters about it has never run dry in all these twenty years; a typical one came as I was writing this. "I am reading *The Bent Twig* for the twentieth

---

* She is now, of course, a leading advocate of peace. Her recent international broadcast in favor of the People's Mandate to the Governments is the best peace talk I have heard for a long time.

time," wrote this apparently middle-aged man in New Jersey. "It's like 'William Tell' . . . I can go back to it over and over again and know that I am in the presence of something true and significant."

In the summer of 1916 Dorothy and I wrote together our little book about suggestion, *Fellow Captains*. Most of my first "poems of wonder and joy" were included in this. We included also several suggestion formulas in free verse. These were not designed only for physical ills, to bring sleep, etc., but also "For a Quick Eye for Beauty," "For a Feeling of Freshness in the Morning," etc. To this book my aunt contributed a formula of her own, "For Calmness"—

> Eyes of my memory and soul,
> Dwell on the picture of Whistler's mother—
> On the long lines of the plain dress
> And the calm attitude
> In the still light in the quiet room;
> Infinite tranquillity.

During that same crowded and broken summer of Dorothy's, between her husband's going to France in April to work in the American Ambulance, and her own following with the children in August, she wrote *Understood Betsy* in a few weeks' time—Betsy, who is coming to be almost as familiar a figure as Tom Sawyer. After it had gone through twenty editions, we dramatized it for use as a school or camp play, with parts for about three dozen children; trying it first in Arlington, Dorothy's home town.

Her son Jimmy had been born at the very end of 1914, when my namesake was four. Both children have the looks of their father, and his vigor and clarity of mind, along with a great many resemblances which I can see to their mother. They have been brought up with a rich background, sharing everything as the family do in *The Brimming Cup*, that glowing, realistic portrait of a many-sided family life. My namesake had from a very early age an ardent intellectual appetite. By seven she read with delight collections of stories for grownups, and even was found reading *The Contemporary Review*. Her brother's tastes are scientific, but his outstanding characteristic, manifested very young, is an inclination to go out of his way to make friends with the stepsons of fortune.

The Fishers were to be absent, as it proved, for three years. Mr. Fisher, rising fast in the American Ambulance, was put in charge of a training camp for the young recruits, then of a string of such camps; and Dorothy left the work for the blinded soldiers to take over the commissary of the Ambulance training camp at Crouy, where my little goddaughter became desperately ill with the first case of typhoid fever on record there. When Sally began to recover, and Dorothy was advised to take her away from the Paris winter, she went with both children to the Basque seaside, near St. Jean de Luz. In that fresh, bright climate Sally was soon so plump and rosy that her mother conceived the idea of bringing as many as possible of the undernourished children of the Paris poor down there to build up their health; and this became the highly successful and much expanded work which occupied Dorothy during the remainder of her three French war years.

In the meantime Carl, Sue and the two children they had then had moved—in July!—into the middle of Georgia. Carl had already left his general practice for X-ray and radium. His precious little quantity of radium, bought for six thousand dollars and insured for three, came to a strange end in the Macon hospital, where my brother had applied it to the arm of a patient, an uneducated old man, who could have had no idea of its value. When my brother returned to take the radium off, the old man said, "Oh, I threw it away. I got tired of the bandage, and I ripped it off and an orderly came in and carried it away."

An exacting search was made. "Detectors" of some sort were sent down from Atlanta, and the sewers of Macon were searched, but the lost lifegiver was never found.

A röntgenologist is occasionally asked to photograph an animal for diagnosis. Injured race horses, for example, often require the help of an X-ray. The strangest patient my brother ever had was a thirty-foot python with an injured spine, which was brought up to his office in a great box carried by four men. "The python was extremely gentle," Carl said; "he laid his head in my hand as confidingly as a dog might do. He seemed to understand very well that we were trying to relieve his discomfort. We only *took enough of him out of the box* to place the injured part on the table and take the pictures of it."

This huge patient, after diagnosis of its injury, was treated with sunbaths; but its hurt proved mortal.

Like all the rest of our family, at home and abroad, my brother didn't share at all in my pacifism. He offered himself for X-ray service, and remained throughout the war on the list of those available.*

For the pleasure of being near the Cleghorns, Aunt Jessie and I went to Macon for several winters. Susan thought the school hours too long, and she and Carl let me teach Dalton and Fannie, who in that way could have their whole afternoons for outdoor play. By the time we got there, the Cleghorns lived in the country at the end of a trolley line, and had chickens and a cow. I had several arcadian winters with the children. Fannie—an ardent, overflowing temperament—was beginning to learn; Dalton was four years older. He liked to think; liked to hear of things strange and far off, and understood things difficult to express.

I received a great deal of education from teaching the children. My worst fault as a teacher, then and later, was falling occasionally into a reproachful, martyrlike attitude. I would sometimes even weep. I was frequently too impromptu and unsystematic. Though this has advantages such as freshness and responsiveness, it sometimes made me vague, and left the children's work too little framed and bulwarked with routine. But I began to feel confidence in myself as a teacher, because the children felt confidence in themselves and consequently liked, on the whole, their lessons. And though my faults, which did so easily beset me, taught me a good deal about

* Ten or twelve years before this, however, his clear mind had realized the full rank enormity of the Boer War, while I, who thought myself so idealistic, had swallowed whole the British justification of it.

teaching, my merits as a teacher taught me a good deal more. Half consciously I began to see that to encourage the pupil is fully half the job of the teacher. And it's so pleasant a technique, to encourage! One encourages almost by nature. It's only the practice, after all, of courtesy toward the children. One takes to this agreeable art *con amore,* and sevenfold so when the pupils are already nears and dears.

People say the newer types of education "demand a great deal more of the teacher" than the old fixed, formal methods. I can't see this. The modern teacher can unbend, be natural. It surely doesn't require as much effort to swim with the current and respond to nature, as it requires to conform to a stiff rule and thus contradict nature. What could be better than the frankness of modern teachers about things they don't know, and its natural result of teacher and children finding them out together?

Dalton, Fannie and I had a great deal of simple-hearted fun when in the middle of the morning we went out to play. I professed to be a wonderful runner and jumper and to Dalton's great mirth gave pompous instructions on jumping off the terrace, and then illustrated by jumping (with the utmost efforts of my short legs) about half as far as Dalton could. Even little Fan surpassed me.

I learned (by their frolicsome reception of my first attempts) how to capitalize others of my absurdities and inhibitions, and to extract a positive advantage out of the things I couldn't do. I began to see, and act upon, the deep meaning of the adage, "The oyster mends his shell with pearl." I'd always liked to "sing" the poetry I loved, by chanting it forth monotonously. Now I found that it enchanted the children to hear one of these absurd performances, about which I'd been rather sensitive ever since discovering how grotesque a musical ear would find them. Fan loved to hear me thus chanting the old burlesque, "When shall we be married, John?"

This little niece, now Mrs. Robert Lester, has made me this year the kind of present one receives, at most, once in a lifetime. She has brought to pass a desire I've vainly cherished for forty years; she has adopted a child. The summit of graciousness, the apotheosis of hospitality, this action always seems to me; and that it should come so near as this gives me a deep contentment, and an especial affection for the great-nephew I've not yet seen.

Fannie and Dalton conducted my education by day and by night. Being so much with them reshaped my thoughts of prayer. From joyfully praying for their health and grace, I came to feeling that they were already naturally at home

"Playing and sporting on the eternal shore."

Fannie and Dalton hadn't been brought up in very close relations with the church. Their mother and father's religion was nearly all action, pure and undefiled.

When they had lived in Macon only a year or two, Carl was appointed head of the Macon Hospital, and accordingly they moved into the superintendent's house, across the street from that end of the hospital which contained the children's ward, and the balcony on which the little patients used to play and sleep in the sun. There was at that time in the children's ward a little boy three or four years old, known simply as "L. M." He had tuberculosis of the bones of the leg. He was a very fragile child, whose recovery seemed rather doubtful to the doctors. My sister's heart had soon, and deeply, warmed to this little boy; she had found out all that could be learned about him, and was turning over in her mind, and finding out by letter, what was the utmost that could be done for him in the state of Georgia. There was an orthopedic hospital in Atlanta, on whose waiting list he might be placed. In the meantime, the nurses had made a pet of him, and he had been kept on as a patient month after month. Good food and constant care were helping him.

He had a winning way—an exceptional amount of come-hither in his brown eyes. By the time Aunt Jessie and I got to Macon, he was calling Susan "mother." She bought his little suits and underwear and looked after all his needs; and she often had a special joy and surprise for him beside. From calling her "mother," he soon began to call Carl "daddy."

184

DOROTHY WITH HER CHILDREN, 1916

SUSAN CLEGHORN, WITH DALTON AND FANNIE

It was not his first visit to the hospital. Indeed he was quite at home there. Several times previously he'd been brought there, and diet and care had built him up; but he was poorly cared for between whiles, and had always soon come back again, newly run down, transparent and suffering. He was a soothing syrup victim; his pain at night had ordinarily been quieted with these sugary drugs. My sister's profound tenderness for children was plumbed to the bottom by this little boy. At one time she thought of adopting him. Finally she visited the private "orphanage" where he'd been neglected so long; visited the hospital in Atlanta where he was successfully treated a few years later; visited the pleasant, homelike Methodist orphanage where it seemed hopeful to place him; visited authorities and lawyers and finally, when L. M. was well enough to be transferred, had herself legally constituted his guardian and retained the post long enough to take him to the Methodist Home, all outfitted with new clothes, and still chirping out "mother" and "daddy" to herself and Carl, while he passed around to the other children the oranges Sue had brought for his little house-warming.

# 11

WE WERE in a pleasant boarding-house in Macon in March, 1917. I
saw the headlines of the Russian revolution over the shoulders of a
fellow-boarder. What a feeling jumped into my heart!

"Ordered to fire on the people, the soldiers folded their arms. They
walked to and fro among the people, fraternizing with them."

If it were a great thing to have lived to read Frost and Masefield,
what a moment was this! Age cannot wither it.

But now my three-years' stubborn incredulity about the continuance of the war, and above all about our government's ever entering
into it, crumbled down like the walls of Jericho. I hadn't known
(especially since becoming a Socialist) how much there still was to
crumble; how much old-fashioned faith in the Declaration of Independence, the first eleven amendments to the Constitution, and a
host of accepted Yankee habits of democracy. For two years *The
Tribune,* my aunt's guide, philosopher and friend, had been ardu-
ously pulling and hauling its readers into a "war psychology." In the
night one might worry about this, but by daylight it had always
looked too preposterous. Too preposterous that Theodore Roosevelt
should shake a fist in the President's face and thunder out that it was
the President who was accountable for the sinking of the Lusitania;
that the President was haunted by the ghosts of those who went down
with the great liner; making a fierce pun on the name of the country
place where the Wilson family spent the summer,

"These are the shadows proper to Shadow Lawn!"

I had, like hundreds of thousands of others, pinned an unreasonably
high faith on Mr. Wilson. For some strange reason I hadn't taken in

until now the fact that he paid no smallest attention to the wrongs of Negroes. So far as I know, he never used his office or personal prestige to lighten by one straw the burning injustices they live under, "to keep the world for the white." This, as I came to see in 1917, and blushed not to have seen sooner, is the final judgment bar for every man who rises to high office in the United States. It is the real "acid test" Mr. Wilson himself used to speak of, meaning something else.

When he was reëlected, I of course, like multitudes of my fellow-countrymen, thought this was a security for peace. How many of their votes had been given in response to the widespread appeal, "He kept us out of war"! (Not my vote, to be sure, though many thousand Socialist votes were cast for him.)

But now, on the very day after I'd repeated, in my line-a-day journal, the assurance in the daily papers of immediate recognition of Russia, I wrote,

"Pacifists, sick at heart, expect war."

On April Fool's Day,

"Clergy preach on the Christian duty of war."

On Good Friday, in a black box,

"House 373 to 50 votes war, at three o'clock in the morning."

Jeannette Rankin, the first woman in Congress, was one of the fifty who voted for peace. So was Mr. Kitchin, the majority leader, Mr. Keating, the leader in the fight against child labor, and Mr. Lundeen, the new Minnesota member, who had had the originality to take a referendum of his constituents on our going to war, and found a majority of them opposed. No other Congressman, so far as I know, took the risk of following his example.

The Easter message of the newspapers was

"Army Buys Three Million Trench Bombs."

A week from that day I wrote in my line-a-day, with a marginal finger joyfully pointing,

"Socialist National Committee, meeting at St. Louis, declares for peace."

All this month Aunt Jessie and I had been in Washington, coming

187

up from Macon at the end of March. As soon as we got there, I hunted up the Emergency Peace headquarters on Pennsylvania Avenue—a cold empty shop, the windows covered with peace news, clippings from the papers, which were constantly being read by passers-by. Mr. Lochner and Emily Greene Balch were there, making peace armbands. When we got enough made of these, we sat on the counters and talked. Miss Balch was still, I think, a Professor at Wellesley. She was soon to take up an international life, and eventually to be the Secretary of the Woman's International League for Peace and Freedom. It was Mr. Lochner who afterward went abroad on Mr. Ford's peace ship, that effort to save the lives of young men which aroused mirth among some people.

On the day after Mr. Balfour and the British mission arrived to assist us into the war, my line-a-day says;

"Congress votes seven-billion loan to the Allies."

That month in Washington is clear enough in my memory. I remember my going to see Mr. Lundeen, on account of our early Minneapolis days, and other members of the House and Senate who represented states in which I had lived, to find out what they intended to do about conscription. I remember our peace demonstrations, and our organization of the No-Conscription League on the Capitol steps. But once out of Washington, I find it hard, in a hundred ways, to separate the events of 1914-17 from the events of 1917-19. They were really two wars; the European war, and then the one our government took us into. Not that it matters about the small things I remember doing—when I lettered and pinned on my coat the first of my homemade badges, a scarlet "Love Your Enemies," which I wore through the rest of the war; or when I took up to the office of *The Manchester Journal,* to have reprinted on leaflets I could enclose in my letters, the account in *The Tribune* of the ghastly bayonet drill at Plattsburgh, which visiting mothers fainted at, and which the next day caused the suicide of a young man there who couldn't escape from the drill. I don't know whether I joined the Fellowship of Reconciliation in the first or the second war.

I don't know whether it was in the first or second war that I became acquainted—by letter only—with Badger Clark. I could tell by looking over the files of *The Century Magazine*, for I began the acquaintance by writing a letter to him after reading a poem of his which appeared there, called "My Father and I."

"My father prayed" (it began) "as he drew a bead on the graycoats
Back in those blazing years when the house was divided.
. . . Prayed, while hoping the ball from his clumsy old musket
Might thud to the body of some hot-eyed young southerner
And tumble him limp in the mud of the Vicksburg trenches."

And it went on to point out that while this veteran's son might follow the colors if they called him, he would be obliged to stop praying when he did so, with this farewell to Christianity,

"Jesus, we part here.
My country calls for my body and takes my soul also."

In answer to my letter I received a live wire of a pacifist letter, full of youth, humor, fire and electric tingle—so capital a document that I wrote once more to ask, might I get it printed? and a second tingling hot, merry and reckless letter came in reply, saying "Yes—print 'em anywhere you like, from *The Atlantic Monthly* to *The Police Gazette*." I thought of *The Survey,* and being in New York at the time, walked over to their office with the two letters coruscating under my arm. "We'd be glad to have them both," Mr. Kellogg said, "but why don't you offer *The Century* the first chance since they printed the poem?" On this advice I took the letters to *The Century,* and they printed them together in their next issue, and sent Mr. Clark, as I remember, twenty-five dollars. On this he sent me a third letter as impossible not to have printed as the other two; and this I took to *The Survey,* where Mr. Kellogg printed it after Mr. Clark, at the editor's request, had enlarged it and given it a title—

"Cowards and Fools, Fall In!"

It was so stirring an article that orders came in from far and near for bundles of the number containing it, and also some letters angrily objecting to it; Dr. Rainsford, in particular, the doughty old "muscular Christianity" rector of St. George's Church, canceled his subscription on the spot, as I remember.

My correspondence with Mr. Clark continued for several years. His letters poured out from an apparently inexhaustible fund of sincerity, shrewdness and high frolicsome spirits, all employed with natural literary judgment, taste and sense. Phrases of some of them remain familiarly in my memory. Especially I recall what he said when President Wilson took us into the war. "As I look back, along the line of Wilson's speeches, they seem to mark a sort of Dantesque descent. He has hung back; he has looked earnestly for a way. . . . The peace without victory speech was his last longing look upward. The armed neutrality speech showed his countenance set pretty steadfastly toward the blue flames at the bottom. Then in this 'great state paper' he reached the nethermost circle, and there spit on his hands, seized a butcher knife and called upon his God, just like a headhunter or a European monarch."

From time to time, however, he would say something of this sort;

"I wouldn't be able to resist the band, and a lot of flags flying—if I were called up in the draft I'd remember my old cowboy days, give a whoop, jump into the saddle and be off."

I didn't believe this, and thought it was only his sociable habit of making contacts with all and sundry readers. But when the draft extended to men of his age (the thirties) it proved true. He complied, and more or less willingly entered the service.

One of the first things I had done, when we came up from Washington to New York on the way home, was to pay a visit to the Fellowship of Reconciliation office, and the adjoining one of *The World Tomorrow,* which at that time was called *The New Era.* Norman Thomas had founded it. My visit at these offices was my first acquaintance with him. I've seen him many times since then; sometimes sitting by the fire, or out on the grass, at our school conferences at

Manumit; talking to crowds, debating with Scott Nearing on Communism; speaking at the meetings of the Fellowship, or the League for Industrial Democracy. The impression is always the same. Integrity, vigor, freedom, clearness, knowledge, sweep—and something one can only call devotion, rooted deep in the fastnesses of the heart.

To see Norman Thomas at his best I believe one couldn't have chosen a better place than the luncheons, about 1921, of *The World Tomorrow*. He was then no longer the editor of the magazine he had founded, but his interest in it was far from having waned, and his counsels were still at its service. He always came in late; and the conversation was often eddying about some side issue, while Anna Rochester and Devere Allen tried to extricate us; and then Norman Thomas came in, sat down, and somebody told him what we were talking about. I think it was the nearest thing I ever knew to pure intellectual joy, to hear him disentangle us and draw us all, liberated, back to the central theme.

I found myself, when we got home to Manchester, the only pacifist in town. There were, however, friendly listeners. And in Zephine, seven miles away, I had a comrade. She and I talked timidly that year about soap-boxes. She was more courageous than I in contemplating them, though I'd been much nearer to soap-boxes than she. I'd often listened and sometimes replied to them in Union Square. I could imagine even with pleasure, (for unlike Zephine I love the limelight), going on talking, once I had a few people gathered and listening. But how get started? how buttonhole the original passer-by? Oh what a gulf, once you consider it, between being asked, arranged for, to speak at club or church, and baldly hoisting yourself in harsh loneliness upon a box or curb, to throw out filaments of speech to catch the attention of some cold, fishy-eyed stranger who goes on his way contemptuously and leaves you leaning toward him? Probably that isn't exactly the way it's done. But neither of us had ever attended a course at the Rand School or elsewhere in street corner speaking. However, we both tried to get our courage up with some sort of nebulous public appeal in view.

As soon as Carl wrote that there would be a camp for drafted men near Macon that winter, I realized with a sinking heart exactly what I ought to do; go out to the camp, scatter peace leaflets about and be in jail by sundown. I knew I couldn't do it, even though I made a point, that next winter, of seeing the "woman's cell" at the Macon jail. (It was a nice room.) I might have got up my courage—I greatly doubt even that—if it hadn't been for considering my brother's extreme disapproval and my aunt's sure fit of despair. But no. I think I should have found some other excuse, lacking these.

That year Wallace and Zephine went to France to help, Wallace in the Y. M. C. A. and Zephine with the blinded soldiers; and in cold Paris, so short of fuel, the trouble with her lungs appeared.

Dorothy had gone. Zephine, my complete fellow pacifist, had gone. And yet I never felt any call to go to France, or Belgium, or sick and starving Serbia, or even to anguished Poland, where both sides were rolling each other back and forth over the land and punishing, each in its turn, the already ravaged population for having harbored the other army.

No, what called to me with a voice I longed to answer were the weak, hasty, confused, courageous pioneering efforts which scattered individuals and penniless, new-born, shortlived organizations were making for peace. All I did was to join, send my quarter or fifty cents for a subscription to the tiny paper, write a letter to the newspapers, to the President, to the Department of Justice protesting against the arrests of radicals, to the War Department inquiring how many conscientious objectors had died or gone insane in prison to date; how under the Constitution they could be tortured as they were? I recollect several answers to these letters. One or two gave me quite frankly the numbers of those who had died or gone insane. Another implied that such tortures as I had indicated were not being used. This reply I sent to Norman Thomas, whose brother Evan was at that very time, I believe, in prison as a conscientious objector; and he replied, in effect, "When such a custom is about to be modified or abolished, the authorities sometimes deny its existence." It was only a day or two

192

after I received this comment from him that a small item appeared in the papers headed, "Military Prisoners Will Not Be Tied To Bars Any Longer."

The practice of tying military prisoners to the bars of cells (it said) and all other methods of severe corporal punishment had been ordered abolished by the War Department.

And beside this call rising in my ears of the pioneer pacifists, as weak, and therefore as demanding, as a baby's cry, I was still hearing the old cry of exploited animals (which were now, we heard, beginning to be used in chemical warfare research by the War Department; in the interest, now, of destroying life instead of saving it). And I heard the cry of poverty from a thousand mouths, from Labor in steel towns, coal towns, lumber camps, child workers in mills, beet fields and canning factories; Negroes humiliated, cheated, driven, terrified, shot, hung and burnt, or in the chain-gang, loaded and bruised with spiked iron anklets, working under guns, in terror of the stretch and the sweatbox, on the sweltering roads of Georgia. I heard the cry of prisoners in infected jails, in dark punishment cells, in death cells, watching the electrician set the current in order in the chair.

Only one of my burning poems is about Negroes. But it's not half burning enough! It only points out that

> He who is forbidden
> To share our policies,
> By that exclusion,
> As by a long handle
> Twists and turns them.
>
> He who is excluded
> From our society—
> The act of his banishment
> Shapes our order.

I called it "On Reading Many Histories of the United States," and it was included in *The Enchanted Years,* a volume commemorating the centennial of the University of Virginia. For some time I felt a certain amount of complacency in this poem, and considered it as having said something. Then John L. Spivak wrote *Georgia Nigger*. Beside that testament of horror I realized how pale, academic, had hitherto been my measure of revolt against Negro wrongs compared with what they are. Who can write anything about them, ever again, to compete with *Georgia Nigger?* Every Governor of a state which tolerates the chain-gang—every mayor, alderman, and village magnate, every judge, magistrate and justice of the peace, every member of a jury, every member of a church, ought to read *Georgia Nigger*— and the sweatbox and the stretch and the chain-gang itself would be gone with the thumbscrew and the rack.

But in the very winter when my eyes were scorched by reading John Spivak's book, a letter came through the mail of which the very heading healed my eyes as they read it—

ASSOCIATION OF SOUTHERN WOMEN FOR THE PREVENTION OF LYNCHING

These militant white women are organized in all the southern states. They investigate on their own responsibility and publish their findings, as damnatory as ever were printed. They call persistently and courageously on their governors to protect the Negro. It's some good, even in this regard, to have lived threescore years.

When I say that peace effort in the United States was weak, I am making a generalization of my own—we had nothing to compare ourselves with. Countries where Labor was strong had had an engine ready to convey the peace feeling of the people to the authorities. We remembered how, on the night preceding Germany's declaration of war, there had been thirty crowded street meetings in Berlin demanding peace. We'd watched Karl Liebknecht in Germany and Jean Longuet in France, (the leaders of the minority Socialists) standing like lions against the war, with dumb passionate crowds of workers crouching behind them. In England, where the Fellowship of Reconciliation had been founded, so many Quakers were imprisoned for peace that the largest Quaker Meeting in England was held in a jail.

IN MY THIRTIES

On the other hand, the Socialist *majority* in this country had pronounced against the war; it was the minority of the party here (with John Spargo at their head) who supported it. To be sure, a time came during the war when the majority might have reconsidered their decision, with a possibility of changing their declaration—or so some Socialists thought—but by that time the savage law had been passed inflicting twenty years' imprisonment for criticism of the war, and no comrade would favor a conference, lest he expose others to this penalty.

Then, too, we had in this country the People's Council, a gigantic bean-stalk, branching out overnight with fresh thousands joining. It was holding great national peace councils in east, north and south, each much bigger than the last; and in September 1917 it was going to Minneapolis for a monster meeting, which I played with the financially extravagant idea of attending as one of the fifty delegates-at-large. But the size and rapid increase of this popular peace party attracted serious attention by this time from the friends of the war, both federal and state, and the Minneapolis meeting was suddenly refused by the Governor of Minnesota, over the willing consent of the Socialist Mayor of Minneapolis; it knocked at the doors of Chicago, where it precipitated another conflict between the state and city; was invited to North Dakota by that calm libertarian and good old-fashioned American, friend of every generous cause, Lynn Frazier, then the Governor and now one of the Senators of his state; and in the end of the autumn, after a Secret-Service-shadowed, melodramatic meeting in Chicago, withered away under the persecution it had aroused, and I suppose its strength went into the various smaller but more permanent, tougher, and less spectacular peace bodies.

# 12

## THE JAIL

Is this a clinic, then, for ailing souls?
  A shop for damaged manhood's skilled repair?
Life-saving station on the shores of time
  To save time's shipwrecked sailors from despair?

Or is it but a refuse heap, to breed
  Filth and disease to threaten all mankind?
A furnace for the shreds of self-respect?
  A slaughter-house for crippled souls and blind?

WHAT little service I could do for Labor, beyond a verse or two, was
to come a few years later, in a Labor movement school. I never seriously thought I could succeed as a volunteer picket or a union or-
ganizer. Race relations I could only mend in my own contacts, showing courtesy and respect. But I thought I saw a way to respond to
the bitter cry of the prisoners. I was in revolt within against the whole
penal system; against, in fact, the whole principle of punishment—I
felt as Margaret Wilson did when she wrote her noble book (long
afterward), *The Crime of Punishment*.

And I could see a way for a person like myself, without money,
influence or experience, to begin. I would write a letter to *The Survey*
telling how indecent and how useless, to me, seemed the whole scheme
of hurting the criminal in order to make a good citizen of him—or
of others; how (as I thought) the morally sick should be studied and
treated as carefully as the mentally sick or the physically sick, and

196

with as single an intention to cure them. I would try to show that while the morally sick might need as careful restraint as the mentally sick, in order to safeguard society, there was no more reason in the one case than in the other to mete out harsh conditions to them, or hold them up to public disgrace. In short, as I wrote this letter, I was trying to show how caked with folly and harm is our inherited idea— without basis in modern psychology—that those who do evil deeds should be evilly treated by society in return.

At threescore I would not subtract a pennyworth from this position, but would emphasize the obvious abnormality of those who can deliberately plan a crime involving suffering to others for their own advantage; an abnormality which we all feel, in a natural recoil, as from a dangerous lunatic, while at the same time, for purposes of punishment, the law assumes that these persons are essentially normal. And so I would suggest, in writing my letter again, that psychological clinics should succeed the courtrooms, as well as hospitalization the prisons—a modern manner of taking the Christian advice, "judge not."

Mrs. Walter Cope of Germantown answered my letter in *The Survey*. She was, and had long been, Secretary of the Pennsylvania Prison Reform League; but she was convinced that prison reform was pouring water in a sieve. She invited me to come to her house in Germantown in the autum, to meet a group of persons interested and experienced in prison matters, and to try, as I'd hoped, to form a new body of protest and revolutionary change.

This result was dazzlingly above what I'd hoped for from my letter. And when I reached Mrs. Cope's house, I saw in a few hours' time what a woman she was, how wise, how humane, and what a range of feeling and knowledge she had. All that she ever did for great causes in public ways never subtracted anything at all from her warm human encouragement and comforting of those who had also ventured into the fray and been wounded or stranded. Her opinions were decided, even fiery, but her kindnesses were all alike, uncalculating, unrestricted. The steel glint in her gray eyes was warm, not icy, and the steel string in her voice was part of its sweetness. How many times, on later visits to her, I've seen her secluded in her diningroom (a convenient place to give a bite or sup casually to her visitor) talking cordially with some rash young crusader for civil liberties, some strike picket or pacifist out on bail; a stranger to her, coming without other credentials than his social passion and practical courage.

On the night of our meeting, how fast her black dress swept about the room from one colleague to another! I knew already the names of many who were there. Among them, I particularly remember the speech and personality of Mary Winsor, the suffragist. She spoke especially of prison punishments. "If for one moment," she cried, "a judge in open court sentenced a convicted man to floggings, to bread and water, chains, a dark cell—any one of the common prison punishments, that happen every day!—sentenced him to be infected with tuberculosis, syphilis—the spectators would rise in a tumult, the papers would print it in scareheads, the pulpits would brand it, and in less than a month laws would be passed against it! But all the judge says aloud is 'Ten years.' You have to know the inside of a prison to know what that ten years may mean."

One among the prison protesters there that night (a guest of Mrs. Cope's, so that I saw him again at breakfast) was Winthrop Lane, whose articles, "Uncle Sam, Jailer," were already appearing in *The Survey*. These accounts of the Federal prisons such as Leavenworth, etc., were sending a thrill of shame through the socially minded world. They were the fruits of a trip Mr. Lane had made to see these fortresses; fruits of his patient, dry, tongue-controlled perseverance in finding out, seeing for himself, hearing from the wardens' lips, what tortures were in general use.

When our meeting closed, I was overwhelmed with distress; a sense of failure rushed over me, along with the certainty of my personal responsibility for it. At a particular point, a clear chance had been given me, I felt, to organize the interest and the potentialities which Mrs. Cope had assembled here; and I had laid it down. How or why I had done so I couldn't think. Outwardly, of course, it was from ignorance how to begin, lack of experience in gathering up the feeling of a meeting; but inwardly it was cowardice and dread of doing it wrong, that had let the moment pass. Only two or three times in my life have I felt such amazement and horror at my own behavior. I seemed to have betrayed Mrs. Cope's efforts and to have made the great refusal.

If ever, it was then that I experienced what those unfortunates feel who see all their moral life through a glass, darkly, and whose unsuspected weaknesses suddenly betray them into irrevocable harm.

I am expressing better, now, what I then felt than I could have expressed it at the time. I falteringly said something to Mrs. Cope—a very small sample of what I was thinking. If she had such a thought about the meeting, she concealed it from me, and picked up the pieces as well as she could. Before he left the next morning, Mr. Lane accepted a sort of commission to consider our hopes and let us know, a little later, how we could best proceed. (My own original idea had been some informal banding together, without officers or dues, of all persons who strongly wished for a revolution in treating criminals. I'd thought that each of these members should be a member only while he continued to visit and find out all he could about his local jails, and while he also brought up the matter of their improvement or abolition at least every year before his church, club, grange, local newspaper, etc., and wherever he had an opportunity.)

Mr. Lane, for a long time, didn't write to us. Some adequate reasons prevented, I remember. But when he did write, the effect was to postpone indefinitely the hopes I had been cherishing. I can see now, that all I really needed was obstinacy in trying out my ideas. They would eventually have led me somewhere, and borne fruit in human amelioration. And why I had no more perseverance at this time I can't think, any more than I can bring realizingly home to myself why I never as a young girl made any plans to go west and keep house for my father.

I only acted out in my individual life what I had thought of as

199

the rule for a society, visiting all the jails I could, wherever we were, and trying weakly to interest others and give my findings local publicity. In Macon I used to go every week to the county jail. The warden, "jailer" he was called, let me take in fruit, pie, magazines, tobacco, paper and stamps, and carry out the prisoners' mail. The Helping Hand, a young girls' club, used often to finance my baskets of oranges and pie.

My first introduction to the jail I obtained from one or two Methodist women who were in the habit of conducting a weekly service there for those of the prisoners who wished. I went there with them and took part. There was in the jail no chapel, diningroom, or general room of any sort that could be used for such a meeting; we had to kneel and sing in the narrow corridor that ran before the cages in which the men were penned. In these cages they lived day and night, winter and summer, without respite and without going for a single instant into the sunshine. Their food was passed in to them, and they ate it in the presence of their toilets. This food was provided by the "jailer" at his own discretion, I believe; I am not sure, but I think, that the arrangement was for the county to make a yearly allotment to the jailer for the prisoners' food; if he could save anything on quality or quantity, he received the benefit in his private purse. So far as I could learn, the food consisted of one or two cheap kinds of meat, dried peas or beans, cornbread, coffee and molasses. No fruit, in that country where peaches lay unharvested under the trees for the taking; no milk, butter, eggs, no green vegetables any more than fresh air.

I made a great many visits to the jail before I ever knew of what was called the "old part." I assumed, all that time, that I was seeing all the prisoners every week. When somebody happened, one day, to speak about the "old part," I went to see the jailer. "What prisoners are there in the old part? where is the old part? can I go in?" "Oh, they're misdemeanor prisoners, thirty or forty of 'em—Niggers—in for a short time, a week or two," said he. "No, no, you can't go in—they're a rough lot—wouldn't take a woman in there!"

"Well, I'm no young girl," I said. "I'm old and tough."

200

"No telling what they'd say," he replied, shaking his head. "Curse and swear, or worse, probably. If I should let you in, I'd go with you and protect you."

"Well," I said, "I haven't got any pie for them, or any stamps, or magazines. I've only got these violets, about two violets apiece."

They were poor little pale violets, with stems an inch or two long; wild ones, the first of the year.

We went in to the perpetual twilight of the old part, where, in cages much less spacious than those in the "new part," dark forms and faces were glimmering, partly visible. The men seemed sad, gentle and polite; each one accepted his two violets. "Thank you, ma'am."

The next time I went, the jailer let me go into the old part alone. I managed to have a greasy doughnut or wedge of pie apiece—dismal stuff, costing more than fruit, but they liked it better. They were, again, sad, reserved, friendly. They talked little; most of their strength they seemed to be using to endure the monotony and gloom.

There were a dozen "murderers" at that time in the Bibb County jail; all, I think, were white. Most of them were extremely human. Their crimes were all of the hip-pocket kind, impulsive killings, for which a fist fight would have been a satisfactory substitute, could they but have demeaned their manhood to obey the law against private weapons. Mr. Wilkins,* in particular, who had had two trials and one "hung jury," and was awaiting another trial, was the kindest of men. He would never have been in prison if he had never possessed a revolver. He had shot another man in the most picayune quarrel imaginable—a dispute over a hen. Once, when a young Italian traveling musician who knew not a word of English, and hadn't a cent (a stranger in Georgia) was arrested on a charge of intended rape, Mr. Wilkins appealed earnestly to me, as he'd never appealed for himself, to take up the young man's cause.

This young Italian's case found friends among the many kind people in Macon and was the occasion of a friendship I have always continued in spirit with Mrs. Lee, the wife of the then rector of St.

* Not his real name.

201

Paul's Church. She cordially agreed to appear with me in the court-room when the young musician's case came up for trial. We went together to see Judge Nottingham, who had been retained for the defense. What he said I have always remembered. "Ladies, the best help you can give this poor fellow is to go over and shake hands with him before the eyes of the jury. Let the jury see that the prisoner has friends—respectable women."

But the case of this youth never came to court; it was *nolle-prosse'd* —a happy ending.

Not so with the ghastly case of Jim Denson, a Negro from another county who was rushed away from a crowd of lynchers to this jail. He was under sentence of death when he came.

I saw the account of his case in the Macon paper the night before I was going to the jail. He was a penniless, friendless boy under twenty. He was accused of assaulting a white woman over seventy. I don't remember whether or not the paper said he had confessed, as they call it. The judge had appointed a lawyer to defend him; the lawyer had said "We make no defense." Not a word of defense was made, while his life was pronounced away. I believe the judge had asked this ignorant, untaught child if he would waive his legal rights. What conception could he have had of a word like "waive"? He obediently said "Yes, boss," and was sentenced to be hung.

When I asked to see him, after visiting the other men as usual, the jailer said "You've gone right by him, and given him pie." I went back and asked the men in the Negro cage, "Which of you is Jim Denson?" One with the aspect of a roughly carved image in stone said "I is."

I don't know what words came into my mouth to say to a young son of earth who had five days to live. I remember asking him what church he belonged to? "Never been no church." How far had he gone in school? "Never been no school." But he could read and write? No. "Never learned nothing."

He wouldn't mind my sending a minister in to see him? "No

ma'am." Was there anybody I could write to for him? mother or father? sisters or brothers? Mother dead; "I wishes I could see my father." He gave me his father's name and address, and I wrote—wrote more than once; but Jim Denson's father never came to see him. No answer ever came. Did nobody ever read his father the letters I wrote? Had he no way to come? Would no one bring him? For the two years Jim Denson lived in the Macon jail, I think he never heard from home.

At random, after walking past two or three of the Negro churches in Macon, I selected one and went in to see its pastor. I found a quiet, dignified man, as remote as a human being could be from the "preacher" of the funny stories. He received my anxious account of Jim Denson with perfect quiet sympathy. He knew of him already. The Negroes were quietly raising money for a lawyer for him. Collections would be taken in the Negro churches next day. And when I asked, with the unquenched horror of my first girlhood knowledge of a Negro burned, "But if he gets a stay of execution—if he has a lawyer to defend him—will a mob take him out and burn him alive?" he answered,

"No—no, I think you needn't fear that—I think your fears are exaggerated."

Eventually Jim Denson had a lawyer, a white lawyer, a well-known criminal lawyer. He received stay after stay, pleading for a new trial—that is, for a trial. Could he be thought to have had a trial, when there was nothing but an undefended charge and a sentence to death? But he never received an order for a new trial—he was never tried. Like Sacco and Vanzetti, like Mooney, like the Scottsboro boys, his blazing wrongs were brought to the attention of authority after authority, and every man of them so used his power as to cause that friendless boy to die.

In the end, when hope was over, Jim Denson was taken back to his "home" county to be resentenced. Lynchers assembled again, and this time captured him. He was put into an automobile at night with

203

three white men. They had a noose already round his neck. Perceiving that they were all intoxicated, he worked one hand loose and got it up to the rope round his neck, and worked that loose. He worked it off, and jumped from the car. He ran on all fours along the ditch he'd landed in, was shot at, dodged the bullets, ran through woods, a field. How could he even run, just out of two years in jail where no fresh air or exercise was ever allowed? He asked a white farmer for something to eat—the farmer shot at him. Hungry, exhausted, he struggled on. The sheriff pursued him with bloodhounds. They found his trail, and one of the hounds caught up with him. Jim Denson patted the dog, talked to it, and it grew friendly and followed him. Another bloodhound caught up with him, made friends with him and followed too. The third came up—he couldn't tame it; it bayed and brought up the sheriff with the handcuffs.

Jim Denson, as he was brought back to jail, asked the reporters who came out to meet him,

"Boss, you reckon they'll hang me now?"

"No, Jim, reckon not," the white men answered.

For a day or two it was thought that they wouldn't, now, hang him. But whatever authorities were asked to change his fate, again found it their pleasure and wisdom to make him die.

He was hung.

It seems to me that his two years under sentence of death may have been the best two years of Jim Denson's life. Apparently for the first time, he then found somebody who took an interest in him. There were people really willing to spend a dollar or two to save his life. He was worth fighting for.

I think his wit, courage, coolness, endurance, after two years in that dreary jail waiting to die, showed that he had risen in knowledge and self-confidence there. From a youth that was more barren and forlorn than even these barren years of doom, something had glimmered round him, some sense of his value. He had heard the voice of the community saying, not indeed the noble words of Walt Whitman,

204

"Despairer, here is my neck!
By God, you shall not go down! Hang your whole weight upon me!"

—but something with a faint resemblance, a kind of prophecy of that.

Prophecy of some sort there must have been in those days, if I could have heard it, for a few years ahead in my life was coming one of the most heart-refreshing visits woman ever paid to jail. In our own state of Vermont, at the very time when Jim Denson's expropriated life was being violently taken from him by the third snatch, the Woman's State Reformatory was being returned from Windsor to Rutland, and the Governor was asking Lena Ross to be the head of it.

Seven or eight years after that, Dorothy told me that I ought to go and see it; and I went up to Rutland, crossed the river and the green lawns of Riverside and entered the human dwelling place that Lena Ross has made of the old gray cell block which had been delivered into her hands. She took me over the whole place, and I saw the convicted women of Vermont and the federal women prisoners from all states east of the Mississippi—not languishing, idle and half alive, in frowsy cells, but working busily in a great laundry (which pays almost the whole of the running expenses of the prison) with wide open windows untroubled by bars, open to the sun and air, carrying baskets of clean linen to hang out in the grassy drying yard, taking pride and pleasure in their skill and success. I saw them going in to dinner in the cheerful diningroom with skyblue walls hung round with pictures of the sea and ships, of children and mothers. I saw them reading and knitting in their social room; I heard them in the chapel (whose lace altar cloth was their work) singing with great voices; and (a little reluctantly, even after all this) I went to see their cells. Miss Ross doesn't call them cells, any more than she calls the inmates prisoners. "Don't you want to see," she asked, "the girls' bedrooms?"

I needn't have hung back, or remembered the greasy gray untidy forlornnesses so drearily familiar to me. On every bed, smooth as a nun's, lay a snowy bedspread. On every bureau was a photograph or two, a pincushion or a book, a little dish of flowers. Through the corridor that ran in front of their doors they couldn't help seeing the beautiful sweep of mountains to the east, and receiving the morning sun.

Thousandfold recompense for my useless letter to the Survey, my trifling visits to the Macon jail! What I couldn't help to do, incompetent self-hinderer that I was, nevertheless was being done. Here and there, sparse and precious as the first flowers of the year, human hearts were rising, with wits and powers to match, trans-substantiating the crime of punishment into the cure of souls.

Just before I went home from Riverside, Miss Ross's secretary handed me a letter from a western judge to somebody in Washington, who had enclosed it for Miss Ross to see.

"Women from hereabouts," he wrote, "who have been sent to the state reformatory in Rutland, come back after serving their terms so changed and rehabilitated that their neighbors sometimes write to me to ask what's happened to them. They come home and make good neighbors and good citizens."

The largest of my puny efforts toward the penal revolution came a few years later, when I organized the committee who tried to abolish the death penalty in Vermont. Dorothy and Zephine both served on this, and Dorothy wrote a letter which we circulated widely, and not only we, but the national League. A goodly number of well-known Vermonters like Walter Hard, Charles Crane and Professor Perkins served on this committee and furnished it with capital ammunition; but we lost our bill by a substantial majority while New Hampshire, with no campaign at all, nearly tied on the same question.

And yet Vermont almost never has an execution, and all its state penal institutions are enlightened and humane. One would have supposed Vermont a promising candidate to follow the fifty-year-old example of Maine, and the seventy-five-year-old example of Rhode Island.

206

# 13

It seems to me now that 1918 was the height of two great waves of excitement, two rivers meeting, breasting each other, weltering together and mingling inextricably the passions, thoughts and reactions of which they were composed; the river of the workers' sense of power, pouring out of the channel of the Russian revolution, and the river of national militarism, struggling on in the maniacal strength of unreason and fear.

A *War Journal of a Pacifist* which I kept in the summer of 1917, (April to September inclusive), is sprinkled over, toward the close, with signs of the rise of the Bolsheviks, which took place in October, immediately after I closed my *Journal*. Within the next year, of course, Labor throughout the western world was to be invigorated to the marrow of its bones by the spectacle of Russia.

How great was the change in tone of the strugglers for peace! For the last four years they had offered mediation, appealed to the conscience of the world, made "pleas." Emily Greene Balch has put them together in her book, *Approaches to the Great Settlement*. The federated Masons had made a plea, forgotten now, offering their services for peace, as a great international body. The Socialists in all countries had struggled all through the summer and fall to get passports for their delegates to Stockholm, so that they could agree on terms which could then be brought forward simultaneously in their parliaments. And the Pope's great letter, solemn and Christian, had issued in the middle of the summer of 1917. These three international efforts, "the Black, the Red and the White Peace," so much more powerful than offers of mediation from a single government, could not have failed,

(I almost think) if they had been made in the brusque tone of 1918 instead of the deferential tone that still held over in 1917. When it had been seen in Russia that people could stop fighting, with or without the sanction of their commanding officers; that they could walk into the palaces and turn the rulers out, and open and publish the secret treaties, how natural it was that fraternizing in the trenches should become so widespread, and break down "morale"! It was natural for the strugglers for peace to grow bold. The Black and the White peace came no nearer, but the Red peace came on by leagues, with strikes and bread riots, and the beacon fire in Russia blazing up behind them. They felt a now-or-never haste as the Russian revolution was attacked by one White army after another, backed by the Allies. To see our part in this, is there a better book than *Jimmie Higgins?* The war power of the world seemed to rear its tidal wave against the workers' furious will to peace,

"And all the world was in the sea."

What heights the war current rose to! That food blockade of Russia, that blockade of medicines and anæsthetics, in revolt against which a body of American women raised money to send anæsthetics there, to relieve the mediæval sufferings of surgical patients in the Russian hospitals. How savagely peace motions were repelled by the newspapers, up to a month before the armistice; "We are too busy to be bothered by talk of peace," "Does a judge hold a peace conference with the criminal?" "Hang the Kaiser first and receive peace terms afterward."

Though peace was the natural client of radicals, that very alliance (I thought) made the warring governments try to break it up, and carry peace away from its red connections. But they took a savage method. Late in the summer of 1918 I find in my line-a-day a vast German strike, in several cities at once, seven hundred thousand men and women. It was only broken by the order that "all who do not return to work on Monday morning will be shot." At the same time, in this country, the I. W. W. were practically outlawed, and a hundred of them were convicted in one mass trial. Who doesn't remem-

208

ber these violent laws? to criticize the government, flag, army or navy was made punishable by twenty years; so that when Gene Debs was tried on three counts for his Canton speech, he might have received sixty years' sentence, and the judge was thought magnanimous to inflict only ten. Taking example by such frantic laws, what a wave of tarring and feathering went over the land! Several Negroes were burned at the stake "in the public square."

Like the rain of meteors in Rome on the night before Cæsar was assassinated, were all those natural convulsions that took place now in 1918. That was the year of that unimaginable earthquake in China which engulfed such multitudes of people, and carried away a hill, carried away a road, with the rows of trees that shaded it. India, from which wheat had been exported to feed the war, was in sight of a monstrous famine that would starve tens of millions. A shipload of munitions exploded in Halifax harbor, and wrecked the city, throwing down the buildings on the people in the streets, which were full of crushed bodies; and on this horror a four-foot snowstorm fell, through which the rescuers tried in vain to find the living and the dying.

I was sitting in our parlor in Manchester one afternoon, overwhelmed by the war and these fearful concomitants; tired to the bone of thinking, sorrowing, hoping, raging. My lap was full of the ephemeral pacifist papers, *Four Seas,* the last bulletins of the dying People's Council, *The Public, The New York Call,* etc., and letters from Zephine and Kate Codington, my great Macon friend and fellow pacifist. At the bottom of my thoughts was great anxiety for Zephine. Wallace was bringing her home, under a foreign doctor's verdict that she had tuberculosis. They were landing in New York that day or the next. I was longing to see her. I felt spent, useless, lonely in my passion for peace, and sick to death of myself. I dropped the papers on the floor and went upstairs.

There was hanging or rather pinned on the wall of my room a small penny picture of "Christ Tempted," by Cornicelius—a picture in which I felt great power and companionship, so that I had written a sonnet about it. Coming in now, so weary and heavy-laden, my eyes fell at once, as they usually did, on this dark, struggling Christ, who seemed so near and natural. But greater, much greater than usual, was the power which seemed to issue from the picture and to focus back upon my heart and life the hopes that were wandering away from me. I stood still a long time, looking at the picture, perhaps an hour. I realized the experience behind Masefield's line, which previously had seemed exaggerated, "I stood in bliss at this for hours." I sat down on the floor and began to pray, in the manner which had lately become customary with me, pushing away my tiny temporary concerns and titillating surfaces of consciousness and entering gradually into a state such as the latter end of a Quaker silence. But on this day of my illumination I entered on a quiet state immediately. I began to pray for the President; that into his heart might come an overwhelming will for peace. I did feel some power rousing into my prayer. But instead of going on thus exerting my inward power, I was drawn beyond all partial or particular effort, into a state of joyful peace. As this, this silent flood of joy and calm beyond all things temporary, rose deep beneath and bore me up, my eyes for some time poured out tears, cool, pleasant tears, not salty or burning, like the tears of pride and sorrow. "Bliss!" I thought; "this is the serene and overmastering bliss of immortal life." My fingers, as if it had been habitual with them, made the sign of the cross over and over again.

This calm, capacious joy continued a long time, another hour or two. When it released me, there was no sense of ebbing, no letting down; but through the putting on of supper, dishwashing, walking up to the village in the evening for the mail, and for the summer evening's sweetness, the same bliss and calm continued, wondering yet familiar, strangely homelike. In the morning I awoke with it, and anticipated with extraordinary pleasure the leisure of a time of prayer. It was then that I began to go out for a morning hour of prayer every day, when the breakfast dishes were washed and the house in order; this would be between nine o'clock and ten. I went to the beautiful hillsides of the cemetery, from which all the mountains were visible, east and west; often, at that early hour, with mist still rolling off into the blue like blowing clouds of snow. I sat on the grass where that flight of steps goes down through a thicket of cedar to the brook in the ravine; and now I understood what Lady Julian and other mystics had meant by "seeing into heaven by looking closely at a hazel nut," for since my illuminated afternoon I could feel the growing life of the grasses round me mingle sweetly with my life. The life of earth was too near and commingling for any dread of dying; I began to cherish a pleasant wish that we could all die lying on the ground, as Father Damien and Walt Whitman wished.

When I prayed, my house duties, my writings, little public tasks, etc., fell into a smiling order, quite carefree. If I'd forgotten an important letter, on which someone's happiness might hang, it then came pleasantly into mind in ample time; if not, it often turned out to have been cared for otherwise and better. If I wished to see a particular person, often I "happened" to leave the cemetery as he passed the gate. Some power was surely released which ordered life much better for me than before—"whether in the body or out of the body I cannot tell."

I don't know how to express this experience truly in any less sweeping language. And yet it is certain that coincidentally with this quiet and joy I did at times become hot, hurried and cross—did pin my efforts to temporary successes, and become painfully downcast when they failed. I did feel the familiar chagrins, discouragements, conflicts, petty despairs. I yielded to them, but they mattered less, were easier to bear, neglect and forget. Intolerable shuddering chances, as that someone dear to me might die with some painful slow malady, became infused with some ozone of bearability, some *power for us both to see joy beyond.*

By prayer I could also release some unheard-of current of encouragement and soothing into family life, and into my calls in the homes of friends beset by poverty—unheard of, I mean, in my awkward natural manners. Something, whether in the body or out, caused me often to say wise, refreshing words without forethought.

In this illumination of mine religion became really childlike and illimitable—still difficult to follow, but easy beyond words to understand! a single principle, in no way depending on historic origins or personalities, books, traditions, training, intelligence, character or morals; a purely inward act, an instant's will to unselfishness, a *reach toward loving,* which instantly reaches back to us, embraces and makes divine.

> "Why labor at the dull mechanic oar
> When the fresh breeze is blowing
> And the strong current flowing
> Right onward to the eternal shore?"

# 14

On coming home to Dorset, Zephine began to be better. Dorset is much more than home to her; like Arlington to Dorothy, it is really her larger self. When she is well, the community has a thousand welcome claims on her; now that she was ill, she came back to it, found herself able to rest there far better than elsewhere, and life began to flow back into her body. As the summer went on and she gained so much and so fast, we began to think of the possibility that the French doctors had overstated the condition of her lungs. Now after the lapse of sixteen years, it seems certain that they did so. Or else her inward harmony was still more potent than we thought.

Seeing her color and strength come up was a keen joy, and I exulted in reporting it to Dorothy's anxious inquiries. One happy thing to tell her! Dorothy's letters at this time were occasionally rather panting, as if with carrying a huge load of vicarious sorrow. The well-known photograph taken of her at that time, so lovely and tender, is very sad. She was deeply worn, and weighed less than ninety pounds.

While those two mingling torrents of passion, Labor and the war, were composing themselves into peace, people like me, who for three years had been unable to understand why the war went on, had now become convinced that peace was farther than ever away. (Dr. Carrel had recently prophesied that the war would last for fifty years.) Still, I did write down, in my line-a-day, the Austrian appeal for peace, and the German government's consternation at it; trying, all the time, not to expose my heart to the hopes for peace that blew by us in the gale.

We were in New York by the first of November, when I printed, in my line-a-day, in exulting capitals,

## RED FLAG FLIES IN VIENNA—
### WORKERS OF THE WORLD, UNITE!

with trumpets roaring in the margin, and banners flapping across the page, displaying the Socialist emblems of the torch and the continents clasping hands. On the second I wrote

"Revolution sweeping Hungary."

On the seventh, Aunt Jessie said at lunch, "Let's go over to Brooklyn and pay that call today." The journey involved a change from one subway to another in the heart of downtown New York; and losing our direction, we found ourselves in Wall Street at the height of the paper snowstorm and waded ankle-deep in the improvised confetti that fell steadily from the windows above. While we were still bewildered, trying to find out what it was about, the evening papers came out, carrying the two headlines cheek by jowl,

## PEACE DENIED! ARMISTICE NOT YET SIGNED!
and
## RED FLAG FLIES IN KIEL!

What four days those were for Socialists, between the false and true Armistice days, the days of the German revolution! All that has happened since, from the "peace to end peace" to the Nazi purge a year ago, can't pull those days entirely down.

"Fri. 8," (I wrote) "The Revolution spreads in Germany—the mutinous fleet puts to sea under the red flag!
Sat. 9. The Kaiser abdicates.
Sun. 10. The red flag sweeps on to Berlin; Stuttgart, Frankfort, Leipsic, Cologne, hoist the international colors!"
"In four days," (I wrote, bursting through my line-a-day) "the deadly fear that the Allied troops would be used as the hangman of the

Russian revolution has been swept away. Two Socialist states will be too strong together to be put down!"

A night or two after the real Armistice Day, the Socialists had their peace parade. It was the first political parade I'd walked in since Harrison's election. We met at the Rand School in Fifteenth Street. Seeing with envy the transparencies and homemade paper signs many of my comrades were carrying, I asked the bearer of
"You Can't Imprison an Ideal"
if I might walk beside him? This young man gave an unsmiling assent, and I took my stand at his elbow.

My comrades were very grave, almost subdued. They looked, as Socialists usually do, rather pale, hardworking, sober folks. However, when in our march up Fifth Avenue, we reached the Waldorf, where the waiters were on strike, and paused to cheer them, an electric thrill ran through our column. Some of the bystanders caught it, and cheered with us. We stayed shouting and cheering there for some time, then proceeded to Fifty-Seventh Street, where we turned west. Our celebration was to end in a meeting at Carnegie Hall. No sooner had we turned the corner than a little body of men in uniform attacked us. My partner, who had never once allowed me to carry his sign, even for a single block, was wounded in the hand, and blood flowed from it. Even then he wouldn't let me take over the banner, but held it aloft in the other hand. But our ranks had been disorganized by the attack, and by the nearness of Carnegie Hall, into which everybody was hurrying to hear the speeches. I saw two more khaki uniforms coming toward us, and ran over to them and seized one of them by the sleeve, without premeditation saying in ladylike tones "Please *don't!*" They hesitated and then turned back. I was rather thrilled to have been in the mêlée, small as it was.

So far as I know, the Socialists never organized another parade in New York for ten or twelve years. Peace was followed by the days of "witch-burning" and red-baiting, round-ups of radicals, who were loaded in trucks and dumped into jail by hundreds. Dr. Elizabeth

215

Baer of Philadelphia was rushed to prison without warning at midnight because she was a Socialist officer. The twelve Socialists elected to the New York legislature were unseated. All this had its usual effect upon the Negro. There were eighty lynchings that year, and seventeen of them were burnings.

That was the year when Carl and Susan's youngest children were born, the twin boy and girl. I was transported with this bounty and distinction which had at last fallen on our family. It rewarded a life-long desire of mine. Twins, we'd always known, ran in our family. Our father had been a twin and our mother's first children had been twins. I'd always thought it very hard that with twins to right and left of us, Carl and I had never seen, much less been, them. Now I was very much uplifted and felt a strong desire to run through the village ringing all the doorbells. I did rush from the telephone down to the kitchen, bursting open the door and shouting "Twins! Agnes! We've got twins!"

To my dismay, our temporary household assistant, Agnes, a woman of great dignity, rose slowly from her knees. She had been in the midst of prayer, and her dark eyes (she was a very handsome woman) regarded me with amazement. Even then, shocking as it was to have rushed bellowing into the stillness of prayer, I could only bethink myself of a word or two to begin an apology before the twins burst through again, and I said in a rising voice of irrepressible excitement,

"But, Agnes, you *must* excuse me—we've got twins!"

We had twins, but they were not identical twins. Lucy Ann and John Cleghorn, even at six months old, had personalities very different indeed. If you sat down with a twin in each arm, Lucy would sweetly relax and bask, dwelling in profundities of infant thought; Johnny would spring up and down in endless efforts to be off and away on his adventures. Their photograph sitting together in a baby-carriage showed these characteristics. John's infant eye appears to wink, and he has a sly and merry look. Lucy Ann is blooming and serene. She is a little like my mother.

216

DOROTHY (AT LEFT) IN THE DOORWAY OF THE "BRICK HOUSE" THE OLD HOME OF THE CAN-FIELDS IN ARLINGTON—NOW THE COMMUNITY HOUSE—DURING A COLONIAL EXHIBIT.

These admired and highly prized twins of ours set me thinking afresh of something I'd thought of before. "What will you tell the children?" had been one of the forms of war propaganda; "What will you say when in days to come they ask you, "Daddy, what did *you* do in the war? What did *you* do, mother?" Pacifists, of course, had applied this question to themselves with a difference. "What did *you* do, mother and daddy, to stop the war?" "Were you one of the people that tried to down war, Aunt Sally? What did you do?"

"Well, children, nobody could write anything in those days without putting in war or peace, and I put peace into everything I wrote, and so none of it got printed." That was what I would have liked to say—and how much more! But that at least. Was it too sweeping? Perhaps.

Here were my three books, the harvest of five years. One was my little six-months' *War Journal of a Pacifist*. I knew I couldn't place that for many years to come. This Journal was in no sense literary. It was only a record, from a minority angle, thousands of miles behind the pacifist front or any other, of such facts, often small, but to my mind significant, as floated by me in the air like straws in the gale. I couldn't think anybody would publish it now, with its unpopular point of view, or would ever publish it for any merit except the recalling of forgotten facts; and for that merit I must wait for the facts to be forgotten.

*Her Late Thirties* was a small novel. It recounted how a business woman in East Orange had fallen heir to a house in Vermont, and how she accumulated there first an old cousin, a violent-tempered old gentleman, and next a young relation of high-school age, over whom both she and the old gentleman became so warmly parental that all three together they composed a family of sorts. Into this family life irrupted the war; the boy was carried away by the old tribal passions; the heroine became a pacifist; and at this moment of inner and outer conflict, the love of her youth, a middle-aged invalid, a courageous idealist, reappeared in her life and helped her understand the possibilities of faith in and freedom for the young.

This novel had been submitted to two or three publishing houses. One of them had given it a very friendly reading. Judging from the first part, they had let me feel quite confident that they would publish it; saying, in fact, that it was a good deal better than its predecessor. But on reaching the later chapters, they had abruptly changed their minds and returned the manuscript. They hadn't said they were refusing it on account of its pacifism. They explained that the end was very inferior to the beginning and middle. But the end was the pacifist part.

Then there was my little History, *Children's First Life of the United States,* into which I had let loose a number of things I'd always missed in the histories the schools were generally using. For example, I put in a whole chapter every now and then about the contemporary clothes and cooking and tools and games and furniture—and so far as possible, the contemporary notions—the everyday life of city and country. And, remembering how crude was the idea of Indian culture in which I had spent the imagination of my own young years, I opened my book with an account of the Inca and Maya attainments—the roads, the calendar, the astronomical pyramids (which I'd only thought of, when I was young, as temples of human sacrifice) and the decimal quipus; the arts, too, the Mexicans' floating gardens and roof gardens, the metal work and rich clothing, the sculptures; and when I came to Cortes and Pizarro I let the fur fly about their gruesome cruelties, and their imbecile destruction of priceless Indian monuments. I pulled out from the shameful obscurity in which he dwells in our school histories the noble name of Las Casas, and lifted into the light—if my history had ever been published—the thrilling story of Tuzulutlan. To think, I said to myself, that nobody has told the school children of the United States how at the very time when Magellan was sailing round the world four Dominican friars under the fiery Las Casas carried out with the sole help of four Indian peddlers the brotherly peace of Christ with the unconquerable Land of War!

In my own youth I had felt that the history of any and every other

218

country was more romantic than ours. In middle age I saw that some of this misapprehension was due to the businesslike view of life which puts into our histories every money-making invention, every political fray and every war, and leaves out all the musical, poetical, recreational, spiritual and international history of our country. And I saw that some of the dryness of school histories came from their undue brevity (which again was due to learning the whole of these books, instead of reading them) and the cramped limits to which romantic elements like the Underground Railway are kept. This wild story and the whole of the Negro history of the United States, I thought, needs to be told at full length. Of course I was in no position to do this properly; but I could move vigorously in that direction, and I did. So far as I was able, I opened the floodgates to the bold enterprise, the wild courage, and the calm presence of mind, of those hunted pilgrims to freedom of the Negro race. It was not my fault if a high tide of admiration didn't rise in the minds of the rising generation for their black heroes.

I also tried, on my small scale, to follow those historians who were beginning to include Labor history in their narratives. I wanted to show the endless struggle between the worker and the owner for the fruits of industry. I wanted to expand the meaning of the word "loyalty" in the minds of children from its usual narrow sense into the widespread and many-sided emotion it is; showing the loyalties within Labor unions, the class, race and religious loyalties of Indians, Jews and Negroes; the loyalties of immigrants to home and parents, and to old, beautiful cultures; and the kind of loyalty the strong often feel toward the weak and the inarticulate. And I wanted to show clearly what cold-blooded cruelties, the infliction of what long-drawn agony, the complacently regarded fur trade really means—something closely akin to the slave trade in its callous exploitation of the helpless.

Such notions, hot with feeling, were in my mind as I wrote my little History; and in my chapter headings and quotations introducing them—quotations selected with loving care—I tried to do more than indicate the chapter's story. I longed and tried to have these golden sayings interpret and lead the child's heart beyond the facts to a concept about them; not a finished concept, not the same for every child, but something unchangeably sympathetic to human values, and capable of expanding with years and knowledge. Of all my quotations there was one which seemed the most perfect for this sort of undogmatic influence; and I used it at the head of four different chapters scattered through the book; it was William Watson's quatrain,

> "Momentous to himself as I to me
> Has each man been that ever woman bore.
> One moment, for the twinkling of an eye,
> I felt this truth; one instant, and no more."

My little History underwent the same experience that *Her Late Thirties* had undergone. After reading the early part, a firm of publishers practically accepted it. We even held consultations about illustrations and considered whether two editions might be desirable, a schoolroom one and a more attractive and expensive one for private use. But again, when the last chapters were reached, the manuscript was promptly rejected. Again no mention of pacifism was made in the publishers' refusal, but I was told that the later chapters became too scattered in interest for possible publication.

Well! here was my harvest, and here was its reception by the friendliest publisher I was likely to encounter. I'm not sure yet how much it was pacifism that caused my books to be refused now, whereas before the war they were all accepted. Perhaps the ending of *Her Late Thirties* was sentimental. My *History* does branch out, as the nation has done, like the mouths of the Mississippi. On the other hand, common sense tells me that pacifism had a great deal to do with the rejections. I am the surer of this because I wasn't urged to rewrite and improve the latter part.

What I thought at the time still seems to me just and probable; that pacifism wouldn't have kept my books out of print if they'd been very outstanding, brilliant, powerful books; yet that they were quite good enough books to have secured a publisher if they hadn't been pacifist.

So far as telling the children goes, however, it doesn't matter whether or not I have any fruits or records to show that I was one of the early pacifists. We were both wrong, militarists and pacifists, about the children's making any of those imagined inquiries. These rising generations are very different, as everybody says, from what we were at their age. They view the World War very differently from the reverential view we took of the Civil War—they view the Civil War very differently too. They are never going to ask us what we did, in my opinion. They probably won't ask us anything at all, except to give them room. They may ask each other, "What shall *we* do, if anybody starts it again?" And if there is one place in which their courageous impertinence and self-sufficiency should rejoice our hearts to the brim, it is here, where all possible sang-froid they can muster is needed to resist the old sentimentalisms and the rouge and tinsel of patriotism.

Still I hope my own nephews and nieces will remember that there were early pacifists, whose hearts, living or dead, are with them whenever they serve notice, like the Oxford Union,

"We do not intend to die for king and country."

There was one experience, I thought, that might do to tell the children. But only as a comic interlude. I received one visit from the Department of Justice.

It was while we were in Macon. Aunt Jessie and I had an apartment of sorts; she was ill, and I was struggling to get half a cord of wood with which to eke out the ton of soft coal dust which was the only other fuel available (and for which, indeed, I had stood in a long line for two hours in the City Hall). The agent of justice was a young man and very pleasant and polite. He'd come, he said, because of a letter I'd written to one of the New York papers—or was it to the Department of Justice?—ridiculing the idea that Communists were enemies of society, and denouncing the persecution of them.

"You say in this letter," said the agent, ingenuously, "that you know some of these Communists personally."

"Yes, indeed, and they're the best kind of people," I replied warmly.

"Well, I'd like very much to have you give me their names and addresses," said he, taking out pencil and notebook. "Are they Macon people?"

I didn't suppose there were any Communists in Macon; at any rate, I knew none there. My pacifist and humanitarian friend Kate Codington was the nearest to one that I knew, and she was remote indeed from Communism, not being even a Socialist. But after saying there weren't any there, I couldn't forbear asking the young man whether he really supposed I or anybody like me was going to assist his Department to throw our friends into jail?

He responded genially to this, and we spent a pleasant half hour together. I found him as willing a listener to my views as even my tongue, "hung in the middle and wagging at both ends," could wish. All the time we talked, I was remembering that Mrs. Cope had given me a copy of the letter which her brother, Francis Fisher Kane, had sent to President Wilson on resigning from the Department of Justice. In a good opening, I asked him if he'd read it?

He said he was, and he seemed to be, innocent of all knowledge of that noble letter, one of the best documents in American history, and by far the best remonstrance anybody had made yet against the red-baiting frenzy of those years.

"Oh, let me give you my copy!" I exclaimed. "Everybody in the Department of Justice ought to read that—how is it any of you have missed it? a letter from the inside—from your own Chief! about your own Department!"

He promised to read it, and I trusted that curiosity would induce him to, if indeed he really hadn't. For that matter, it would bear reading twice.

I had letters, too, from the Department, asking with perseverance

222

for information damaging to some radical or other. It was an enjoyable correspondence, for such inquiries always give one a welcome opportunity to furnish the government with warm encomiums of friends and colleagues.

And that's all!

Only that after the war I still couldn't sell my books, couldn't sell my verses half as well as before. They came back, and continued to come back. My notebook had fewer and fewer *SOLD's* printed up and down the lists of titles. My little earnings, which had been three or four hundred dollars a year, fell to eighty dollars.

I don't know and can't remember whether I ever thought that now the war was over, I could go back to writing the verses I'd been accustomed to write before. Perhaps I did. Perhaps I thought the magazines which had welcomed them once would soon relapse into welcoming them again. Perhaps I thought the magazines would remain the same! Perhaps I even supposed—many of us did—that the world would subside again to about what it had been in the summer of 1914.

I had always assumed that if I couldn't extend my small income a little by the writing I was going to keep on doing anyway, I could probably find a situation as a teacher. My notion was that probably the Seminary would open its door to me. I regarded my summer tutoring and my three winters teaching Fannie and Dalton as teaching experience. I never supposed that I needed a course in a Normal School, or that a college degree would have been of any particular help in finding work. Now that I was "making up my mind to teach" (as if the decision lay with me!) I developed a theory, expounding it occasionally before a family audience, that whereas most teachers of English are not acquainted with the processes of composition from the inside as writers are, one like me, who had long been trying to write, would have a more practical approach. My natural enthusiasm rose gladly, of course, to this idea, but I still, after a few years of teaching experience, think it a sensible one.

# 15

WHAT I found true in my middle forties when I turned confidingly from one kind of work to another, might perhaps prove true for other ages and stages— Don't try to overcome and go against yourself; don't try to do just as well as characters of an opposite type the work, so foreign to you, that comes so easy to them; but boldly advertise your real capacities and see if what you can gladly give isn't wanted somewhere in the world.

Here was I, no longer young, educated in the most sketchy manner, warmly affiliated with several despised and suspected minorities, able to teach—if at all—only one thing, and that a subject everybody else could turn a hand to. Perhaps my childlike unawareness of the difficulties I was likely to encounter was itself an asset.

Or was it that simplifying serenity which had dawned upon so many of my days since my religious illumination? Was it that occasional intuition, conferred by prayer?

We crowd around the wholesale lots of opportunity like shoppers at a bargain counter, and think that our best chance to find a working foothold is where there are the greatest number of footholds (often much alike). This seems sensible to us, but it leads us often away from consideration of what we have an inner desire to do. Our best opportunity is not so likely perhaps to be found by the hundred as in one delicate fitting together of special need and congenial talent. What each man and woman needs is not a thousand chances, but one right, satisfying chance. It is as my great-grandmother replied when Aunt Fanny, in her giddy youth, asked, "How many offers of marriage did *you* have, grandmother?"

WILLIAM FINCKE

HELEN FINCKE

"One!" said Olivia Mallory, "and I took it. I would have been ashamed to have any more."

I don't know exactly how to apply this counsel of mine to an industrial town with most of its openings for young people in a glue factory or collar shop. It sounds very foolish, to be sure, when confronted with mass situations. Let me withdraw it from such pretensions—let me leave it for "him that can use it"; there is life behind it and it contains some sense. Though it isn't in accord with the economic structure, nature approves it.

I may, however, be only rationalizing my good luck.

When the Seminary failed to take advantage of the great opportunity of having me teach there, I wrote to a teachers' agency, and received a blank which caused me a good deal of wonder. I'd never supposed my personal appearance would be inquired into; and what to say to the inquiry, "Can you keep good discipline?" I might have answered "Perish the thought," but instead I cautiously admitted that I was not what could be called a good disciplinarian; on the whole, I wanted to rely on interesting the pupils. Holding back my answer, for a photograph to enclose, I bought a *Nation* at the Equinox news-stand one evening when Aunt Jessie and I went up to watch the dancing. In it I saw an advertisement of a school which I ought to be able to reproduce exactly, for I long remembered it word for word. It was one of those advertisements of which William and Helen Fincke alone had the style; as untypical an advertisement as could be imagined. Between the lines, as plain as the smell of a meadow in summer, breathed a warm comradeship, a frank, immediate confidence in man, for which nothing in my experience of this world, cordial and pleasant as I'd always found it, had prepared me.

"That school," I said to myself, "sounds like the Fellowship of Reconciliation. What if I could get a job there?" It was a frankly eager, though careful, letter that I wrote inquiring. Though I knew Norman Thomas only a little—it was before my *World Tomorrow* days—I gave his name without asking permission. The sense of personal friendship which pacifists felt for each other in those days was very strong and warm.

Mrs. Fincke replied, asking me to come at the school's expense, stay a night and discuss the matter. It was in Katonah, New York. Yes, it *was* a school of the Fellowship of Reconciliation type. Norman Thomas had said a good word for me.

Two miles out of Katonah, up a winding road through overhanging woods, arose a house like Mount Vernon. On its piazza were the couple who (I didn't know then) had turned their own house into this visionary school and were supporting it out of their modest fortune.

They told me in cordial full detail about the school. Indeed, yes! it was pacifist; two teachers for the coming year were conscientious objectors, who had served one, and been sentenced to twenty years. "Bill has been in jail too," said Mrs. Fincke, looking quietly pleased. "Only a few days, to be sure. Free speech—a test case for the Civil Liberties."

Mr. Fincke's delightful grin appeared. It seemed to take you confidentially into the rich foolishness of treating his achievements seriously, when as a matter of fact he only did what he enjoyed doing. I thought, however, "Well! I never saw a man who looked quite so boldly at the world!" It didn't quite suit my—what to call them? predilections.

The whole object of the school, they said, was peace and brotherhood. "Bill turned pacifist in France—and I turned Quaker while he was away," said she. "He'd gone over with the first unit, from the Presbyterian Hospital, on a boat that was torpedoed and sunk in the middle of the voyage."

"Yes, I turned—lock, stock and barrel," Mr. Fincke said, "when I saw what war was doing to us, body and soul—I was a minister," he interpolated with a wink that said, "You might not think so."

"Well, then, what were the best licks we could put in for peace— that was what we asked ourselves when I got home," he continued. "I didn't think my preaching was the best possible lick. We decided

226

to start a community school—" His wife shaded her eyes from the sun, and he got up and pulled the porch shade down, with just the immediate quickness and decision which seemed to illustrate the story they were telling. "—where we could live," she concluded, "the kind of life that was the most opposite thing we could think of to war."

I said to myself "Do I wake or sleep? Is it possible that chance has brought me into a band of people living like this?"

Stammering with joyful haste and faint remnants of incredulity, I asked "But how? How do you do it? Live how? How share?" And I said under my breath the golden rule of Socialism, "To everyone according to his need; from everyone according to his ability."

They gave me a picture of the school life. Its government, democratic of course, was divided into "delegations" (the Quaker word), eight of them, from the Delegation of the Inside Work to the Delegation of Peace and Sanctum, which safeguarded the individual liberty and peace. The Chairmen of them were elected by universal suffrage at a monthly meeting; and everybody in the community served on one or another of the Delegations. Everybody did his share—on a revolving basis—of the manual work. Everybody joined in recreation together, and all sat down together at meals. Nobody was left out, anywhere.

My never-sated hunger for inclusion received this description as a cup of living water. I had come where there was no Pale.

—Who and how old were the students?

Mrs. Fincke began to tell. She gave me thumbnail sketches of girls and boys, no two in the least alike in personality or background, scarcely alike even in age. She gave me vivid personal motion pictures of them—what Sophie had said when she lost her pocketbook, what Ed or Archie had started at school meeting—original, Franciscan, surprising things. There were about twenty-five of them, and they ranged in age from thirteen to twenty-six. Classes were only eight or ten in number; they were held indoors or out, in walking groups, around tables, sitting on the floor. The curriculum, beside usual studies, had Labor-problems courses, courses in working-class history, and applied religion. The young conscientious objectors, burnt up with the idealism they'd been caged and tortured for, had invented such courses and were going to give them the following year.

The school was one year old—or would be in October. It had been begun, with joyful haste, immediately after the war.

We had dinner in a room with two fireplaces. Our whole house at home had but one. Two fireplaces in one room! "Oh, well, don't lot on that," said Mr. Fincke merrily. "Even with both of them roaring, it's cold here in winter. Prepare yourself for that—freezing cold!"

"What a thing to say!" I thought. "He'd discourage some people."

We had a homely country dinner at a plain long table—great platters of fresh corn on the cob, and every vegetable from the Brookwood gardens. I was introduced to Nevin Sayre, then at the beginning of his life campaign for peace education; to Bill Simpson, a fresh-complexioned young clergyman turned Franciscan radical; Sam Hasanowitz, a burning-blue-eyed young Russian Jew, a pupil for the school year and farmer in summer; John and Ben, seven and five, the two younger of the Finckes' four sons; Billy and Tod, the two older, sixteen and fourteen, tall, laughing and musical; "Petie" the governess and Kitty the handsome little white-haired cook and competent factotum; and Spencer Miller—we had no Mr. or Mrs. at the table. He was a fair, athletic young man, wonderfully quiet and courteous, with a manner such that whatever he said, as "Will you have some butter?" seemed to be saying instead,

"It's a wonderful thing to be a human being; and you are one."

Spencer Miller, young as he was—nowhere near thirty—had already been Secretary to Thomas Mott Osborne at Sing Sing, and had served a year as Acting Warden; the youngest warden, it was said, of any great prison in the world. His extraordinary gentleness and confidence had great power over men of a hard and stormy past. Occasionally, during the following year, discharged prisoners came to lunch with him at Brookwood, where he was a part-time teacher.

228

I saw him once among the prisoners at Sing Sing. They crowded round him, swallowed him up in a flood.

When dinner was over, Mr. Fincke said cordially;

"Miss Cleghorn, will you and Petie wash the dishes?"

Petie and I became readily acquainted during our dishwashing. She took the stranger's unfamiliar help as a matter of course, and told me small items about Benny and John, the school, etc. Petie, (Miss Florence Petersen) was the daughter of a Danish clergyman in the West Indies, and an English mother. She spoke like an English-woman. I thus began with her a long, warm friendship. We were many a time to burn midnight oil together.

It was years afterwards that Petie told me that the Finckes had found me somewhat old-maidish and stiff looking—had wondered whether I could fit into the free and easy community. But they were the kind of people who like taking such chances. With my usual peasant-like simplicity and naïve self-assurance, such a fear never crossed my mind. From every moment that I spent there, I burned the more to stay.

After dinner several colleagues arrived, among them Nevin Sayre and Norman Thomas, and a conference began which I gradually realized was partly about me. Billy, the eldest son, took me out on the grass with the two dogs, and we carried on a desultory talk. Nature, while making this youth singularly handsome and imposing, had made amends to him by conferring upon him a bright disarming smile.

In the course of time, I was called into the assembly. I sat down, feeling by no means strange, anxious or embarrassed. "Dad" Fincke, as everybody was calling him, said in his free, comradely, direct fashion,

"Well! We'd like to have you. Our regular salary for teachers is a thousand a year, but we haven't got that much left, and the only thing we can offer you is half pay and half time. What would you think about that?"

I said it seemed a great deal of money to me—five hundred dollars and living in. Even for much less than that, I'd be exceedingly glad to come!

They reminded me how much there was to do in a community school—cooking, dishwashing by turns, sweeping—everybody took hold; giving the children castor oil when they had sore throats— "Your interest in mental healing wouldn't prevent that?" and "Dad" said with his comradely laugh, "You'll never be able to keep down to part time! What'll become of your half-finished novel that you told us about?"

"Oh, I'll get time for that if it takes the whole night," said I, hardily; and I really thought so. *The Wests and the Warrens* had been occupying my thoughts for six months incessantly; a story of two families joined by friendship and marriage, of whom one ilk were natural radicals, forever moving their conceptions westward, while the others were by nature forever running away from the new and bold, back to their rabbit-warrens—I fancied the moderated symbolism of these names. "Yes, I'll find time for *that*," I repeated. "I'm awfully glad you're going to take me, for I'm crazy to come!"

With these people you said right out what you had in mind. It was to me an entirely new phenomenon—a group of people living in such carefree comradeship. New as it was, a New England spinster could plunge into it as a duck into water. No "adjustments" here—no "getting wonted," just the easy art of being natural.

In early October, when the school had been going on for two or three weeks, its one-year-old birthday party was held. It was my turn to be one of the cooks, and the feast, though simple, kept such amateurs in large-family cooking busy. I came in late to supper, rolling down my sleeves, and was no sooner seated than called on to "say something." Without knowing anything to say, I rose and said from the depths of my heart,

"I find myself extremely happy."

So deeply did I feel this that it sounded like a line of poetry in my own ears.

The center and soul of our life was school meeting. It took place on Wednesday evening. Everybody was always there, occupying chairs and the floor, according to taste and opportunity. Two or three boys lighted the fire, and it blazed up jovially in the livingroom fireplace; so that even if a window-pane had been smashed that day by a couple of big boys skylarking, the room still looked, and on the whole felt, warm. All the delegations reported. First there were the Inside and Outside Work. (Everybody helped on the outside too; there were chickens, pigs, horses, a cow or two; the root-cellar was being built, the road up from the highway was often worked on, we painted the Shanty, one of the dormitories embosomed in the woods, and tidied the barnyard.) Then we had delegations on Education, Recreation, Punctuality (who rang the bells), Repairs, Finance; and I was recurrently the Chairman of Peace and Sanctum. The reports were anything but dry, anything but impersonal. They reflected warmly and freely the writers' dispositions, and freely brought upon the carpet the conflicts that had risen that week in human relations. Nobody ever veiled these momentary crises; they ran their course in full daylight, and no suppressed resentments resulted from them. Accustomed as I was to the decent, colorless anonymities of ordinary meetings, I remember how startled I was when Paul and Mary brought up their grievance about the dishwashing, at the first meeting of the year. They acknowledged that they'd forgotten to do the dinner dishes, but claimed that the Inside Work Chairman ought to have reminded them, instead of smugly leaving the tables unset until the "Punc." delegation rang the supper bell, thus making the whole school wait for supper while the delinquents washed the dishes, and rousing, thus, unnecessary public resentment against them. I'd been a member, myself, that week, of the Inside Work Delegation, and I'd rather gleefully consented to the Chairman's dramatization of Paul and Mary's neglect. But when Paul so clearly stated his and Mary's opinion that this was making the worst of their forgetfulness instead of the best, I saw the matter in a different light; nor did the community laugh at him, or bid him sit down. They listened seriously; and the

231

dudgeon on the one side, and the self-righteousness on the other were both aired away.

Reports could be made revealing and dynamic. My first report on Peace and Sanctum was not yet written when Helen Fincke, running her arm through mine as we left the diningroom, said "Sally, how about this—I've been thinking about it all the morning—Whittier's verse,

> '—Let our ordered lives confess
> The beauty of thy peace.'

Could you tuck it into your report?" I saw that such reports could do much more than report.

Twice or three times in my life I've seen one or two controlling personalities create a prevailing atmosphere among a more or less haphazard assortment of persons of both sexes, whose ages and backgrounds vary widely. Once in a New York boarding house I saw a sweet and joyous little old maid, homely, penniless, and with one arm partly paralyzed, create out of her own luxuriant kindness a true family condition, I could almost say, an affectionate family life, among her changing troops of boarders.

"Dad" Fincke, rising in school meeting with his enticing wink and grin, expressing his vigorous opinions with his eloquent hands and energetic voice, diffused about him—what made Brookwood; its brotherly, confident freedoms, its energy, its open-mindedness, its swift, warm concern for what the other was thinking and feeling; and we all breathed it in, and lived on it. Helen Fincke, when she spoke in her low voice, released upon us her beauty and grace, inward and outward, and her deep thoughts and intuitions. She raised our eyes to wider horizons, opened windows, renewed the air.

At school meeting, when reports and "old business" were over, "new business" let loose all sorts of ever-changing, often Franciscan experiments in ordering our life. Early in the autumn, we passed this rule;

When anyone was absent from the diningroom at the time Dad

232

Fincke said grace, those who were present at the absentee's table should wait with food cooling and untasted until he came in.

"What if he never comes?" asked two or three voices at once, as soon as the chairman said "Discussion on this motion?"

"Nobody at the table will have anything to eat," replied the mover, unflinchingly.

The motion was thoroughly discussed before we passed it.

Sam Hasanowitz, who sat at my table, disapproved of the Brookwood meal-times. He had already made a speech about it in school meeting. "I'm not hungry," he had said, challengingly, "at half past seven in the morning! I get hungry at about ten o'clock, and I like to get myself a bite at that time. Then at noon I'm not hungry either! I get hungry at about three. At supper time I'm not hungry! I like to eat something just before I go to bed." He looked round with his hot, bright blue eyes. "I don't see anything wrong in my having a bite when I need it!"

I suppose Sam voted against the motion; but he was an ardent idealist, loved the ground Bill Simpson walked on, and found in the word "coöperation" his most religious symbol. He may have voted for the motion.

At all events, it was but a day or two before Sam was late, very late, for breakfast. None of us ate either our apple or our oatmeal. Whoever was waiter at our table that week had no dishes to scrape and carry to the pantry to be washed. We all rose when the rest of the diningroom rose, and went first to our morning sweeping and then to morning meeting. Sam was at morning meeting, and made, as he often did, a speech. "What we need," he said—and amplified—"is coöperation." His speech was very good. No one tittered. Sophie was our table head—a student from last year, a girl who had great influence. After morning meeting, she took Sam by the arm and led him to the diningroom. There on our table were the eight apples, the bowl of oatmeal, the bread, the milk, untouched.

"I am sorry!" Sam said. He said it with humility, and it was eloquent.

This rule—not a hundred per cent efficient, even with the quick and responsive Sam—must have satisfied us, on the whole, as a community expression on our prevalent unpunctuality, for we kept it in force for what at Brookwood was a long time; several months. It was not so Franciscan as another rule, which had been passed the previous year in regard to neglected house or outdoor duties. By this rule, no one who had forgotten a fire, or any other community service, was allowed to do his neglected work; only a volunteer was permitted to do it. Dad Fincke used to relate with relish how he had been the first to fall under this ban. "When I found that I'd forgotten the furnace," he said, "I started on a rush to see to it—but no! I had to stand by and see a volunteer do it for me. You can't imagine the feeling it gives you!"

We had several plays that year. Helen directed *Cathleen ni Houlihan* and played Cathleen. I remember our having *A Night at an Inn.* I enjoyed the spirit of these young amateurs more than I had ever enjoyed going to the professional theater. I was prepared by my natural liking for realism to appreciate the Russian theatrical idea of non-professional acting which has become familiar now. Finish and polish were not what I liked best, but fire and spirit, and naturalness, and freshness. I didn't however feel any wish whatever to try my own hand at a part, much less at directing a play; and when the teachers volunteered to furnish amusement for the community one Saturday night by a version of Bluebeard, and I was told off for Sister Anne, I was rather embarrassed. Anybody who knew me would have said "Oh, don't try to have *her* act!" However, I contrived Turkish trousers out of my bathrobe, and tried to feel like Sister Anne, as she ran to and fro with terrified glances out the window; and to my amazement I enjoyed this minute dramatic experience, and remembered it with enjoyable surprise.

My teaching responsibility, outside of special tutoring for two or three boys, was to assist Fred Leighton, who had been engaged as teacher of English and Social Problems. Fred's heart was in the Social Problems courses he had invented; he carried on very interesting discussions in these, and aroused lively arguments. I used to go in by the library fire to listen to them. Fred was one of the two conscientious objectors about whom Helen had told me on the August day when I first went to Brookwood. He and Duane Swift, who taught mathematics and what science we gave, had become acquainted in prison. They had been sent together to Alcatraz, in California, where they had been put into cages so constructed that a man could neither stand, sit or lie down in comfort. Fred was a Chicagoan, and had known of the pacifist movement; Duane was a southerner, who had worked his own way, in solitude and silence, walking alone in the woods, through the alternative of killing other men or becoming what the government considered a criminal. "I never knew there was anybody else in America that felt the way I did," said this southern boy, "until I was in jail."

Gradually, during the autumn, the English teaching fell into my hands. It was new to me to organize classes, even very small ones; but it was vastly interesting to me. I found every atom of teaching pleasant, down to correcting spelling papers; everything but the wandering attention of my pupils; but in the diversified field of English it's not hard to fit every pupil out with work he needs in a form he doesn't dislike.

I started a regime of daily themes, and found that "Pat" Ehrlich could deliver excellent oral ones; that Tod Fincke, at the very moment when he laid down his bitten pencil in despair of writing a theme because he "couldn't think of a thing to write about," was bursting to relate to Mary Fraser and Teresa Boehm an incident he had lately witnessed at a concert; and hanging around to listen, and observing the good proportions with which he constructed his tale, and the way he capitalized the humor of it, I was able to say at the end, "Well, Tod, you've done a very good D. T. for today, anyhow." I took the teacher's voyage of discovery to find the pupil's confidence in himself. To lead young people to explore their own possibilities now began to seem to me worthy of some better title than "encouragement."

Most of the Brookwood students were ready material, especially those who had been there for a year already. Accustomed to the warm, mellow climate of the place, they didn't need a long, patient endeavor to convince them that they could express themselves. And I had a pleasant time with the "required" reading. Fred and I had agreed to present it in four lots—novels—essays—solid reading—poetry and plays. Each sort was on a shelf where the boys and girls could browse and choose according to taste. With the essays I had a particularly good time; for having put Lamb, Hazlitt, Matthew Arnold and Emerson—all small, cosy books—on the shelf, with a sign that said, "Read a little of each, then read as much as you like of the one you like best," I found that each of them had found a lover. Arthur Folgner took to Lamb and read a dozen of his essays with spontaneous enjoyment. Pat, who was only thirteen, chose Hazlitt (the essay on "The Fight" was the first he read) and wrote an appreciation which began, I remember, "It was a great day for English literature when William Hazlitt first opened his eyes." An intellectual Jewish boy took delight in Arnold's *Friendship's Garland*. Emerson, of whom Sam Hasanowitz had never heard before, took such possession of him that he wrote me a note in substance thus;

"Having found Emerson, I never intend to read anything else."

Love of poetry was a strong bond between Helen Fincke and me. We often read it together in the evening in the Finckes' livingroom at the top of the house. She read in a low voice, full of feeling for the beauty of the lines. My own reading was too emphatic. The harmonies which touched my soul I seldom rendered forth by my voice. Though I had heard, and loved, beautiful reading of poetry, I didn't yet appreciate the elements of pause, hush and delicate changes of tone.

Helen and I not only loved poetry alike, but we loved two of the same poets. We were both very fond of Matthew Arnold. She could read "A Summer Night" or "The Buried Life" very well. Especially we shared an enthusiasm for Masefield. This autumn she was reading *Enslaved* aloud at bedtime to four boys in their early teens.

236

Dad Fincke, who rose early in the morning and was vigorously active all day, often lay down on a rug and went to sleep while we were reading poetry. I could never bear to have him waked. It seemed to me that poetry could have no better use than to thread its sounds and meanings through a man's deeply needed rest.

Many beside me were happy at Brookwood. Chance comrades there felt a loyalty for it which to outsiders might seem tropical. "Isn't it silly," somebody said once, "that every time any two of us meet in a doorway or on the stairs we have to say 'Hello, Marion,' 'Hello, Romeo,' when it's the sixth or eighth time we've passed each other that day?" I didn't think it was silly. I liked the Brookwood climate.

H. W. L. Dana, who gave a course there in the spring, told me he never had felt so much at home in his life before. "I think it's because we have no servants," he said.

At the end of that year one of the girls said to me, "What's the name, now, of that novel you've been writing?" I tried in vain to remember *The Wests and the Warrens.* The very name was gone from me. I hadn't written a line on it for months. I never took it up again. Brookwood had taken the color all out of it.

When I went home from Brookwood, I was occasionally asked, "How do *you* get along with the big boys?" Until I was asked, I'd never thought of the big boys as a special problem for me. I liked them very much. They were indispensable members of the community and shouldered all sorts of work and responsibility; though in an adolescent fashion, frequently forgetting or neglecting a job, but usually trying to get even with themselves after doing so.

And I was often asked, "What do you do on Sundays?"

Sundays were free and pleasant days at Brookwood. We had a morning meeting a little longer than on the other days, and there was plenty of time for winter sports. We had wild, dangerous coasting down the winding ravine, safe skating on a flooded field, and sometimes snow-shoeing across lots to the village. Visitors came up from New York on Sundays, for it was only forty miles. On Sunday evenings we had something special, a picnic in the spring, a discussion perhaps of what the big boys meant to do if they were drafted in another war, or something else about religion in action; or else Dad Fincke would read from *The Unknown Disciple*. He thus read, one evening, the chapter about the highroad to Damascus, the passing traffic in caravans, and Jesus going in on a summer evening to a neighbor's house and talking like any other simple, friendly, feeling man, with the little girl of the household.

I don't know why that evening has remained so clear and dewy in my memory beyond others—it was probably an unusual harmony that filled the room and made a golden bead of time. Changes were coming, of which we all knew, which we were all taking part in; but they were going farther than we thought. Such Sunday evenings, of which we supposed there were many more ahead, were to be very few.

# 16

ALL this year anxiety had been nibbling at the hearts of Bill and Helen Fincke. This experiment in brotherly love, into which they were pouring the flood current of their lives, was still too precarious. It was now, in its second year, still too changeable. The staff was changing; Helen Little, the housekeeper and domestic science teacher, broke down in health and had to go away—came back— broke down again. A love affair took Fred Leighton away. Brent Allinson (the young man whom President Wilson had appointed to a consulship in Switzerland, and who had been arrested on shipboard as a pacifist, and sentenced, like Fred and Duane, to twenty years, of which he had served two) came to us fresh from prison, and was happy at first, but perhaps found Brookwood too free and easy, the students too democratic. They thought him fastidious and formal and were inclined to guy him as an aristocrat. He went; Bruce came; and with each change there was a rearrangement, and what was much more important, a change in the composition of the community. With our fluid, experimental customs, this meant an immediate change in our life.

Expenses were somewhat unpredictable. The Finckes were seeking to stabilize the school in this and other, more important ways. They went on trips to speak before Labor bodies, in hopes of Labor union support, with union scholarships, the school being turned more definitely into a Labor school, with perhaps a measure of union control; a plan that foreshadowed Manumit. They realized that no such change could be made without sacrificing some part of the fraternal freedom, the open-handed generosity, that mellowed and beautified

239

Brookwood, pouring like sunlight over its everyday tasks and human frailties.

The Finckes were not Socialists, but members of the Farmer-Labor party. They had been at the Chicago meeting with the Committee of Forty-Eight when that party was born, and Helen had run for a state office on that ticket. At Chicago they had become acquainted with Toscan Bennett of Hartford, a former corporation lawyer who now had entered the Labor movement and was absorbed in serving it. Helen and Bill went over to see the Bennetts at Hartford and the Bennetts cast in their lot with Brookwood, moving over with their three adolescent children, Toscan, Kate and Tan.

There ensued six weeks of incessant conference about transforming the school into an adult school for prospective Labor leaders. The prospect seemed rosy and I believe there was none of us who didn't feel enthusiasm for the change. The Labor College has justified us, with thirteen years of solid, often brilliant service, and nearly half that time the harsh years of the depression. In the last three days of the spring vacation, we had a final memorable conference, with Labor and educational leaders and sympathizers coming up from New York, among whom I especially remember Arthur Gleason, whose illuminating articles on the state of the world everybody was reading in *The Tribune* and elsewhere, and who was so soon to die and lay down a pen nobody was able to take up.

A. J. Muste was also there; a man about whom we all knew that he was the pioneer who had organized the underpaid textile workers and led them in that successful strike in Lowell, where they maintained non-violence, though A. J. and others were beaten up by the police. I remember well my first sight of A. J. It was in the dining-room, and my first look at his thin face was when his peculiar smile was irradiating it. There is a combination of several rare qualities in him. He has the clearest realistic sense of what poverty is, how its pains and penalties feel—a quick flesh-and-blood realization of these things which Bill Fincke also had, and which constituted a close bond between them. Indeed I've observed nothing in my whole life that forms a closer bond than this.

But along with this, A. J. possesses a mystic realization of infinity. He is deeply, irrevocably aware of the presence of God. In his smile both these things show as plainly as a human face can show them; the tenderness for the disinherited, and striving effort with them, and yet this joyful consciousness the while, of

"—life eternal moving through and under."

My most prized recollection of A. J. Muste comes from the early days of my acquaintance with him. We were reading poetry one evening at Brookwood in the first autumn of the present Labor College there; a group of the new, grown-up students, active union men and women, who expressed a general, but no particular, liking for poetry. The poems I chose to read that evening were none of them the ones I loved best. I was afraid (fatal cowardice in human relations!) to bring forth what in my heart I thought the best. With a craven notion of "giving the majority what (I thought) they'd like," I read some tuneful, pleasing, fairly poetic numbers, of which I was rather fond. A. J. arose, when his time came, and with a stride or two of his long legs approached the bookcase; taking down the Oxford Book, without preface he began to read Vaughan's

"I saw Eternity the other night
Like a great ring of pure and endless light
All calm as it was bright."

I felt instantaneously how the bold proffer of the best we have is everlastingly right. Those who were listening seemed all to feel the pure power of the poem, the deep experience that must lie back of such words. I was at once shamed and exultant, and received from that event a mighty piece of education.

It was no wonder Bill and Helen Fincke singled out A. J. as the right head for the new Brookwood. It took time to convince him

241

that he ought to leave the Textile Amalgamated in other hands and turn to Labor education. When A. J. consented, it was in great measure because he felt the powerful possibilities of working at such a task with Bill Fincke. The bond between them was deep and firm.

I was re-engaged as English teacher; and as one approaching a quicksand blindfold, I proceeded through the summer, with sanguine serenity, to arrange my work for the coming year on the basis of my undoubted success the year before. When I thought of the difference there would be between teaching irresponsible, impulsive adolescents and mature men and women, with experience in life, ardent for the Labor movement, it was only to rejoice in the prospect. I knew they would like to study, wish to write,—enough said. I looked forward to a delightful and successful year.

But I was very much dashed when, late in the summer, I learned that the Finckes weren't going to be living at Brookwood. Helen, warmly and energetically as she had used every resource of her fine mind to help transform the little school into the Labor College, felt quite unable to fill an active post in it any longer. Here was a daunting and totally unexpected decision! "I'm at home with boys and girls between ten and twenty," Helen said; "I don't know how, don't feel the power to try, to work among grown-up people." It struck me as absurd that she, who seemed to me so adequate, could feel such helplessness; I thought some other string had been touched discordantly. She was firm. She and the boys would go away; Billy was entering college anyway. They would take a house at Bedford Hills. "But Bill is staying," she said. "At least, he'll drive over from Bedford to Katonah, stay the week, and come home for Sundays."

When she said this, we were sitting in Dorothy's pinewoods, having a picnic with Dorothy; the Finckes had driven up through Vermont for a summer holiday. The rest had gone off to swim; Helen and I were alone. I remember how the August air cooled round me as she spoke.

On the September evening when I drove up to Brookwood, there was no one to be seen in the house, and I went all alone into the

242

big room assigned to me, the room four romping boys had had the previous year. What a hush and coolness all over the place! I searched about for A. J. and his wife, for the Bennetts—not for the Finckes! The air in the house as the door opened had told me they were already gone. When I did find the Mustes and Bennetts, who were in the midst of a conference downstairs to which they welcomed me, the room in which they were sitting seemed a new room I'd never seen before in the house. To this day, I cannot, in memory, locate that room. I remember it all by itself.

Well, then, the people who had made the atmosphere of "old" Brookwood were gone. Bill, the Mustes and Bennetts said, would be driving over to spend the next day, would be there, off and on, "all that week." *That week?* No more? No more. He was one of the Directors now, Executive Committee, something of that sort. He would be coming over once a month or so for a meeting.

I didn't realize until much later how heavy a personal blow Bill's departure was to A. J. Muste; how much more strange and hard it made the natural strangeness and hardness of such a task as his, the new head of a new school of a new kind, a body all of strangers to be drawn into an entity, a mutual life. At the moment I was too occupied in trying to adjust myself to feeling lost and strange, and to my bewildered, troubled realization that something lamentable had happened there that summer.

When I went over to Bedford Hills and asked, "What, what has happened?" Helen said, "Ask Dad," and Dad Fincke said, not without his smile, "We've been evolved out."

I knew, later, a little more. There had been a sudden, careless, but unmistakable intimation from one of the warmest backers of the new Labor College that all the Finckes had done in founding "old" Brookwood seemed more a drawback than a help.

This extraordinary misprizing of a value the rarest and deepest remains to me a wonder and sorrow beyond most others of its kind in a lifetime; and so it was to all the rest of those who cared most about the new Brookwood. But it seems to me that the smallest

243

intimacy with human blunderings (and above all with our own) takes forever out of our vocabularies the words "to blame." In Harriet Monroe's magazine, *Poetry,* I once read a poem which described a man's incredulous gaze at his own hands, which had done an evil deed as if without his consent. Thus I conceive it must have been with the event at Brookwood which Bill Fincke briefly and gently called "evolution."

There was no withdrawal of the Finckes' interest from the new enterprise; only the most cordial furthering of its success in every way that could be contrived in accord with the new plans which they soon began to consider for a fresh educational start, to utilize their own energy and ideals.

But here I was beginning again as a stranger in the very walls where I had been so familiarly at home, to which I had thought I was returning as a habitué, a family friend. No new house can be as new as a former home in new hands!

My work, too, soon took on the character of an untried and unexpected task. The Labor students had already begun arriving before I arrived at Brookwood. Their ages ran as high as forty, but the majority were between twenty-five and thirty-five. They represented, as we had hoped, a great variety of trades. Two were young coal miners from Ohio, (the most immaculate young men I ever saw) two or three were machinists from Pennsylvania; there were several skilled textile workers from the south, who knew a great deal about fabrics and patterns of weaving; then there were seven or eight young women, members of the International Ladies' Garment Workers' Union, (generally called the I. L. G.) and other unions; and there was one painter, a delicate looking man, who "bore in his body" the cumulative poisoning of his trade. He it was who had the most literary mind. He read a great deal, and discriminatingly; and there was a book half constructed in his imagination. There were several lovers of poetry among the students, and I remember that one of the miners had a great liking for Swinburne. Several of the I. L. G. girls had been

244

at summer school at Bryn Mawr the previous summer. One of them, I especially remember, had turned with instant joy to the literary courses there. I remember how she described her glowing sense of illumination at reading Arnold's *Sweetness and Light*.

There was of course among these Labor-conscious workers, these demanders of "the good life for all," a large proportion of ready speakers, people used to making points, holding attention, etc. They were highly articulate in this, sometimes in another field. And of course they wanted to extract the utmost value from their two-year course. Why, then, was my attempt to carry on English classes with them a failure? Why could I never draw them into my nicely laid out courses or capture them by flexible approaches?

At the time I thought, almost with resentment, that it was altogether because they were what I called Labor Puritans. They wanted literary feeling, personal expression, not for life in general, but for the Labor movement alone. To this they were consecrated like Cromwell's Ironsides. It was wonderful, it was sacrificial, but it was altogether different from what I'd conceived. What I'd conceived was a state of mind so free that to them it would have appeared treason, or at all events, an aimless and dilettante state. And perhaps they were right. They were the ones to be satisfied. They were the ones who knew best what they wanted. It was not they who were ignorant—it was I who knew too little of their responsibility, and what they had to meet.

The fact was that my plans and my powers were not what they could see their way to make the slightest use of. They needed a teacher as intimate as they were with some part, at least, of the great movement they were dedicated to; a teacher who could carry them straight ahead in the arts of public speaking; who in writing would help them turn out better editorials, appeals, résumés of Labor history, controversial writing; who could assist them to contrive Labor dramatics, turn out humor and perhaps fiction, but all with the one end; and who at the same time would also enlarge their general interest (as I wanted to begin by doing) outside the Labor field. General reading, etc., they were eager enough for, but only after their really vital needs should have been met.

When, not without sorrow and wounded pride, I gave up the ghost of my teaching at "new" Brookwood, the students were delighted with my successor. She was Josephine Colby, a woman younger than I, but ever so much more experienced in just the right fields. She has been a tower of skill and strength at Brookwood ever since. "Polly" Colby is versatile, competent, cultivated, and warmly human. I felt rather reluctant to meet her. My honest love and hope for the Labor College, and concern for A. J.'s effort, were having to contend with the inflamed condition of my *amour propre*. However, Josephine Colby came into a committee room in New York where I was in conference with others, and came directly up to me with a frank look of pleasure. She too had been invited to serve on this committee, which was choosing fifty books for Labor education in literature. For an instant, my cordiality to her, though ready, was perfunctory; but only for an instant. She was too much for me—I had the surprise and joy of spontaneously liking her.

I'd come to New York to look for a job. Aunt Jessie had written "Do come home," and Dorothy, "Come up and visit me." Helen Fincke had said "Come up here, and you and I will write a memoir of 'old' Brookwood." Carl and Sue had written to come south. I didn't expect, of course, to find a teaching job in the middle of November. What I thought was that I could fit in neatly somewhere as a mother's helper, and have some time to write. I went at once to stay, while hunting work, with Anna Rochester and Grace Hutchins.

Anna's mother had died. Left thus alone, she had resigned from the Children's Bureau and come to New York. At a conference in Massachusetts she had met Grace—a woman of her own age, a like background, and many of the same qualities. Both were large-minded, yet finely exact in small things; generous, yet very fair to all sides of a situation; compassionate and full of delicacy and respect, yet roundly uncompromising; and both were Socialists.

Grace had long had, and Anna soon shared, an intention to found a small community of women to practice social justice. This very autumn, 1921, they had rented, refreshed and furnished with their own comely belongings a house on West Twenty-Seventh Street between Eighth and Ninth Avenues. When I joined them, three of their possible five companions were already living there; and I was the possible fourth, if I could find work.

But I couldn't find work. Nothing in the line of mothers' helpers, much less a governess or teacher, offered. And now I found a singular change taking place in my attitude toward the world. Remote as I was from the danger of being cold or hungry, open as several kind doors were to me, beside Aunt Jessie's and Carl's, I still began to feel a kind of desperateness rising in my heart. My relations with my environment, hitherto so placid and cordial, began to creak and come askew. Recklessness came creeping into my mood, as a bitter juice might trickle into a cup of sweet milk. I began to feel devil-may-care. As I inquired for work, and everywhere got a steady negative, I thought, time and again, "Why should a healthy, honest woman, who can work, and knows how, keep begging the world to use her? Let them come and find me when they get round to having some use for me in the world! I'll sit down on the curb in the sunshine and wait for 'em."

The League for Mutual Aid, of which I am a member, received me with the utmost cordiality, and found me two jobs. They were purely housework, and I didn't take either of them. If they had been in country places I should have been much tempted. But a curious homesickness came over me when I thought of housework in a dark city apartment—hanging clothes out over a sooty yard—a feeling of prospective imprisonment. I shrank from thus mewing myself up, and for the first time in my life, felt a dislike for strangers as such.

Nothing in my life seems to me more valuable than this brief interlude, this softened version, of hunting a job. I received more education from it than I could have done from reading a thousand books, even on this subject. A few years later, at a meeting of the Vassar

247

chapter of the League for Industrial Democracy, I heard Priscilla Smith, a senior there, describe her own experience during a six weeks' taste which she and other students had taken the summer before, of living on their own manual efforts, and the ordinary pay for such. "When I had been two or three times refused work," Priscilla said, "by indifferent managers in factories, it began to be fearfully hard for me to try again. I had to screw up my courage to climb those dark stairs to another dreary loft, and receive another refusal." Well did I know what she meant—well understand how much our smooth, courteous self-confidence, in the comfortable classes, depends on our safe footing on a little margin of dollars at the bank! Many a time during the depression I've thought, "If these things were so in a green tree, what of the dry?"

Alice Beal Parsons, then in New York with her little flower of a child, beginning her literary career with free lance writing, was a friend of Anna's. She too was looking for a job which would give her a small steady income, the while she wrote in free time. One day a possible job as secretary came to her ken. She was so generous as to offer it to me first, a kindness I shan't forget.

One day Grace and Anna laid before me a two-part job they had invented to fit me. It was to be financed by themselves. I was to spend half my time writing for *The World Tomorrow,* and half in informal usefulness among the neighbors, especially the children, in West Twenty-Seventh Street; remaining, of course, a member of the Community House. They represented with all their kind eloquence how valuable I should be in these capacities—work they'd both felt the need of somebody to do—work I could do to the queen's taste. I needn't think they'd thought this up to help me out—oh, dear no—I should be filling real vacancies.

I was happy indeed to accept their sisterly offer, and spend six months (until time to go home in June) in trying to make good in these two capacities. Both "jobs" were thoroughly enjoyable.

The editors now of *The World Tomorrow* were Anna, Devere Allen and Nevin Sayre. The numbers were devoted each to a single subject—race relations, company unions, family life, youth and peace, etc. The articles were asked for. The authors were seldom paid, but they generally consented to write, and put in generous time and effort. My principal work was to endeavor to captivate the imaginations of young people by recounting great adventures in brotherly living, drawn from anywhere in history, the obscurer the better. Three among this series of heroic true tales were subjects later of my ballads —Harriet Tubman, the caisson worker, and the Dominican friars.

*The World Tomorrow* differed from *The Nation* and *The New Republic* in its warmer and more religious attitude toward human nature; it was more ready to encourage, more inclusive toward all varieties of man. Though able, it was not as able in the literary sense as *The Nation*. Its book reviews were good, but not as good as *The Nation's* or *The Freeman's;* they were a little more pedestrian. But *The World Tomorrow* as a whole had a much broader outlook on the life of man. When the depression finally made an end of that noble magazine, there was a sense of desolation in the hearts of its old lovers. There's nothing now so daring and constructive. Its criticism of cruelty and foolishness in high places was second to none. One of its best features was the page (generally done by Anna but kept up long after she resigned) "Not in the Headlines."

The other half of my "job" was especially pleasant. I did whatever I could find an opening for. I might visit someone's daughter or brother on Ward's Island, bring children into the House for games on a rainy afternoon, get the promised ice-cream for those newly returned from St. Mary's Hospital with sore burning throats from tonsillectomy. No two days were alike, but there was always something I could do and be welcome. And again, as at Brookwood, I was given a vote of confidence and turned loose by my employers to do my best.

The life of the House was full of grace and pleasantness. Its plan was that each woman of us should have a job, and that all together we should carry on the cooking and housework in our free time. We should each live on a working woman's pay, a decent minimum, which with care and honesty was fixed at eighteen dollars a week. We each took our weekly turn as dinner cook, which carried with it the marketing; and if the cook saved anything from our joint market-money, she divided the rebate among us at breakfast on Sunday morning when we each paid in our quota for the coming week.

I remember that when I was cook I sometimes came out flush enough on Saturday night to have strawberries out of season, or even ice-cream. I'd thought myself a pretty fair cook, but Grace and Anna, with a quarter my experience, proved infinitely better. They turned their fine minds to their cooking, and served delicious meals. They were used, too, to the hot intensity of gas, whereas I baked according to the milder warmth of coal. Once when Miss Julia Lathrop was coming to dinner with Anna, I baked my scalloped oysters so solid and dry that Anna suffered, I know, real distress at serving them to her beloved guest; but she said nothing, and I was too mortified myself even to thank her for the eloquent kindness of her silence.

Sunday afternoon was our day at home to all our joint and individual friends. Grace Hutchins was exceedingly attractive as a hostess. Her graceful old dark blue silk, her fine white collar set off her rosy comeliness. I think of nothing more often about the House, I find, as years close over the few months I spent there, than Grace behind the teapot on our Sunday afternoons.

I made two great friends among the House Companions; Lucie Myer, a teacher, a woman with a serious countenance but a daring and delightful brand of humor, and Stella Lundelius, then a Henry Street nurse, whose fair face and nature make me think of Lowell's lines,

> "She is most fair, and thereunto
> Her life doth rightly harmonize."

Among the particularly interesting people I met there often was Solon De Leon, (the son of Daniel De Leon, who founded the Socialist Labor party). Solon at that time was spending his firstrate knowledge and ability as editor of *The Advance,* the organ of that mighty union, the Amalgamated Clothing Workers. I also once heard there the arresting thoughts of W. M. Leiserson, at that time the impartial chairman of the Amalgamated's Joint Board, the body which settles all disputes between the union and the employers in the clothing trade, where they never have a strike. If genius consists in the power to see analogies, Mr. Leiserson is a genius. "The rise of Labor to a voice in industry," said he, "is the modern rise of the House of Commons." "I wish," thought I, "W. M. Leiserson would write a history of the United States." I thought with impatience of the little one I'd written.

Upstairs in the House was a chapel. We often had prayers there, and once a Quiet Day. In after years, when Grace and Anna went to Russia, they were caught up there into the revolutionary flame, and coming home, found themselves infinitely removed from churches, and from the unqualified pacifism in which I still, and more than ever, believe as the real revolution in human relations.

"At dead of night their sails were filled."

During my year at the Community House my poems began appearing rather often in *The World Tomorrow,* and I wrote some interpretations of religious doctrines in the terms of community life —but strongly flavored with Brookwood atmosphere and memories —which suited well the spirit of the magazine, and wouldn't, I suppose, have suited any other. One of these, called "The Incarnation," I've always liked.

> Sometimes to me, as sometimes to my neighbors,
> There comes a thing I call an incarnation.
> Whoever has it tries to tell about it;
> He tries, in vain, to let the others see
> How indescribably divine it was,
> And how its beauty and delight unselfed him,
> Making him bathe in streams of paradise.
>
> There was an autumn afternoon last year
> When everyone of our large family

But Helen and myself had gone away
To see a football game; and we had meant
To finish in the kitchen very early
And spend the afternoon out in the woods.
But every moment's housework that we did
Disclosed the need of something more to do;
The clock crept round to three and round to four
And there were still the garbage pails to wash.

We went, with our acidulated patience,
Out to the garbage pails. We stood and felt
Something come streaming round us from outdoors.
The light was gentling and the air was sweet;
The birches trembled and the green grass shone.
In came a heavenly childhood to our hearts.
We stood and felt that holy childishness.
It was intense, calm, magic, simple and strange;
Pure sweetness in the core of homeliest use.
What happened—how it happened—if we knew!

The garbage pails in this poem shocked Aunt Jessie as nothing, not even my Socialism, had shocked her before. "Put in something else," she entreated me, "no matter how homely!" She couldn't bear to put the divine beauty to such a test, and felt, I believe, that I'd affronted it.

# 17

"However, Anna and Grace," I'd said in the fall, "you know the Finckes may buy a farm and start another school—they've taken their share out of Brookwood so as to get back into the field of Labor education. If they ever offer me a job, I know I'll want to take it, whatever it is."

In the spring the Finckes did buy a farm, a dairy farm in Dutchess County, and stocked it with Holstein cows. They found, by means of one of their unique advertisements, a likeminded family to come there with them. These were the A. B. Clarks, young people with three children. Alfred Clark was a highly educated farmer. "He'll be the manager," Bill Fincke said, "and I'll work under him." I went up for a Sunday in April, met these Clarks, and saw the fields, hills, woods, and the little potential schoolhouse where I could teach (such was the plan) the four boys on the farm, the two young Finckes and the two young Clarks, all between seven and ten. My mouth watered to be teaching again. I loved every detail of it. "Teaching," I began to say, "has it all over writing. In teaching you're at close relations with human nature. Your failures are despairing, but your successes dispose of them in the twinkling of an eye." I often thought "I'll write a sonnet on teaching, with this for the last line,

> One swallow makes a summer in my heart."

Helen and I laid out the pleasant plans. I would go home for the summer and come down from Vermont in September "with my joggerfy under my arm." "And after a year or two of that," said Helen, "I believe Bill and I'll be able to start another school. He wants to make the farm pay, first."

253

I had a happy, vivid year and a half in that tiny school, sometimes succeeding, sometimes despairing. All my faults and all my merits as a teacher stood out in the baldest possible relief. In spite of hating it so violently, I slipped occasionally into trying to "make" the children do their work; invariably this failed, and invariably I thought "Thank God, it never works!" and began afresh to teach in the only way I ever wanted to teach, by interest and partnership. The boys were exceedingly alive. John Fincke, the eldest, was the most so of all. It was good for his intense, driving nature, highly motor-minded, to be so much with the elder Clark boy, who had a great deal of Quaker poise and serenity. The chief event of the tiny school was due, however, to the two younger boys. Benny Fincke's rich and whimsical imagination conceived the idea of giving a play "to show the history of the earth." Perhaps he'd been fired by Van Loon's *History.* "We'll show it all in flames, as it was in the beginning," he proposed, "by pinning red paper streamers on our shirts, and turning summersaults all round and round the floor. We'll show the first creeping, crawling things, and the monkeys turning into men." "Oh, yes!" his mother exclaimed; "one of my accomplishments is knowing how to make up like a monkey. I'll help you with that." With her help, too, he worked up a scene showing an Egyptian Pharaoh dictating hieroglyphics to a scribe. In a burst of enthusiasm, he said "We can have a wonderful Hebrew prophet! Richard can be the prophet. Did you ever hear him talk in all kinds of languages? He can make up languages as he goes along, reel off syllables without ever slipping into a real word. Give us a sample, Rich!" The seven-year-old Clark boy did indeed have this extraordinary ability to do something no grown-up person can possibly perform—utter a succession of infinitely varied sounds without a single actual word. He accordingly impersonated the Hebrew prophet, and the flow of his extraordinary Hebrew continued, with proper gestures, for a long time, an unduly long time, so that a diversion had to be made to get on to the later scenes, and show the death of Socrates. Here, too, Richie took the title part. The other three, draped in curtains and table covers, enacted the

254

last gathering of the friends of Socrates, and Richard, with a dewy smile, drank the hemlock and tranquilly fell dead on the floor.

Such were the pleasures—the troubles soon seemed microscopic—of my one-room teaching at Manumit Farm. In 1924 we started Manumit School.

The rolling country round Pawling is beautiful, more countrified than trim Westchester. In early morning, when all kinds of country are lovely, hushed and washed, newborn, the low hills round our low-lying cluster of barns and houses were touchingly beautiful. When I was not in Vermont, they seemed as lovely as Vermont. Our brook at Manumit was beautiful, flowing southward under the sycamore-shaded bridge, with a late-afternoon sky reflected in the water; anybody would linger there even in spring, when the children rushed so often up the wooded "Cobble" hill before breakfast and after supper. There was beauty in the old farmhouse which was our main dwelling and the small old house where the Clarks then lived, still called by their name; beauty too in the new house the Finckes built, down in the very crook of the brook's arm, as it were. This house they called the Mill, because a mill had stood there in the farm's early days; and they used the old grindstones for their doorsteps. A small view of this house is in the Encyclopedia Brittanica. There was but one ungainly building on the place; it was the hurriedly built gymnasium, with boys' dormitories upstairs.

Everything promised well for our venture. Manumit would be another Brookwood, but anchored more firmly against the winds of change. A community school again, with the same fraternally shared work and play, the same Franciscan freedom from locks, keys and penalties, the same school meeting, so lively and outspoken, the same liberties and responsibilities to balance each other; but a steadier underpinning, a body of Labor and educational backers for the founders to depend upon, and—if possible—some Labor union support.

Our students were all to be children, none younger than nine, none

255

older than fifteen. Like Brookwood and like Quaker schools and colleges, ours would of course be coeducational. Two-thirds, we hoped, would be workers' children, who—to fit their fathers' incomes —could come at a price lower than cost; the figure was originally a dollar a day. And though we welcomed Jewish children, we meant to have the school not entirely filled with them, but to have fifty, or anyway forty, per cent of Gentile children.

Our capacity was early filled—we had dormitory room for only twenty-five. As we had foreseen, many Jewish parents were interested. They seem to be more attracted than other people to educational ventures. But we had plenty, too, of Gentile applicants. In the first year there was no Negro at Manumit, either as student or staff member; later we had both.

Our curriculum we divided into five fields; natural science, social science, mathematics, English, arts and crafts. In every one of these we hoped the farm would come into use in dozens of ways. We could foresee plenty of problems, researches, dramatics (with an outdoor theater) and endless arts and crafts rising out of our hundred and seventy-seven acres, our fifty cows, our garden and fields, woods, ice-pond, brook and pastures.

The best beauty at Manumit, we knew, was sure to be the life and nature of the Finckes themselves, pervading everything as it had done at Brookwood. Whether rising in the same careless, natural way at school meeting, to recall to us all, by some significant detail, what the school was for; or summoning everybody with enthusiasm to harvest the squashes, or pick the tomatoes by lantern light before the first frost; improvising a part in a play or charade at a Saturday night frolic that was starting off slowly; talking by the Mill fireside, so humanly! with a boy or girl whose father had lost his job, or who had tangled himself in some quarrel, deception or trouble; in dozens of ways their influence, we knew, would reach farther among us, be more welcome, come more natural, than anything else could do.

Founders as they were of the school, we knew they would never come into a faculty meeting and say, "We wish to have it thus and so."

MANUMIT

WHEN I WAS FIFTY

We were all called in council over the curriculum, the admission of each child, all the school plans. Our faculty meetings were often enlivened by a burst of pros and cons. Teachers argued freely and warmly for their views. It took a straight majority to change a plan we once had made. Helen Fincke could be convinced; Bill often was. With ardor defending his views, shaking his finger, raising his voice, he kept, nevertheless, a beautifully open mind. I've many times heard him say, "Well, I was wrong," smile, say no more, wink, perhaps, at his own earnestness, and take hold with a will of the plan he'd lately been opposing.

Everything promised well for Manumit. Yet the school was planned in a shadow; there was sadness all that year at Manumit. The Clarks' rosy, hearty little daughter had been ill since the new year, and died in the summer. It was about this little Emily, the farm's darling, whose tiny life had just spanned the two years of my life at Manumit, that I afterward wrote "The Moon and Emily."

> When Emily was only rising two
> Her father used to lift her on his shoulder,
> Late in her little evening, early in ours,
> And carry her to whatsoever window
> The moon was shining through. Emily could say
> "Moon! Moon!" before she knew another word
> Except, of course, the cotyledon words
> "Mother" and "Daddy."
>                              She was such a child
> As it befits to live to green old age,
> Earth was to her so welcoming and homelike!
> She seemed so native to the hearth and meadow!
> Even in tumbling she was confident
> And lifted up a face surprised with laughter
> To the tall brothers. "Emily," I thought,
> "Will marry young, and rear a troop of children."
>
> I think of Emily when I see the moon.

But there is something obstinate about me;
My wits are stubborn, and will not invest
The shadowed part of the moon with any substance.
No; the moon swells and shrivels to my mind
As to my senses; sometimes it rolls by
Gold as a melon rolling from the vine,
Honeyripe; and behold it comes again
Shrunk on one side, and like a withered gourd
Left in the fields of sky. If I could once
Decisively and vividly imagine
The truth about that shadow on the moon—
How it's our shadow, of which the moon's unconscious,
From which it takes no sort of vital change,
But rolls into the shadow and rolls out
And still remains the unmutilated moon—
Then I could think the same of Emily.

Between her second birthday and her third,
She, who had so far waxed, began to wane.
We saw her waning, as we see the moon,
And all her rosy substance thinned away
As the moon thins; and like the dark of the moon
Came over us the dark of Emily.

There is a line, that comes somewhere in Chaucer,
Expressing, in an accidental way,
What I am told, and partly understand
About this death, of moons and of beloveds;
How it perhaps is a recurrent season,
Transiently falling when our shadow falls
At a certain angle. Here's the line I mean;
"Up rose the sunne, and up rose Emilie."

—*The World Tomorrow*

This was the first poem which I wrote in the double sense of human life closely and deeply interfused with nature, the underlying and overlapping of the transient and the timeless. In this habit of thought, which had become fixed with me, I was very much under the influence of Ouspensky's *Tertium Organum*. First heard of at Manumit, this book had come within my reach at Dr. Worcester's reading rooms at Emmanuel Church in Boston, and in fifteen minutes of waiting there, my chance opening of it to the chapter of geometrical indications of a fourth dimension had filled me with deep excitement. I now had read it all at my own leisure, very slowly, and with profound pleasure, which perhaps no other book in my life has equaled. Though it seemed to me speculation, it was the most significant and expanding speculation I'd ever read or heard. It actually cast a light, I found, on life, death and destiny.

Bill and Helen were a happy man and woman on the day the school opened, a warm, sweet September afternoon. Like Brookwood, Manumit opened with a frolic and a picnic. It was warm enough to swim, with the late sunlight on the pool; and the children rushed into their bathing suits and into the water, screaming and laughing; it was one of the gleefullest moments that sparkle in my memory of a beautiful, demanding, succeeding, heart-rewarding year.

I had charge of English and dramatics, and half charge of a small dormitory of "youngers." We were then using here, as at Brookwood, the Dalton Plan, by which the classrooms become studios where students of all classes work separately or in voluntary partnerships as they choose; consulting the teacher whenever they wish, for he is always in his workshop in working hours. I like the Dalton Plan much better than any other I've ever seen in practice. It's wonderfully flexible. It releases both student and teacher from incessant close bondage to the clock, gives the broad stretch of time the enthusiast likes, and yet allows the methodical mind to subdivide as meticulously as he pleases. Its monthly units better provide for thoroughness than the menace of a thousand examinations. It seems to me to prevent pretty well those deadly slid-over pockets and vacuums in knowledge to which children are so helplessly liable under other plans. But what I like best about it is the freedom and the practice in managing their own time which it gives the children. Drawbacks it has. Practically all children slip behind the year's work —the contracts, I find, are sometimes laid out with a margin to allow for human nature in this regard. The student does lose a good deal of organized group activity, though there's nothing to prevent him from joining with two or three others to work together.

In teaching English I found the Dalton Plan perfectly delightful. A boy or girl came in sometimes all on fire with a poem he was writing; sat down, scribbled, sucked the pencil, came over to read it to me as it stood thus far; enjoyed my pleasure, asked a few questions—but sometimes not; and was off again to the quiet far end of the table. A girl or boy came in, wanting (perhaps having asked for it in her monthly contract) to "get up a play," or "give three or four scenes." She sat down with an armful of books and a sheet of paper, to select. A couple of children who were choosing poems for a Manumit Anthology, or the like, ensconced themselves with *The Home Book of Verse, This Singing World,* etc., making busy notes, colloguing in whispers, nodding and shaking heads at each other, showing me their results. They were acquainting themselves with the style and sense of half a dozen poets. I was a lucky teacher, for the low-ceiled, rather dim, but cosy and intimate Library of the old house was my classroom. It had a fireplace, a long table, a wide settle, arm chairs, and a window-seat; the shelves were low and reachable and there were a good many good books.

At Manumit we had once more the Brookwood delegations, now calling them by the more usual name, committees. It was the highest honor in the school and the heaviest responsibility, to be Chairman of the Inside Work. We quite as often elected a boy to this post as a girl, and once or twice a girl was simultaneously chosen Chairman of the Outside Work, and had, with her committee, to assign such jobs as feeding the horses, cows and calves, clearing the stones from the fields, shucking corn, filling the silo, or running the snowplough, while some tall lanky Inside Work Chairman was assorting the sweepers, moppers and dishwashers.

We crowded round the Inside Work assignments when they were posted on Sunday nights, and pored over them to see and remember what we were down for. There always ensued a rush of complaints, especially from the youngest children; the Chairman usually received them patiently, but sometimes he resigned in protest. "What you put me down again for on dinner dishes? I was on dinner dishes *last* week! Don't you think I want a change?" "Vegetables!" a small child would protest. "I don't want vegetables—I want hall, stairs and side porch to sweep! I told you that before you made out the assignment!" and sometimes she would add "—you dumb-bell!"

Something symbolic of school life, perhaps of all life, happened to me that winter. Raymond Fuller, the science teacher, (the man who had told me about *Tertium Organum*) set up one clear frosty night a telescope that Solon De Leon had lent the school. At supper Raymond announced that he would show, that evening, to those who cared to cross the brook to see it, the planet Jupiter with all of his four moons showing. I resolved to go, cosy as the fire in the library felt, and big as was my pile of spelling papers to look over. "Raymond," I thought, "has troubled himself to set up the telescope, and the other teachers surely ought to show an interest." In such a dutiful and sanctified mood I went over the bridge; the night was splendid, and began to animate my mind—the sharp fresh air rushed into my lungs. Putting my eye to the telescope, I found my whole conception of the stars suddenly expanded, the sky and its spaces made unexpectedly real. Before I went to bed I wrote "The Mother at the Telescope," which *Harper's Magazine* afterward published.

> I saw the moons of Jupiter!
> The cloth for tea was just laid on
> And toasting of the cheese begun,

When out of doors I sensed a stir
And one child calling "Wait for her!
O mother, come and see this star,
Brought down as close as lanterns are!"
Apron and all, I ran to share
My boy's great moment.
                                        What a night!
Frost, a new moon, sweet biting air,
And through the telescope, I swear,
A fragile berry filled with light!
I saw it with these very eyes!
With such near-sighted eyes as these,
That had been watching bits of cheese,
I saw the drop of light that swung
Its four faint sailing moons among!
The moons were only half the size
Of scales of minnows. "And that star
Has me transported twice as far
As Jupiter from earth," I said;
For in my veins and in my head
Great joy and wonder blazed and shone
To think what I had looked upon—
Moons of a planet in the skies
Seen with these kitchen-gazing eyes!

That year, too, I wrote "Nightfallen Snow." Like all my poems in
these years, it represented my overbrimming sense of unity between
the life of man and the (possibly conscious) life of nature.

These nights of snow are loving to the air
As the still mother of a grieving boy;
For so they fill the air with soft concern,
Imponderable, irresistible,
And draw the numbing hardness slowly out,

And slowly weave a gradual sweetness in;
So spending, on its harsh and hungry gloom,
The last calm silver penny of reckless love.

O perfect strength of soft, unstrenuous snow!
O mouth of beauty whispering in the night!
Aeolian snow, that thrills against the wind,
That drifts on hidden grace and lights it up
With shreds of many rainbows blending white!
O wild and revolutionary snow,
That tosses utter newness round the world
And lays it on the nations in their sleep!

—*The Atlantic Monthly*

It was in these years too that I wrote "The Life of Water," to express yet once again the bright joyful sense of unity in nature, and its intense aliveness.

A chord sounding thus in the depths of the heart is made up of more notes than one. Perhaps the chief note in this newly keen sense of mine of the oneness of life came from the new unities and fellowships of my life as a teacher. In such a school as Manumit there's not only a strong fellowship among the teachers themselves, but a still stronger one between teachers and children.

Of this I think Walter Sassaman was the best example we ever had at Manumit, except the Finckes themselves. Even during the first winter, absorbed as I was in my own work and vicissitudes in classroom and community, and blind for the most part to everybody else's achievements, I couldn't help exulting in the brilliant way in which Walter was blending his teaching of the social sciences with the spontaneous creative impulses of the boys and girls. I don't know how he did it. Not from experience or training, for he hadn't been trained as a teacher, he was very young, and this was the first of his teaching. Evidently it was parcel and part of a genius he has. Or perhaps it was owing to the fact that at this time he was in the act of

263

falling in love with my young friend Stella Lundelius, whom I had known first at the House that Grace and Anna had started in New York, and who had now come to be the school nurse and dietitian at Manumit. They were married the next year.

Something convivial and hearty about him created a kind of campfire of the spirit. I remember once coming suddenly on a spring day out of the house at Manumit, feeling my heart chasing the summery wind as it blew over the grass, and seeing Walter coming forward in the line of impassioned rope-skippers in front of the dining-room door. It was his turn to cut in and out of the double ropes in one of those elaborate fancy jumping sets the children had—almost a folk-dance, and with just such an odd, pretty name of its own—and as I watched him sporting thus with the children in his rich fraternizing gusto, I understood in a flash how this fellowship would naturally flower in his classroom successes. And I went on to think, with an electric thrill, "Has everybody else been too absorbed, like me, in her own attempts, to realize what threads the others have been interweaving with ours?"

We were soon to share a general feast of one another's achievements. Late in May we had a series of delightful evenings when we took time to tell each other in detail about our teaching. These evenings followed delightful days, the most halcyon of my working life. In May the children at Manumit were extra happy, in somewhat the idyllic way that Wordsworth describes; they did "like young lambs bound As to the tabor's sound." They bounded out of bed early in the morning, rode the farm horses, rushed up the road for lilacs, ran up Cobble Hill and snatched bouquets of jack-in-the-pulpits. We could have our classes out of doors, read our plays in parts, rehearse, even take a Regents' sample examination sitting on the grass. When it was time for outside work, we weeded long rows of tiny vegetables in fresh earth, or pulled the rosy rhubarb, of which we could have four helps at supper; at the mid-afternoon bell we rushed into the swimming pool and seemed to bathe in wine. Then came the evening, when our pleasure rose so high at each other's successes and at bringing the harvest of our own. Manumit, a little more earthen than Brookwood, was still too good for earth.

When we came back to school we found that during the summer vacation a small ailment with which Bill Fincke had been annoyed—a mere chronic lameness of the neck—had proved to be part of a probably incurable malady; leukemia, in its gravest form.

None of us found this at all possible to believe, except Stella Lundelius, the school nurse, who knew what leukemia was. But, as in such cases from the beginning of time, we knew that we should have to come to believe it.

The school was falling round us. "Brightness fell from the air." We didn't tell the children.

Bill was forty-eight, and what a *living* man! His energy was at once dashing and enduring; there was a spring, glow and gayety in the way he worked; his spirits never seemed to reach a low level. And at first it seemed incredible that he was ill. Neither he nor Helen spoke of illness or anxiety, and both were as much absorbed in Manumit as ever. The endless smoking and talking of the teachers at faculty meetings went on as late; and in the mornings when Bill tried to sleep, the forgetful big boys shouted as loudly to the cows, as they drove them under his windows to pasture; they whistled and roared out silly songs in the young height of their spirits. They didn't know how much it meant when Helen gently told them "Dad wasn't very well." But in January the children had to know. They could see for themselves that he was growing very weak, turning very white. One last walk he took, slowly, alone, round all the barns and houses, looking, as Daniel Webster had looked, in a like case, at every cow and horse, every snowy field. He and Helen went away. They took an apartment in New York, where doctors were near.

Dr. Linville came to be Director—not "in their places"; nobody used any expression like that. We went on as well as we could with our classes and with the community, and on our week ends we went to see Bill and Helen. Norman Thomas went to see them, Nevin Sayre, John Haynes Holmes, Scott Nearing, A. J. Muste, Yale and

Union Seminary friends. The children went, in their Easter holidays; and in the spring we took down Mayflowers, rooted and mossed, growing in dishes; we took daisies from the home fields. In the fall when school opened again, we took down Manumit corn, melons, and apples.

Bill lived until the second May after that lighthearted one when Manumit was one year old. He was so strong that twice, for a long spurt, he'd seemed to be getting well. In the last month of his tranquil slow drowsing away from life, I thought often of Arnold's lines

> "And the width of the waters, the hush
> Of the gray expanse where he floats,
> Freshening its current, and spotted with foam
> As it draws to the ocean, may strike
> Peace to the soul of the man on its breast
> As the gray waste widens around him,
> As the banks fade dimmer away,
> As the stars come out, and the night wind
> Brings up the stream
> Murmurs and scents of the infinite sea."

# 18

HELEN FINCKE has never returned to Manumit. After Dr. Linville, Nellie Seeds, Scott Nearing's wife, became Director, and stayed there five courageous, hardworking years. Generous, appreciative, very mindful of Labor and the social hope, she was good to work with. Her whole heart was in the school.

Scott Nearing, though usually on his travels, speaking all over the country, or collecting materials for a new book, every now and then appeared at Manumit. Vegetarian that he is, his vigor was unbounded, and he was out by five o'clock at latest on a spring or summer morning, to hoe corn for a couple of hours before breakfast. The children liked him very much, and willingly worked with him in building dams for their skating pond and swimming pool.

My first sight and speech of him had been at the opening of Manumit in 1924. We were having a week-end conference of Labor leaders and educators, and others interested in the school. On the Sunday morning those of the gathering who were prolonging their conversation at the breakfast table were suddenly presented by Scott Nearing (who had finished his own breakfast and washed most of the dishes) with a huge pan of lima beans to be shelled, which he set down before them on the table with humorous energy, along with an invitation to make their fingers useful as well as their tongues.

The Directorship of Manumit, when his wife undertook it, was her own job, and she tackled it on her own responsibility. (Nellie Seeds is and was a Socialist, and has never followed her husband into Communism.)

Among the teachers who came and went, George Hamilton, my

fellow-Vermonter, and I became the permanent ones. George had come there as a farmer, and his manifold abilities only glimmered forth gradually upon us through his extraordinary capacity for silence and for standing in the shade. We were half way into our Labor pageant before we found out accidentally that George was an experienced manager of pageants. We were several months finding out that this thorough farmer, able to take a hundred dollars in prizes for Manumit at Danbury Fair, was at the same time a better teacher than most of us, and that what he did for the children was worth far more than what he did for the fields and the dairy. When George spoke at faculty meetings he seldom gave his opinion, but cited instead the facts he based it on; and this he did with great and humorous impartiality. And when he had furnished us with his opinion, if anybody launched an opposing fact at him, he was enough of an Abraham Lincoln to say, "Yes, that's so," without any rebuttal.

Yet his feelings were strong, and ran along one main channel—he was the quiet, efficient friend of every under dog.

I remember asking him, when he first came to Manumit, if he were going home to Vermont for his week-end? No, to New York, he said; there was a meeting of the Friends of Freedom for India. He is a complete, unhesitating pacifist, both in public and private; a War Resister. He is that singular being, a Green Mountain Socialist farmer; not a parlor one, but a dues-paying party member. And when I asked him once, in some momentary discouragement, "What in the world is it, George, that keeps a teacher going?" he replied, in a matter-of-fact way, "Eternity, I guess."

He never, I am sure, thought of other reward for what he did than the doing; but life contrived that he should find his wife at Manumit.

I wish Bill and Helen Fincke and George Hamilton had really known each other, and wintered and summered together. It would have meant a great deal to them all, and to the children at Manumit.

Something remained of Bill and Helen at Manumit after they went away—remained and didn't seem to diminish.

268

There was a certain boy there who had never seen the Finckes, but who was aware, as others were, of their continuing influence. On a spring evening when a number of us walked up Cobble Hill and rested together by the boulder that commemorates him, this boy, walking homeward, said to me,

"I feel like writing a poem. I think I'll go off in the meadow and write it now."

"A poem—what about?" I asked; and when he told me, I found myself inclined to write a poem about his poem, and to call it

## A POEM IN AN ENVELOPE

On the evening of that day
At the end of May

When in the early shadow
We crossed the meadow,

Climbed to the reared-up stone
Standing alone,

And sank in our grassy places
With quieting faces,—

Then into the open heart
Of a boy who was there
A poem began to start
And enkindle the air.

"This is a lonely grave,"
The poem began,
"A lonely and happy grave
Of a wonderful man.

One day some children and I
Were passing by,

And we quarreled along the way
About what we should play;

But when we came up quite near,
And found we were here,

We looked at each other, and then
We were friends again."

This John Payne is one of many figures of Manumit children who
throng my memory more vividly, intimately, than I can ever tell. One
or another among them, by day or night, steps forward from among
the rest, becomes very vivid to me for a day, or a week, just as his
problems might have made him do in his school days; and then again
retires into the composite, as he would have done then. I remember
with joy another young poet among them, Nadya Romanenko, one
of the "Olders." She came rushing upstairs into the "Middler" dormitory one evening when the girls there were taking their bedtime
showers and I was trying to speed their dawdling splashes. Nadya
had a half-written poem to show me, an ardent lyric of the sea. It was
full of wildness and joy. She stood with me amid the spray of the
showering girls while we read it together. That hour, that sudden
pleasure, has become the cap sheaf of many such memories which I
cherish, of the children's spontaneous poems, and my mother-hen-
like joy in them.

Nadya was one of several Russian children whom we had at our
school. One of them who strides into my recollection with just the
free, rapid gait which marked him at Manumit, was Andrey Tutysh-
kin, the fourteen-year-old son of a Russian doctor. Andrey had spent
all his school years in Soviet schools. He came to this country for six
months with his father, who came to attend a medical congress.

Andrey knew scarcely a word of English, but kept in his pocket, or rather open in his hand, a tiny Russian-English dictionary; and soon he could manage to make us understand most of the crowding things he wished to say. With the object of learning English very fast, he spent a good deal of time in my classroom. The chief thing he undertook there was to write first in Russian, then carefully to translate into English, an account of Lenin's funeral, which he had attended.

"In front of me in the procession," he wrote, after telling how bitter cold was the weather in which those hundreds of thousands stood waiting to see the dead face of Lenin, "there was a very small boy with a governess. As soon as the little boy came up to the body and looked at it, he called out,

" 'Lenin! Get up!'

The governess hushed him, and the guards shook their heads. But he called out again, as he was taken away,

" 'Get up, Lenin!'

It seemed as if he meant to say, 'We need you.' "

Andrey and Nadya were Gentiles, but we also had a number of Russian Jews, some of whom knew pogroms at terribly close range. Iris, (a Brookwood girl) once wrote an account of her own family's escape from Russia under the Czar.

"We were in the woods all night, hiding. Mother covered us up with a green tablecloth so we wouldn't be noticed lying on the grass. We heard the drunken Cossacks riding and shouting through the woods hunting for Jews all night."

To think, (we said) that the parents of these children have been hunted thus, like tigers, in their own country! Then we remembered how we white people, in our race riots, hunt Negroes down.

Lefty, who took Shylock's part in an abbreviation of *The Merchant of Venice* which his grade was giving, was only twelve; and I cut his Rialto speeches down to the greatest passages only, out of consideration for his youth. But with something which I think was racial fire burning in his beautiful eyes, he said,

"Don't cut them! I want to learn them all!"

In the long tapestry of Manumit children that unrolls before me when I am alone, I often see the comely faces of the three Linville boys; the eldest so delicate, the younger two so stalwart, and all so responsive to the beauty and bravery of life. Henry, the youngest, came in from the pasture to the cowbarns one afternoon carrying a newborn calf laid round his shoulders like a tippet—a Bible picture of a shepherd. I often see him too as he came into community meeting one Sunday to ask if we wouldn't send some of our "dessert money" for the defense of the Scottsboro boys. Fiery Joan Michelson had told him about them, and he had lain awake thinking of them much of the previous night. The dessert money was the fruit of our going without dessert at dinner five days a week—a plan the children had adopted to help the unemployed, by which they had already been able to send them a hundred dollars. They now acceded to Henry's motion, and the dessert money furnished twenty-five dollars for the Scottsboro boys.

Henry was not the only one who liked the farm work and the animals. A good many of our boys, and girls too, volunteered to feed the calves, cut the ice, and work the milking machine. When I saw Byron, his shoulders dark against the bright west, ploughing a long meadow in the late afternoon, I sometimes thought of the plough-man in Masefield's *The Everlasting Mercy*.

Manumit was singularly free from every kind of cruelty to animals. The boys and men never trapped, even with a box, and nobody ever fished, either. Our land was placarded thus, in a form of words composed by Sam Pearl, of Stelton,

"You are welcome on our land as long as you don't hunt, trap or fish. We like the animals; and there are children playing all over the woods and fields."

But the children were sometimes unkinder to each other than they would have thought of being to animals. Teasing, that hateful vice, was brought up in vain at community meeting—it obstinately continued. I remember that when Miss Thomas, the founder of the

272

Fellowship School in Gland, Switzerland, came to see Manumit, the children asked her,

"What's the worst thing in the Fellowship School?" and when she said, "Teasing," our children exclaimed, "It is here, too."

One small boy was so afraid of his tormentors that he crawled into the pantry shelves and pushed the raisin box in front of him to win a respite. Yet he was so courageous that he wouldn't let his father, who came up the following Sunday, pack his box and take him home.

Older children were not immune. A certain big girl suffered acutely from crude forms of teasing, which it made her elders furious to behold. Still I remember this, (and she does too) only as a dark curtain for bright days. This girl, like many others whose appearance is highly unmystical, had a rather mystical spirit, close to the surface, easy to reach. Going up into the woods together one autumn afternoon, we opened our hearts in silence to beauty and joy. Through many hateful moments of unkindness that followed, she was able to turn this key that let her into the wonder and joy of nature.

Of many children whose beauty and grace delighted me, I find myself taking Beatrice as the prototype. She had a face with the pale sweetness and wonder of a Botticelli damsel. In the scenes we gave from Shaw's *Saint Joan,* she played Joan. When we came to the trial scene, a beam of light, by a natural enough coincidence, (for the windows of the gymnasium looked westward, and it was late afternoon) played on her head. It was this girl who exclaimed one evening at bedtime, "Reading Victor Hugo has changed my life!" She and Natalie began to dramatize *Les Miserables,* and persevered as far as thirteen scenes.

Among children thus overflowing with initiative, it would have been a strange English teacher who didn't find a welcome for the best of her devices, whatever they were. Much that the children did was dependent on the teacher only in a negative way—dependent only on her not throwing cold water. The outspokenness and self-confidence that flourished in Manumit no one teacher could have

273

spoiled. Calling everybody from the Director down by first names early put the community into familiar, frank relations; and the floor at community meeting was always open to everybody, (cavalier though some of the adolescent chairmen might be with younger children seeking to speak—especially if the Sunday morning were fine and the horses at liberty to be ridden as soon as the meeting should close). Habits like these nourished free-spoken, upstanding youngsters. When I first went into other schools after leaving Manumit, I was surprised at the rising inflections the children so generally used, the questioning attitude toward the teacher, as if all statements needed her assent to be true.

I suppose I've forgotten the devices I tried which proved unpopular with the children. My four kinds of parties were really very popular, and continued so long after their novelty had worn away. They became, in fact, a Manumit tradition. I called them parties because they were in no sense a lesson, and we never had them in a laborious fashion. One was the Imaginary Speeches Party. We supposed ourselves to be holding a dinner and listening afterward to celebrated speakers. The order of speakers was never planned beforehand. No boy or girl knew when he would be called on or for what sort of speech; though it was soon understood that using the title as a hurdle, the speaker could leap almost immediately into whatever he chose to say. He might be introduced as the archæologist who had dug up an unheard-of city in the desert of Sahara, or the inventor of the new sport of swimming in the clouds. The nonsense possibilities in the imaginary speeches tickled the children very much, and I remember as a high light the capital response Pauline Bridge made when called on as the founder of a society to provide hoopskirts for elderly gentlemen. But sometimes their comedy became clever satire; and once I was electrified by a spontaneous passage at arms between a Communist girl impersonating Calvin Coolidge and another who played up to her as an unknown heckler.

Then there were the Definitions Parties, good evening ones, when everybody who came could present a word to be defined, and general discussion was free about it until it was defined well enough to please the company. We sometimes did, sometimes didn't, compare our definition with the dictionary. I often preserved the definitions we arrived at, for in them was real philosophy. We seldom took tricky words, words only useful as mental gymnastics, but words full of human meaning, such as "work," "pleasure," "freedom," "thought." I remember best a certain evening when a boy of dark, solitary temper came and presented the word "love" to be argued out. I never before or after that evening heard him express so much of his own thought and conviction.

Portrait Parties were largely attended. The "ticket" was a written portrait of somebody else. These sketches were usually very short, but much to the point. The children soon learned that to feature outside appearance destroyed the pleasure of guessing at the subject, and they began to attempt to convey the personality instead. We sat in a circle and read our portraits in turn, with an opportunity immediately after each for the company to guess—proceeding in turn round the ring—who had been described. Last of all, the author told us who it really was.

I always wrote two or three portraits myself; for these parties afforded me a prized means of lifting up into his own appreciation a child who for any reason was down on himself, or obscured by the radiance of others. And I could sometimes, if with a light enough touch, put a finger gently on a callous spot in somebody, and help it to recover sensibility. I developed a real skill in this, and I sometimes thought it was the best bit of my teaching.

However, the Poetry Parties were the best known and remembered of my parties. They were excessively simple, and though to our intents and purposes they were original with me, I suppose they have been given many a time in many a place. In fact the Oxford poetry contests seem to me a glorified variety of the same thing, and I suppose the Athenians may have had something of a poetry party carried to a Greek height. With us they were nothing but an assemblage of students (and teachers often came in too) each one of whom had chosen and brought a poem to read aloud. I used to nominate the first reader, and after taking his turn, he chose the next; and thus we continued, often long past the appointed hour, with real delight. And though some children read very badly, or chose tedious pieces, (for which no one criticized them) some child was certain, before the party closed, to read a great poem, and read it fairly well. It might be one of Keats's great "Odes," it might be a passage of Masefield's *Dauber*. Some of the children had specialties. Gussie discovered A. E. and always carried his poems to the parties, Sparky was loudly applauded for her lively reading of T. A. Daly's Italian pieces, and Ralph Taylor for "The Ballad of East and West." Irving read Shakespeare well. Benny Fincke was excellent in De La Mare's "Listeners." Eugene Soloff could read "The Man with a Hoe" in a way that received the tribute of silence.

I gradually came to realize, though not in the beginning of my teaching, that the real literary effort of a human life is in its conversation. Human happiness only to a very small degree depends on written language or public speeches, compared with its dependence on what is said in everyday life between breakfast and bed. Our influence in the world, our power and beneficence, are bound up in our tongues. It seemed to me, during the latter years of my teaching, that I must give estimates of my pupils' excellence in English chiefly according to their conversation, for in no other way should I be a practical teacher, relating my teaching to life. I began to inquire about the conversation of the girls and boys in the dormitories and at the table. And from this line of thought and inquiry came the notion, so popular at Manumit, so fruitful and influential, of student ratings in the whole field of English, including acting.

My idea of examinations had always been to secure a child's judgment of his own reading, conversation and writing; to find out which of the books he read he considered good, which fairish and which poor; to get from him an estimate of whether his writing this year had advanced over last, and which of his stories or poems this year he thought the best; how he judged his own acting; and even how much he thought he now understood of grammar. The children, thus approached, without challenge and with friendly wish to know what they thought of their own work, took a modest, sometimes too modest view. I remember how Ralph Taylor replied, on an examination paper of mine, to the query "Has your hand-writing improved at Manumit?" (for he'd arrived with a singularly good, almost a man's handwriting, and under our freedoms it had become loose and careless)—

"Great balls of fire, no!"

The children liked the student ratings, and were always ready to do them thoroughly. We only took them two or three times a year. Each in turn left the room so that his classmates could discuss him freely. First his conversation. Did Bobbie Davidson contribute interesting talk to his dormitory, to his table in the diningroom? Was his conversation an affair of give and take? Did he draw others out, draw out their best? When he joined a group, did the conversation rise in value? Or fall? Did it turn silly? Did he change it, or continue and add something? Had Bobbie humor? Could he take a joke? Did he tell a story well? Was he confined to a few words, and did he use them over and over again, or did he occasionally bring in a few new words?

What was the best thing he'd written this year? Could he make a scene live? Were his characters alive? Did his stories peter out in the middle—was the beginning always the best? Had he any passages in which the reader felt that the world was beautiful? Could he describe weather so that you breathed it in? Could he put in real humor, belonging to the story and the characters, or did he only tell it all in a joking way, and interlard old jokes?

How well did he speak in public? Had he made an impression and brought people over to his side at community meeting? What sort of secretary, what sort of chairman had he made?

Then his acting. Did he speak up well and naturally? How much life and spirit did he throw in? Could he take a small part creatively? Did he always claim the best part? Did he hold rehearsals together,

277

or waste time and distract others? What was his best piece of acting this year? (For at Manumit everybody acted. It was never a school where a few clever students carried all the plays.)

What kind of books did Bobbie read for pleasure? Chicken-feed, or something worth while? Did the books he read make his talk any richer? Could you see any effect on his life from them? Did he spread the news of a good book? Had he explored the world of books outside of fiction?

A consensus of opinion was noted down by someone acting as secretary, and Bobbie's rating was immediately handed or read to him when he returned. It was generally quite fair, I thought—seldom too severe. However, I remember that one boy did receive a rather severe report once. His classmates agreed that he was running down all along the line—wasn't half the boy he'd been the previous year. This had a sobering effect. He was a boy of great energy, and by the next rating he received a very different verdict.

Before Manumit opened, I had become enchanted by dramatics—the last thing anybody would ever have supposed I could take a lead in. But almost all the Manumit plays now were under my direction, from the spring festival play or pageant which was the great occasion of the year, to the fifteen-minute bits of plays at the morning assembly once a week. Some of these fifteen-minute bits were great fun; and in many of them we were able to give a taste of some mighty book like *Les Misérables,* or a passage of great poetry like Masefield's "Philip the King." In one of these, Bobby and Natasha did "Young Lochinvar" with such glory, especially when

"He quaffed off the wine and he flung down the—"

(five-cent tumbler) on the stone hearth, that the children called out "Do it all over again!" their highest praise. Another of these miniature plays was the inimitable opening of *Old Wives' Tale,* when Sophia pulls Mr. Povey's tooth unbeknown, and it turns out to have been the wrong tooth. Mr. Povey, a fifteen-year-old boy, worked up his part well, and explored the cavity realistically with his tongue,

278

and the girls were very charming in their imitation hoopskirts. Many plays were suggested by students, and sometimes they took direction of them in no small degree. Little girls like Nancy Muste and Bunny Fuller, capital actresses, helped construct our first and best *Tom Sawyer* play. Our really beautiful scenes from *Saint Joan* were proposed by a boy in Junior High.

Of all our plays, I think the students and teachers would agree with me that *Kropotkin* was the noblest. We took the idea from one of the older girls, whose father had infected her with enthusiasm for that noble autobiography, *Memoirs of a Revolutionist*. Older boys and girls extracted most of the thirteen scenes from the book itself, which we all read in full, and by divisions a small group of six dramatized, cast, directed and took part in them. Almost the whole school came into the cast. I dramatized a few scenes, and took a bit too much the lead at rehearsals at first, until Gladys said to Molly, "*We* aren't needed here—*we* aren't directing this rehearsal—let's leave!" I took the hint, piped down, and all went better.

The great scene in the Kropotkin play was the famous prison escape. Though we had "all outdoors" to enact this in, (for we gave it, as usual with our spring festival plays, in the "woodland" theater) we couldn't enact every particular. Still we followed it very closely. Of the twelve confederates we showed four; the violinist playing Schubert's "Serenade" for a signal, the woodman carrying in the logs, the soldier distracting the guard by showing him a louse (from his own head) under a microscope and the young man sitting by the roadside eating cherries to show when the coast was clear. We couldn't get a barouche for the prisoner to be rushed away in; but we had one of the farm horses saddled, waiting outside our "woodland" theater by the brook, and Sam Nooger, who played Kropotkin, ran out of the gate in his dressing gown, mounted the horse, plunged through the brook, and galloped down the long meadow in full view of the audience on the hillside, who rose to their feet, cheering.

But there was another scene which I liked even better. It came

279

early in the play, when Kropotkin was a little boy, waited on by serfs in the house of the Prince his father. We showed this scene exactly as Kropotkin describes it, the family dining, a serf behind every chair—but one.

"Where is Makar?" asked the Prince.

A serf breathed in his ear

"Makar was flogged today, by your order."

"Tell him to come in, nevertheless!"

The humiliated serf came in and stood downcast behind his allotted chair. Filly Vast, who played the boy Kropotkin, looked at him with eloquent pity. When the family left the table, he ran after Makar, caught up his hand and kissed it.

One year we had a twelve-year-old boy from the textile strike region in North Carolina. His own father had been a strike leader. George Baker was so undernourished when he came, that he gained fifty pounds within a year.

That May-Day we decided to give a play about the Marion strike. We had very little time to prepare, and were trying to construct it out of one rehearsal, with George Baker's advice and help.

"What came next, George?"

"Then the sheriff evicted 'em, you know."

"Just how do they do that, George? What'd he do?"

"Oh, he came round and told 'em, first, if they didn't let go the strike, he'd have to throw 'em out. They didn't aim to let go the strike! So, in a couple of weeks, he came round again—"

"Show us how it was, George! Melvin, you act the sheriff—George'll tell you what to do; and George, you act your father."

George took Melvin aside and instructed him. Melvin knocked on the door and said;

"Sorry, Tom, got to throw you out!"

"*Throw* me out!" cried George, in fierce assent.

"What'd the sheriff do then, George?"

"Whe' all those fryin' pans and stuff we brought over from the kitchen? I'll show you!" George seized and hurled the kitchen gear in a clattering riot on the ground.

"Oh, George! Did they do it like that?"

"That's way they do it."

"Oh, oh! Did your mother cry?"

"Cry! No!"

"Did your little sister cry?"

"Cry? No! She made a face, and mocked the sheriff behin' his back."

Labor feeling was strong—though not universal—at Manumit. I remember that when that delightful girl Helen Danzis was Chairman of the Inside Work, she one Sunday morning made the not unusual report that she had had difficulty in prevailing upon two of the students to perform their "socially necessary" work. "In fact," said Helen, "I really believe they've fallen into the leisure class."

Manumit gave me a year's leave, at the end of the 1920's, the year the depression began. This was to let me teach at Vassar as a substitute for an Associate Professor of the English Department who was abroad for a sabbatical year.

On the first morning when my classes were to meet, I felt rather frightened. It was the first time I had thought of such a thing as alarm. Everybody had treated me with confidence; nobody had said, as it would have been so reasonable for them to say, "Let's just run over your plans . . . hm . . . but how are you going to deal with . . . etc.; aren't you going to cover . . . etc.?" Accordingly I had made my plans with happy care and joy, and it was only now, at the last moment, that I began to entertain the useless and defeating notion of fear. I began to say to myself, "What do I know about college teaching? How little I've ever had to do with colleges! What if I make a bad beginning? What, what if they're sorry they asked me?" I sat down on the stone wall outside the gateway to Vassar's beautiful lawns and trees, endeavoring to pray away my fidgety self-centeredness. Drawing slowly closer to the divine element, I could begin to feel—not merely to admit!—that what mattered was not my pride and success, but that the divine element, lovingkindness, should enter this relation, and all would be well.

I waited a little longer still, to feel—not merely to admit!—that the cobwebs of spiritual endeavor are really the unbreakable iron cables of eternity, and then went with a light heart to meet the three young authors' clubs in which I was to be the senior member.

It was delightful, this year at Vassar. So gracious an experience it was that it undid for me Chesterton's saying, hitherto undisputed, "Ease is the worst enemy of happiness." Fresh from the joyful, demanding tumult of Manumit life, I found this ordered, leisurely year coming in like a square of delicate silk in the midst of a bouncing calico patchwork. My classes were all in the art of writing, and all were elective; the girls had all qualified for the work and every one of them liked to write. I found among these girls a high proportion who showed imagination, fidelity and the sense of form. They varied, of course, immensely, in the shrewdness of observation, and its range, and in that great asset for writing and for living, emotional understanding. One among them, Clara Lyman, possessed sustained poetical power, a joy indeed to me. Several of them wrote so well, so faithfully and discriminatingly, sometimes even with poignant feeling poured in unmistakably from life, that I used to wonder over a manuscript, "Where can she send this? It's well worth printing." The college editors did put a good many of their stories into the magazine. But when I tried to think of them under the covers I passed on the news-stands, I always thought, "They lack, thank God, the metallic, jaunty air so many magazines seem to like, monotonous as it is—they lack all that ever-ready snap and smartness. Nobody but the best magazines would take such candid, thoughtful work; and of course it's too immature for them."

It was during this year that I was trying to engineer our attempt to get the death penalty abolished in Vermont. The national office, with which I was corresponding rather constantly, asked me to join the group who were going up to Albany for a hearing on the matter in New York. Would anybody else from the college care to join us? Two or three faculty members and three or four of the girls did go up to Albany that bleak, damp day, and said a few words in favor of dealing more gently with "poor and sad humanity." We had our hearing before a committee of the Legislature of which the chairman was no other than Senator Baumes, the author of the severe Baumes Laws, which were filling the prisons of New York State so full. I looked with wonder at the calm, not unbenevolent face of the elderly man, at whose initiative it was that a fourth offense—regardless of any other consideration but that of number,—condemned the offender to life imprisonment. We had in our delegation Jack Black, the ex-convict, author of *You Can't Win,* a good speaker, and an inveterate enemy of the death penalty. He was an expressive Irishman, with grizzled hair and deep-set eyes. Standing up to speak, when his turn came, he advanced toward Mr. Baumes, who sat at the end of the long table, and fixing his deep eyes upon him, said;

"I'm what you call a hardened criminal. I'm a fourth offender. I've been out of jail for years now, and I'm going straight."

The bill was lost in New York as it was to be in Vermont, and yet I believe that a referendum in either state would have showed a majority for it. In fact, I think it must be forty years ago that the majority of Americans abandoned any positive liking for inflicting the death penalty. It seems to me to hang on from general conservatism while individually most people would be glad to see the last of it; and if it could be stolen off the books for a single year, I think it would never be returned.

# 19

WHEN I think of my Brookwood and Manumit years, they seem—with all their rough-and-tumble, crowded, demanding, rewarding, creative partnerships with the ruthless, affectionate children, and with my fellow teachers,—the most poetic years of my life. My power of living was filled to the brim, and I felt with joy the swelling expansion. And those inventions of mine, those occasional insights into the children's imaginations: the chances at bedtime or in the middle of the night, or on a twilight encounter in the fields, to say a releasing or reviving word; the rich chances, at plays or parties, to feature the child who's been in the shade; all these things and a hundred others, which each of us can think of who has had some happy intimacy with the young—were, I think, poetic efforts, and they needed no other expression than the daily opportunities of such a life. Constructing them, or abandoning them for new, fitting them as delicately as I could to words, drew in the same way on the emotions and the intelligence. Sometimes they arose, as poems sometimes do, from a spout of inspiration at midnight or early morning.

But there was also a new kind of poem which I began to write seven years ago, in the intervals between teaching; a kind which grew directly from the children, the Labor movement and the war. Or can my ballads be called poems? Perhaps they are too galloping, rough, straight-ahead narratives to be so called. There's nothing finished or artistic about them. They don't even try to gild the lily of the reckless brotherliness they celebrate. I should never have conceived of them if I hadn't become engrossed in efforts to kindle young imaginations with the fires and splendors of the heroes of Labor and lovingkindness; above all, the obscure ones.

284

When I read some beautiful old ballad, brief and poignant, and in my mind compare it with one of my own long, rough-hewn narratives in verse, I feel the difference in every fiber of my poetry-loving old heart.

> "O little did my mother ken,
> The day she cradled me,
> The lands I was to travel in—"

and yet when I am saying before an audience my "Ballad of Glorious Harriet Tubman," (the Maryland slave who raided the plantations with a price of forty thousand dollars on her head) I feel all the honey and thunder of the ballad metre.

> She went again, she went again,
> She carried their slaves away.

When I am coming to the end of "Gene Debs," telling of his two or three years between prison and death,

> Gene Debs went east and west,
> And spoke to the world outside;
> A hundred thousand lovers heard
> Gene Debs before he died,

I can't truthfully say that I think my ballads are poor. They are too faithful, too impregnated with the spirits of their heroes. So resplendent is the reckless tenderness of which they tell, so satisfying to the marrow of man's innermost desire, that words themselves seem to rise, even random words, to the occasion. They are kindled by the blaze of human nature, as if in answer to such a prayer as Jacopone da Todi's

> "Sopr' ogne lengua amore,
> Bonta senza figura,
> Lume fuor' di mesura,
> Resplende nel mio core!"

285

My ballads are real ballads too in this, that they are recitations. They ought not to be read silently in the seclusion of a library, but read or said to others in a place that echoes with the footsteps that tread through them. At first I used in all of them alike the plain ballad stanza, only varying their irregular, fragmentary refrains to try to catch the spiritual theme of my heroes' lives. But in "Joseph and Damien" I used a fifth line, which rhymes with the second and fourth, and gives a pause, thus;

> "Father Damien soon will die."
> Joseph Dutton read the line.
> Whose arm would ease his dying head
> And cross his breast with the holy sign?
> Joseph Dutton answered "Mine."

And in the ballad I am writing now, of Tom Mooney and Warren Billings, I've seemed to find, by lengthening the second, but not the fourth, line, a metre which especially suits the impetuous drive of Mooney's rich, belligerent Irish nature.

> In San Francisco offices
> His name began to cast a spell.
> "Who is this Mooney? Where's he from?
> His name tolls like a bell."

Writing and saying my ballads is almost pure pleasure. In both I feel a thrill of delight. I am so confident that my audience will delight in my heroes, that I could feel no misgivings unless through fearing that I had raised, by my manner of telling, some barrier between them.

Manumit children responded warmly to my ballads. In the fashion of the young, they liked to hear them over and over again. "Harriet Tubman," the first one I wrote, is the favorite. Its opening, though not as clumsy as that of "William Griffin," is fairly clumsy; but once past the opening, Harriet's career fits into the form of a ballad like a body into its own skin. My very long ballad of "Tuzulutlan," (the pacifist exploit of the four Dominican friars) has the best opening of all my ballads, but sags in the middle—a structural fault in the adventure itself, which I wouldn't presume in any way to rearrange. "William Griffin," (a caisson worker of heroic endurance and magnanimity) has the best suspense of any, and is the favorite of boys. The actual achievement of this middle-aged man reads like the piled-up plots of John Masefield's tales.

The shortest of my ballads, the "Camden Boy," is the one with the most familiar background. A Confederate soldier, on the second day of Fredericksburg, risked almost certain death to carry water to the Union wounded, who were being shot down at the foot of Marye's Hill, and who lay there slowly dying and feebly calling for water.

This youth, like most of my heroes, survived his own recklessness. I've wished to show young people the sunny side of heroism, and let them exult in the wild bravery that "gets away with" feats of brotherly love. Circumstances can befriend our goodness and our fearlessness; the luck is not more often with the self-coddler than with the adventurous saint: and when I recite how William Griffin, blind, choked, having saved eleven others, overcome at last when he tried to save himself, fainting and falling, all alone, on the floor of the poisoned caisson, yet even then

> Felt, like a man who has rested awhile,
>   His glorious strength revive,
> Knotted the rope around his chest
> And they drew him out alive,

I love to see my audience respond to "the glory of the gift of flesh." Practically all my heroes were physically strong. They were men and women of outward as well as inward might.

"Facts are the angels of the Lord." The field of human heroism, especially in the ranks of Labor, is white to the harvest of ballads that I hope will be written. I think a tide of such ballads flowing over the modern world would do a great deal for a rich peace and a joyful life.

My ballads have now all been printed in one way or another. They are long, and magazines seldom find room for them. *The Survey Graphic* (which once printed an article of mine called "Shall We Have Ballads Again?" has been the exception; it has printed both "Joseph and Damien" and "Lionel Licorish," (the Negro quartermaster who was the chief hero of the Vestris wreck). The longest of my ballads, "Tuzulutlan," has been beautifully printed. Our endeared old playmate, Molly, had it privately done in Switzerland, procuring for it three mediæval illustrations which exactly suit it. The others have all been done in paper covers. Mr. Coates, of the Driftwind Press in North Montpelier, Vermont, went into partnership with me on "Gene Debs," which he set up and printed, and I sold. We had no copyright, and said so on the flyleaf, adding

"Anybody is free to spread this ballad who likes."

Four of them have been printed by our local press in Manchester (*The Manchester Journal*) in tiny green books, with white paper labels. Costing sixty dollars for two thousand copies, they've sold, at fifteen cents apiece, well enough to pay for themselves twice over. *Portraits and Protests,* as Henry Holt published it twenty years ago, never brought me a cent. I think there's something worth considering in this. After all, why should ephemeral writings be printed so expensively as to prohibit the average man from ever buying them? Printed in cheap, transient fashion, they can be replaced readily if wanted. Those that find a lasting place in public affection could then be printed in a dignified edition at present prices.

I particularly recommend my own procedure to poets. Let your poems be printed in small, cheap forms—their lovers will be glad to buy them thus, when two dollars and a half a copy would make many of us pause. Best of all it would be, perhaps, to have separate poems printed on sheets for which the buyer must provide his own binding or portfolio, as Christadora House, I believe, offers them—this makes possible the delightful idea of "every poetry lover his own

anthologist." Even great poets like Robert
body would like in vellum—why shouldn't
to keep in their houses "Spring Pools," "Appl
in Winter" and "West-Running Brook?"

# 20

During the long middle stretch of my life, when youth was past and age not yet begun, I found myself suddenly loving a man whom I knew, loving him with all the elements of my nature.

Not even in the smallest degree was this love of mine requited. In fact, he had no thought, no suspicion of it; and I could see that in a thousand years it would never occur to him.

He lived a many-sided, difficult, generous life. His nature was frank and brave. Though he was entering middle age, and wasn't entirely unworn by life, his bearing was youthful. He was the kind of man beside whom all the acquisitive heroes, the iron-handed, self-willed, lordly men, the magnificoes and conquerors, who lay down the law to the humble, look very childish. He was a man one couldn't continue to love selfishly, for it was soon apparent that one's selfishness would roll up like a fog and obscure him from sight.

After writing a poem called "Saint Clare Hears Saint Francis," I realized that I had been trying to convey something of my own feeling for this man, but hiding it, of course, under the extravagant language of mediæval ecstasy, and using such expressions, out of keeping with the present day, as I thought a girl of Clare's day and background might have used.

> I stood there drinking up cupfulls of his greatness
>     And of his joy.
> I remember him dancing all along the Piazza
>     When he was a boy.
>
> I was loving his hands and his bare feet, and his shadow
>     And the leper on whom it fell.

290

I was wishing for some rough work to do for the lepers
To serve them well.

I did not hope he could feel me standing near him;
Nor wonder if by long prayer
I could make my love creep into his great horizon
Like a current of air.

Back over me came flooding my love for Francis,
Which, when I pray,
By an Act of Love for all poor desolate people
I fling and scatter away.

I disappeared from my thought, from my sensation;
Nothing was there
But a fire of sweetness following after Francis
From the ashes of Clare.
            —*The World Tomorrow*—

Now I was no longer youthfully looking forward, expecting something better and better from my personal life. I was satisfied with life, like Uncle George and Aunt Mary. Everything had come. When I heard people talking about going away for a change, getting out of ruts, getting a little rest, I thought "How strange!" I was quite changed in looks by loving like this—my photographs all show it. When I was young, happy as I was, my photographs were all unsmiling. But now my plain face, in all kinds of snapshots, had a wide, warm smile.

I was extraordinarily vigorous and couldn't see any reason why I should live less than a hundred years. I said to my aunt, "Let's both live to be very old—let's be 'Those two wonderful old women at the south end of town.'" I was never tired, never ill, and it was difficult indeed to make me cross.

I thought I might possibly die sometime, though it seemed unlikely. I never thought of his dying.

As soon as possible after receiving the news, I went down a certain road and entered a field, where I sat down on the earth and looked at my life to see what it had now become. As soon as I looked at it thus, it seemed to sink quietly away and vanish. Instead of life running strong through my veins, it seemed that I must push the blood along to make it move.

Soon I thought of Dorothy; she would be able to help me replenish my life. When I telephoned "I must see you!" she replied, "I'll drive up for you at once." The morning was a sunny one; we sat in her garden, then walked together. I poured my heart out over and over again, and she poured in the oil and wine, again and again, of her sisterliness. Our long-endeared friendship had reached the height of my utmost need, and was dearer than before. From Zephine, too, I received tranquillity and comfort. In one of her books a passage was written for me, and I read it many a time.

This sorrow wasn't at all what I had supposed it to be. Reading poems about love and death, I'd supposed there must be a sense of beauty even in the feeling of sorrow. I'd thought, in my life-enjoying innocence, that such sorrow was just a mysterious, hushed, solemn kind of—yes, on the whole, of pleasure.

The sensation which I now had, of being all ebbed away must be, I think, very common in such cases, for I have heard many say "I didn't see how I could go on living." And there was nothing new, either, of course, in the struggle I now entered upon, to assimilate death, to integrate life and death together—to realize, in short, (not merely to affirm—I still could do that, for my placid old faith was intact) that the dead are inevitably living. And yet I suppose no two of us, in our grief, follow the general human direction through the same lanes of air. After what I was about to learn through sleep and dreams, I came to feel sure that even those who say they have no belief whatever in survival after death must have it in their sleep, even if it's altogether forgotten while waking. I argue thus from the unmistakable evidence of their continuing to join heartily in life, and to show pleasure and confidence in it, after the center of their being has crossed the line. For it's clear to me that we can no more "get over" sorrow by the mere irrelevant lapse of time, than we can thus get over blindness, or the loss of a hand.

But I was one of those who find themselves profoundly bent upon realizing the living life of the dead. In every oasis of solitude which I came to in daily life, I returned to the bare stone of the fact of death, and pressed, pressed against it to find in it the concealed fact that death is a part of life. My energy, indeed, had not died away at all— I was using intense energy in this effort. And I began, after a time, to feel that the concealed realization was near. Intimations of it, unspeakably swift, flashed and were gone. One day in our orchard the bare stone of grief yielded up its knowledge to me, and I could feel, with unmeasured joy, that life and death are one. It was something irrelevant to logic, but perfectly clear to the heart; an immemorial understanding that countless others must have reached. It was the humble, honest knowledge that by being good to the living we can reach the life of the dead. Something like this one has heard a hundred times in one form or another, has been struck by it, thought it satisfying and known it must be true. But now it was known "in the day of visitation." I saw that all loves are one love, and that this inclusive love is, as our hearts naturally understand, divine, eternal. Love certainly is God.

As soon as my sorrow thus began turning into joy and making a unity of life and death, I began to write a series of sonnets embodying —as it proceeded—my experience. This is the first one.

> I know the way to you, my love, my dearest;
>    It is not going far alone to think
>    And let my heart in long, long brooding sink;
> The way that seems the farthest is the nearest;
>
> The way is very sure that seems a strange one;
>    On every living need to spend away
>    And lavish all my loving every day;
> This is the knowledge and the art to change one

Far from a sorrower to one exulting!
  If only all this grace be truly shown
  For each one's sake, not proxy for my own—
Lest I both Love and man should be insulting—

Yet how from self the self itself to free?
—Love more than mine, flood through my love, and me.

After this opening, a number of sonnets follow which relate the strange, illuminating dreams which all that summer and fall covered my life like a sky full of stars. Three of these sonnets describe, with every effort at exactness, a certain night when my consciousness surely went beyond the limits within which all the rest of my life (even the farthest adventuring) has been passed. And the word "elephantine," occurring in the third of these, was encountered in the dream and remembered from it. Until that night, I'd always considered language the most beautiful, delicate and searching of all the media of art. But in this dream I felt its grotesqueness in the presence I was then in, a presence beside whom my personal self appeared somewhat as a puppy would appear in the presence of Plato.

## SONNET XVI

Near midnight of the ninth day of October,
  Resting a long time on the verge of dream,
  I many times went over that vague stream
And came back into waking. Tranquil, sober,

I was in both the waking and the dreaming;
  Serene to the last ounce of blood and bone,
  But full of wonder at the things there known;
And yet they were in no way foreign-seeming,

But as if daylight thought were far refracted,
  And some changed form of consciousness I took
  Past common consciousness, and there could look
On substance of a fine light strength compacted;

A stuff no senses know, nor tools can touch;
Far more enduring, shapelier stuff than such.


## XVII

I saw it in the form of links, or bridges,
  Firm on the air, extending soon trom sight;
  The nearer trestles of a shadowed white,
The farther fading into scarce-limned ridges.

And what those trestles were needed no showing;
  They clearly were the causeways of man's sleep,
  Where seeking spirits move through their own deep
By soundings and by spans of their own knowing.

So from that night my heart has comprehended
  How, in the senses' sleep, itself can reach
  You, O my love! and far from act or speech
Touch your life's hem, where that far transit ended.

Such drawing of the deep-desired near
Casts a long light, not shadow, O my dear.


## XVIII

When human thought comes back from such immersion,
  Such flight into a deep and meaning dream,
  Some human language on the lips will seem
Left as a residue, a waking version

Of what was there, past outposts of the senses,
  That so expands the heart of man to know.
  I clung to these words, but they seemed to flow
And melt away through all my brain's defenses.

Something was present all the time, that viewed me
  As one most innocently gross and crude,
  My elephantine language droll and rude;
And yet with happy calm that being endued me,

And I was unabashed, content and free;
  The presence and the place not strange to me.

My last four sonnets sum up those numberless intimations of eternity, tinier than the briefest dream, which fell into my life toward the end of that time, like showers of tiny meteors. Then reasoning a little about the human consciousness in relation to death, they finally turn back to the remainder of mortal life, and the old loves and tendernesses of home.

## XIX

Hearing a bird chirp, on a late November
  Morning when I was all alone with thought,
  Opened a door of air, through which I caught
A sense of life my soul and flesh remember.

So the green meadow starred with the white flower,
  Not the white violet or immortelle,
  But such a flower as grows where symbols dwell
In life not measured by the line or hour;

That poem which I read in sleep, relating
  How welcome to those English folk, their dead

DOROTHY WRITING "BONFIRE"

Came to their outdoor meal and broke their bread;
But most of all those flashlike phrases, waiting

Just on the inner edge of the first sleep—
These are as fragments of the bliss I keep.

## XX

Fleeting mementoes, lost, the larger number,
 To waking memory; not to waking life,
 Beneath which, far beneath its tremor and strife,
Move the calm powers and swiftnesses of slumber.

Do these sustain, with deepsea floods of being,
 The topmost tossing of the busy mind,
 The waves of sense that run before the wind
Till, sinking through themselves, and inward fleeing,

They leave the glittering height, the fluttering motion,
 Precarious identity of wave,
 And feel themselves expanding through the grave
Toward the secure vast magnitudes of ocean?

I only know the intimations throng
Sometimes by day and sometimes all night long.

## XXI

Play on my life, now, dearest, with your fingers,
 Since now again I shoulder the old cares,
 Enter the house, go up and down the stairs
Where the old joy, my darling, no more lingers.

Touch with bright hands our life of crowded striving;
 Bright beauty of your liberation, reach

Beyond us in the children whom we teach
And light for them the loveliness of living.

What Dante knew when Beatrice found him,
  When, though his mortal tumult blustered on,
  Deep into Paradise they two had gone,
And all his earthly felt the unearthly round him—

Let this sweet wonder, little understood,
Be deep within our flesh, beyond our blood.

## XXII

O other love, O fond and yearning kindness
  My life turns closing toward more and more,
  Sweetness of home, beloved so long before,
But always then with strange and careless blindness,

I know you now by dreams and intimations;
  By wordless insight running past my thought
  The spirit of your form my own has sought
And found direct, by instant penetrations.

In deeps of sleep I know how one, how only,
  The forms of loving form a single bliss.
  But for one golden instant knowing this,
Life has passed far beyond what death makes lonely.

What sound, what light is like the awareness of
The oneness and infinity of love?

# EPILOGUE

"Unbreachable the fort
Of the long-battered world uplifts its wall."

THESE lines of Matthew Arnold's, which I read in my youth with a kind of shallow intellectual realization, I now realize "as in the day of visitation." At threescore I share their mood, and understand them from within.

What barbarities, I ask myself, of man to man or of man to beast, have been abandoned in my lifetime, and replaced by generous and joyful kindness? A few only. Though some governments—our present one among them—have grown more humane, others are far cruder and blinder, thicker-witted and heavier-handed, than when I was young. War, like a soft-nosed bullet, is spreading decay. Vivisection is increasing. Poverty, whether temporarily or not, has increased gigantically. Negroes on the upper levels of education are better respected; but on the poverty levels where most of them dwell, they are still savagely terrorized; the heroes among them, who like Angelo Herndon risk the chaingang's slow torture to bring the sufferings of the poor to the notice of the comfortable, find no refuge yet from white revenge.

I see what a fatal error it is, then, for us who live in cautious comfort perpetually to repeat,

"Things are slowly improving, things will gradually get better, we must see a long way ahead before we take the next step, we must beware of sentiment, Rome wasn't built in a day."

Alone among us, as we ramble occasionally a few steps ahead

299

toward grace and amenity in human relations, the Communists have snatched the torch and—let the hot oil drip on them as it may—have run with it into the dark places.

But they have carried along with them the evil old spirit of punishment. They have said to the poor, "like them of old time," "Thou shalt hate thine enemy."

What then can be done, if not only our cool, sluggish hearts, but even the warm, courageous ones whom we envy, keep up the old, old Pale?

There is that other mode of conduct, excessively simple to conceive, but in practice demanding all the wisdom man can scrape together— the kind of conduct Gandhi is trying to show his followers, namely the practice of whole-hearted kindness, without stint, at all times, toward enemy and friend. It's a plan envisaged, I think, by the ethics of all the great religions, and practiced by many of their saints. It seems to have a conquering attraction for the human heart, especially of foemen in distress. (It's even comprehensible to animals.) And it seems to work miraculously fast.

It is the possibility of this kind of procedure which has borne up my own heart through these dark years when despair has risen so fast about the necks of the workers of the world.—This, and the continuing sense of the glimmering transparency of death, and the tininess and timidity of our planetary life, compared with our surroundings of infinity.

These years have given me, like thousands of others, some great joys. Gandhi is one; Russia, in spite of its revenges, is another. And it has been a joy to live, at last, under an Administration which— stumbling forward and backward, colliding with all the habits of government, all the habits of business—has still endeavored to make the happiness of man, woman and child its chief consideration. I am all the more rejoiced at this because it has falsified some little prophecies of my own, made in the months before the election of 1932, when I, as a member of the Vermont State Socialist Committee of Women, wrote letters to a number of newspapers declaring that in the Republican and Democratic nominees the unemployed would find only Tweedledum and Tweedledee.

What a pleasure to hear, so often nowadays, from the tongues of friends and relations quite innocent of radical views, the brotherly admission,

"It isn't his fault that he can't support his family."

To have heard this perhaps a hundred times this year makes me gratefully confident that in my country is taking place a profound, bloodless revolution. With this humaner turn of mind, and our present experience of how difficult it is to abolish poverty and war without changing business principles, should it be long, I ask myself, before Socialism comes into practical power?

In these years, somewhat secluded ones for me, I have had more than my share of pleasures and contentments; those whom I love still hale and enjoying, their best influences spreading, the children growing tall and wise, my namesake with a baby of her own, my pupils, but yesterday children at Manumit, standing up today before a legislature against a tyrannical law. I can exult in the words of Job,

"Upon my right hand rise the youth!"

# INDEX

303

British Mission, 188
Brookwood, 225 ff., 253, 255, 256, 259, 265, 284
Brownell, Blanche, 65, 66, 80, 96
Büchler, Mary, 81, 82, 116, 118
Bull Moose, 161
Burlington, 131, 132
burning alive, 59, 60, 209, 216
"burning" poems, 145, 146
Burr, Joseph, 60, 61
Burr and Burton Seminary, 60 ff., 223, 225
Burton, 25, 61, 74, 79, 113
bustles, 77

"Camden Boy," 287
Camden, S. C., 17
Canfield, Dorothy—see also Fisher, Dorothy Canfield, 104 ff., 129 ff.
Canfield, Dr. James H., 104, 105
Canfield, Frank, 104, 105
Canfields, 104, 105, 129
*Capital,* 155
capital punishment, 206, 282, 283
Carl, 15, 16, 17, 23 ff., 26, 40, 43, 44, 52, 56, 57, 73 ff., 91, 106, 113, 115, 116, 121 ff., 151, 161, 181 ff., 216
Carrel, Dr., 213
Cary, Miss Sally, 98
cemetery, 96
*Century Magazine,* 50, 189, 190
Cercle Français, 99
*Certain People of Importance,* 177
Cervera, Admiral, 113
chain-gangs, 193, 194, 299
Chapman, Dr. Frank, 43
Chicago, 88, 195
Child, Francis J., 99
children, 124, 125, 284, 301
children's companionship a cure for sadness, 153
*Children's First Life of the United States,* 218 ff.
children's literary taste, 57, 58
"Christ Tempted," 209
Christadora House, 289
Christmas, 35, 36
church, 21 ff., 34 ff.
church and war, 177, 178
*Churchman, The,* 88
Civil Liberties Union, 226
Civil War, 112
Clark, Badger, 189, 190
Clark, Charles, 254
Clark, Emily, 257, 258

Clark family, 253
Clark, Richard, 254, 255
Cleghorn, Charles Dalton, Jr., 123, 153, 182 ff.
Cleghorn, Fannie, 154, 182 ff.
Cleghorn, John, 216, 217
Cleghorn, Lucy Ann, 216, 217
Cleghorn, Susan, see Susan
Cleghorns, 23, 123, 164, 182
Cleveland, Grover, 20, 40
clinic for suggestion, 147
Coates, Walter, 288
Cobble Hill, 255, 264, 269
Codington, Kate, 209, 222
Coes, Mary, 98
Coffin, Dr. Lewis A., 142
Colby, Josephine ("Polly"), 246
College of Physicians and Surgeons, 115
Communists, 222, 300
Community House, 247 ff.
community life, 31, 226 ff., 260
Company E, Fifth Vermont, 112, 113
complaisance, 87, 88
"Comrade Jesus," 158 ff.
Cone, Mabel, 31, 53, 55, 80
Cone and Burton, 40, 79, 80
Congress of Religions, 95
Congregational Church, 34, 35, 46, 54
*Conning Tower, see* F.P.A.
conscientious objectors, 192, 235
consciousness, control of, 147
consciousness, expansion of, 293 ff.
conscription, 188
*Contemporary American Literature and Religion,* 159
conversation the chief literary influence in life, 276
Cope, Mrs. Walter, 197 ff., 222
Copeland, Charles Townsend, 100, 101
Cornicelius, 209
Costrell, Dorothy, 58
Cousin Charlie, 32, 74
Cousin Ellen, 33, 34
Cousin Isabella, 165, 166
Cousin Jim, 164
Cousin Willie, 73, 174, 175
"Cowards and Fools, Fall In!" 189
Coxey's Army, 91
Coy, 55, 172
Cramers, 44
Crane, Charles, 206
Crane, Stephen, 106
Crawford, 83
*Crime of Punishment, The,* 196
crudity of dealings with the poor, 139

304

308

# SIGNAL LIVES:
## Autobiographies of American Women

*An Arno Press Collection*

Antin, Mary. **The Promised Land,** 1969

Atherton, Gertrude Franklin [Horn]. **Adventures of a Novelist,** 1932

Bacon, Albion Fellows. **Beauty for Ashes,** 1914

Bailey, Abigail. **Memoirs of Mrs. Abigail Bailey who had been the Wife of Major Asa Bailey Formerly of Landhoff (N.H.),** 1815

Barr, Amelia E.H. **All The Days of my Life,** 1913

Barton, Clara. **The Story of my Childhood,** 1924

Belmont, Eleanor Robson. **The Fabric of Memory,** 1957

Boyle, Sarah Patton. **The Desegregated Heart,** 1962

Brown, Harriet Connor. **Grandmother Brown's Hundred Years,** 1929

Burnett, Frances Hodgson. **The One I Know Best of All,** 1893

Carson, Mrs. Ann. **The Memoirs of the Celebrated and Beautiful Mrs. Ann Carson, Daughter of an Officer of the U.S. Navy and Wife of Another, Whose Life Terminated in the Philadelphia Prison,** 1838

Churchill, Caroline Nichols. **Active Footsteps,** 1909

Cleghorn, Sarah N. **Threescore,** 1936

[Dall, Caroline H.W.]. **Alongside,** 1900

Daviess, Maria Thompson. **Seven Times Seven,** 1924

Dorr, Rheta Child. **A Woman of Fifty,** 1924

[Dumond], Annie H. Nelles. **The Life of a Book Agent,** 1868

Eaton, [Margaret O'Neale]. **The Autobiography of Peggy Eaton,** 1932

Farrar, Mrs. John [Elizabeth Rotch]. **Recollections of Seventy Years,** 1866

Felton, Rebeca Latimer. **Country Life in Georgia in the Days of my Youth,** 1919

Garden, Mary and Louis Biancolli. **Mary Garden's Story,** 1951

Gildersleeve, Virginia Crocheron. **Many a Good Crusade,** 1954

Gilson, Mary Barnett. **What's Past is Prologue,** 1940

Hurst, Fannie. **Anatomy of Me,** 1958

Jacobs-Bond, Carrie. **The Roads of Melody,** 1927

Jelliffe, Belinda. **For Dear Life,** 1936

Jones, Amanda T. **A Psychic Autobiography,** 1910

Logan, Kate Virginia Cox. **My Confederate Girlhood,** 1932

Longworth, Alice Roosevelt. **Crowded Hours,** 1933

MacDougall, Alice Foote. **The Autobiography of a Business Woman,** 1928

**Madeleine.** 1919

Meyer, Agnes E. **Out of These Roots,** 1953

Odlum, Hortense. **A Woman's Place,** 1939

Potter, Eliza. **A Hairdresser's Experience in High Life,** 1859

Rinehart, Mary Roberts. **My Story,** 1948

[Ritchie], Anna Cora Mowatt. **Autobiography of an Actress,** 1854

Robinson, Josephine DeMott. **The Circus Lady,** 1925

Roe, Mrs. Elizabeth A. **Recollections of Frontier Life,** 1885

Sanders, Sue. **Our Common Herd,** 1939

Sangster, Margaret E. **An Autobiography,** 1909

Sherwood, M[ary] E[lizabeth]. **An Epistle to Posterity,** 1897

Sigourney, Mrs. L[ydia] H. **Letters of Life,** 1866

Smith, Elizabeth Oakes [Prince]. **Selections from the Autobiography of Elizabeth Oakes Smith,** 1924

[Terhune], Mary V.H. **Marion Harland's Autobiography,** 1910

Terrell, Mary Church. **A Colored Woman in a White World,** 1940

Ueland, Brenda. **Me,** 1939

Van Hoosen, Bertha. **Petticoat Surgeon,** 1947

Vorse, Mary Heaton. **A Footnote to Folly,** 1935

[Ward], Elizabeth Stuart Phelps. **Chapters from a Life,** 1896

Wilcox, Ella Wheeler. **The Worlds and I,** 1896

Wilson, Edith Bolling. **My Memoir,** 1938